Emulating Alexander

Other Books By Glenn Barnett

The Young Nixon: An Oral Inquiry (Co-author)

When Jesus Walked: A Story of the Christ

Zenobia: Empress of the East

Emulating Alexander

How Alexander the Great's Legacy Fuelled Rome's Wars With Persia

by
Glenn Barnett

Pen & Sword
MILITARY

First published in Great Britain in 2017 by
Pen & Sword Military
An imprint of
Pen & Sword Books Ltd
47 Church Street
Barnsley
South Yorkshire
S70 2AS

ISBN 978 1 52670 300 2

Printed and bound in England by TJ International Ltd, Padstow.

Pen & Sword Books Ltd incorporates the Imprints of Pen & Sword Archaeology, At-
las, Aviation, Battleground, Discovery, Family History, History, Maritime, Military,
Naval, Politics, Railways, Select, Transport, True Crime, Fiction, Frontline Books,
Leo Cooper, Praetorian Press, Seaforth Publishing, Wharncliffe and White Owl.

For a complete list of Pen & Sword titles please contact
PEN & SWORD BOOKS LIMITED
47 Church Street, Barnsley, South Yorkshire, S70 2AS, England
E-mail: enquiries@pen-and-sword.co.uk
Website: www.pen-and-sword.co.uk

Contents

For
John–Roger
In memory of a great man

Acknowledgments

Historical research would be impossible without the dedicated endeavours of research libraries and librarians. I have had the privilege of extensively using the libraries at CSULA, UC Irvine and UCLA while relying on librarians for inter-library loans and journal articles (before I had access to the miracle of JSTOR) and leads for appropriate material.

I wish to thank the historians who vetted this work: professors Touraj Daryaee, Stanley Burstein and Afshin Matin-Asgari. They pointed me toward material and ideas of merit and importance in pursuing this subject matter. I owe a debt of gratitude to Mahmoud Omidsalar, a noted scholar of the Iranian epic poem *The Shahnameh* for his insights on ancient Persia. I am also grateful to my dear friends John-Roger and John Morton for their quiet encouragement.

Thanks also to John Chen and Karen Ter-Sarkisian for their friendship, feedback and insights. A personal thank you to Anja Leigh Russel, my one-woman support group.

Finally I have to thank my wife Marie for putting up with my spending much of my day sequestered in lonely research libraries with visions of antiquity dancing in my head.

Preface

I sometimes think that never blows so red the rose as
where some buried Caesar bled.

–Omar Khayyám[1]

For 700 years Rome shared a border with the Parthian and Sasanian dynasties of Persia who were the successors to the Achaemenid and Seleucid Empires. In dealing with them the Romans had always the example of Alexander the Great before them.

Alexander's exploits set the bar for the Romans who wished to emulate him. Generals compared themselves to him and tried to imitate his military conquests. Emperors might dress like him or commission artwork and coins to promote the comparison. Sometimes it was the Roman public who saw their leader as the 'new Alexander' or collected Alexander-themed art work and wore Alexander talismans to ward off evil.

In the fifth and sixth century AD, with Rome in decline, the imitation of Alexander would morph into the flattery of courtiers who would imply that the current emperor was every bit the hero that Alexander was, even though that ruler might never leave Constantinople on campaign.

After Julian there was little thought of Persian conquest except in the minds of poets and writers who still envisioned a world-spanning Roman Empire from the Atlantic to the Indian Ocean.

At the same time the Parthian and, more so, the Sasanian Persians would see it as their duty to regain the territories once ruled by their Achaemenid ancestors. It is as if they wanted to return the world to the time before Alexander. These lands included the eastern Mediterranean as far as Egypt and all of Asia Minor. An echo of this Persian dream can be seen today in Iran's support of Shiites in Iraq, Syria, Yemen, Lebanon and elsewhere.

This book is written to explore the influence that the long-dead conqueror had in the contentious relations between Rome and Persia, how that model changed over time and how it still influences us today. Emphasis will be on the individuals whose actions defined their times. Did they imitate Alexander and, if so, how?

Introduction

So outstanding were the achievements of that invincible warrior
[Alexander] that even after his death his successors held sway over an
alien land for a great length of time and came to wield considerable
power. I think that on the strength of his reputation they would have
remained in power right up to the present day if internal dissensions
and frequent wars directed against one another and against the Romans
had not sapped their strength and destroyed the myth of their apparent
invincibility.

–Agathias (6th Century AD)[1]

With the exception of Jesus, Alexander the Great was arguably the most famous and influential man of antiquity. He gave his name to an age. Even during his life time his propagandists crafted his image, 'as the true successor of Homer's heroes and promoting his claim to be son of Zeus, an aegis-bearing wielder of the thunderbolt before who even the waves prostrated themselves'.[2]

His fame stemmed from his conquest of the greatest empire of his age, that of the Achaemenids of Persia, which he overran and made his own all by the time of his early death at thirty-three years of age (the same age given for the life time of Jesus). Stories of his life became legend, spreading and expanding in Europe and Persia even a thousand years later during the Middle Ages.[3]

The mythical accomplishments of Alexander against Persia, long before Rome first faced off with the Parthians and later Sasanians, would stand as a beacon for Roman leaders from Sulla to Heraclius. In their own different ways many Roman generals and emperors strove to be like him in appearance, popular perception and, if possible, deeds. Even leaders who did not purposely try to imitate Alexander might have been compared to him by poets, contemporary historians, sympathetic propagandists and fawning courtiers.

Modern historians using ancient sources have demonstrated how Roman imperialists repeatedly imitated Alexander. As early as 1934 professor Michael Tierney would note the similarities between Alexander the Great and Constantine, also called 'the Great'.[4]

In 1967 the German historian Dorothea Michel published an article entitled *Alexander als Vorbild für Pompeius, Caesar und Marcus Antonius* (Alexander as a model for Pompey, Caesar and Mark Antony), in which she argued that Alexander was a model (*vorbild*) for three powerful Roman generals. Her work would help to form a focus of study known as *Imitatio Alexandri* or 'The Imitation of Alexander'. But it is not imitation alone that historians are looking at when comparing Roman heroes to Alexander.

Peter Green expanded the parameters in his article 'Caesar and Alexander: *Aemulatio, imitation, comparatio*' (1978) to include rivalry (*aemulatio*) and comparison (*comparatio*) as well as imitation (*imitation*). HH Scullard, anticipating Green by seven years, discussed how Romans compared their hero Scipio Africanus to Alexander.[5] (See below)

Like Michel and Green, most modern historians of the *Imitatio* have confined themselves to the study of the Republican era of Rome. For instance the expanded doctorial dissertation of Diana Spencer (2000) abruptly ends early in the first century AD.[6]

An exception would be Angela Kühnen who has done the most extensive survey to date in her book, *Die imitatio Alexandri in der römischen Politik*. She extends her analysis to the Severans.[7] For the most part though the Principate (first to third century AD), the Dominate (third to sixth century) and the Byzantine era of Roman history is ignored. This is mainly due to the fact that the surviving primary sources give us a more complete picture of the earlier era.

Imitatio historians that study the generals of the republic or the Caesars often confine themselves to a single leader. An early work by GJD Aalders titled *Germanicus Und Alexander Der Grosse* (1961), for instance, compares the first century Roman general, Germanicus with Alexander.[8]

While the *Imitatio Alexandri* has recently become a common theme, some historians, most notably Erich S Gruen (1998), have argued that the late republican generals of Rome did not actually claim that they were imitating Alexander and as far as we know from our sources, they did not.[9] However, Gruen does not take into account other factors such as public sentiment that ancient writers themselves admit to tapping into. Nor does he examine statuary or numismatics for clues. He does not consider the 'rivalry' or 'comparison' aspects of imitation and he does not consider the political climate of the time.

Despite this narrow view, it is clear that over the centuries Roman generals and emperors adopted Alexander's habits, appearance and eccentricities in their art, statues and coins. The traits of Alexander included the leftward tilt of his head, the slightly parted lips, curly hair and association with the gods. The eleventh century Byzantine historian Michael Psellos wrote that 'Alexander the famous Macedonian had a crooked neck', which would account for the tilt of the head.[10]

The traits of Alexander that are represented in his coins and statues and copied by Hellenistic and early Roman leaders and generals are thoroughly discussed by Professor Andrew Stewart in his magnum opus, *The Faces of Power*.

Julius Caesar has often been compared to Alexander as early as his own life time by Cicero and later by future generations of ancient writers such as Lucan, Velleius, Appian and Julian. Gnaeus Pompey wore Alexander's aging cape while Caligula wore his breastplate. Augustus placed statues once owned by Alexander in the forum.[11] Any emperor or man of wealth visiting Alexandria in Egypt had to visit Alexander's tomb. These actions served to honour Alexander while associating the current emperor or general with him.

The civilian population also venerated Alexander as witnessed by the likenesses of him found frozen in time at Pompeii and Herculaneum. The most famous of these is a 19x10 foot (6x3m) floor mosaic commissioned around 100 BC in a private home known as *Casa del Fauno*, 'the House of the Faun'. This romantic mosaic, made after a Greek original (or looted from Greece), was buried by the eruption of Mount Vesuvius in 79 AD and survived for two thousand years to tell us of one Roman's fascination with the Macedonian king.[12] It depicts Alexander charging at the Persian King Darius III in the decisive moment of their climactic battle.

We also have surviving examples of fourth century clay disks with Alexander's likeness used by the people to gain admission to the games or plays during the time of Constantine. Andrew Stewart discusses several Roman-era Alexander-themed art works now in museums, while another art historian, Niels Hannestad, has written of the imitation of Alexander in Roman art.[13]

There was at least one aspect of Alexander that was not appealing to Romans of the Republic. He was a king. The senate and people of Rome, prided themselves on having overthrown their own king. It would not do to boast about being like a king or to adopt the monarchal trappings of the Macedonian king.

This was also true in the early period of the Caesars. During this time the kingly diadem, a silk head band worn by Alexander as a symbol of his defeat of Persia and later by his successor Hellenistic kings, was shunned by the Romans as a symbol of kingship. Julius Caesar famously refused it more than once.[14]

It wasn't until the third century AD, with the rise of the powerful Sasanians in Persia and the eastward shift in Roman power to a Hellenized Constantinople, that the diadem would again become fashionable.

The imitation of Alexander was bequeathed to the future Byzantine/ Sasanian relationship when the monarchal forms of kingship were emphasized at Constantinople, while the denunciation of Alexander (who was considered by the Persians to be a Roman) was fashionable in Sasanian Persia.

From Constantine (r. 306–337) onward, court functions were ossified into pious rituals. It was considered mandatory for fawning functionaries to flatter the reigning monarch with obligatory, but often empty, comparisons to Alexander.

During the long history of Roman culture there were both blatant and subtle ways of imitating Alexander. Popular comparisons through art, coins, good luck charms and public sentiment were just as important as an imperialist's bravado. Alexander's influence runs throughout the seven hundred years that Rome and Persia were neighbours and adversaries. That model changed over time and perpetuated itself into the future. Echoes can be found in the Egyptian adventure of Napoleon and the American intervention in Iraq and Afghanistan.

The sources for this study include ancient and modern scholarship. The weakness of some ancient sources is understood. The only ancient sources available to us is that fragmentary portion of the whole that has arbitrarily come down to us from antiquity.

Modern history too has its limitations. While historians have produced libraries of books about the Roman experience, much of this scholarship centres on biographies and the western empire.

The Parthian experience is considerably less documented and understood. We have almost no contemporary information on any single individual of the Parthian era other than Greek or Latin material written by their enemies. Their rivals and successors the Sasanians added little and the disinterested Persian poets of the Islamic period barely know of them at all.

The *Shahnameh*, the national epic poem of Iran written in the eleventh century, contains but two paragraphs directly relating to the Parthians with the author Ferdowsi admitting, 'I have heard nothing from them but their name'.[15] Without much to go on, modern studies tend to focus on the study of numismatics, archeology and cultural themes, ie art, architecture, religion, agriculture and trade.

The modern English language writers of the Persian experience use a variety of different spellings and reign dates for the Persian kings. For example, one Sasanian king whose name transliterated from coins as 'hwsrwd' or 'hwsrwb' has been rendered into English in many ways, including; Husrav, Khusrau, Xusro, Khusru, Khusraw, Xusraw, Xosrow, Chosroes, Khosrow and Khusro.

Parthian names are easier because most of the time they were rendered in Greek on their coins. For the sake of consistency the names (and reign dates) of Persian kings used in this study, unless otherwise noted, will follow the example of the late Richard Frye, the dean of Persian historians, in his *The Heritage of Persia* (1993).

Chapter 1

Rome and Parthia

Rome

> Alexander, if he had to match himself with the Romans,
> would have made them fight hard for supremacy.
>
> –Julian[1]

The Roman sources that we have access to, were of two minds about Alexander the Great. On the one hand he was looked up to as an example of military greatness to be emulated. On the other hand many were of the opinion that if he had attacked virile Italy instead of docile Asia he would have been defeated by the Roman army of the time. Both attitudes were still current during the time of Constantine.[2]

Italian professor Marta Sordi has suggested that Alexander may have had plans in place to invade Italy when he returned from Persia.[3] He certainly did have eyes on the west. When he accepted the surrender of Tyre in 332 BC he declared war on Carthage, Tyre's ally.[4] The Carthaginians took the threat seriously enough to send spies to ascertain Alexander's intentions.[5] As late as Byzantine times, a Roman historian would mention it in passing.[6]

They weren't the only ones who were concerned about Alexander's western plans. According to Arrian, the Libyans, Spaniards, Celts, Italians (possibly the Romans, though Arrian doesn't say) and Etruscans also sent ambassadors seeking friendship.[7]

Justin goes further, saying of these ambassadors: 'So powerfully had the terror of his [Alexander's] name diffused itself through the world that all nations were ready to bow to him as their pre-destined monarch'. We also know that while Alexander was in Persia his naval forces were active in the Mediterranean Sea as far west as Crete and the Peloponnese.

The attitude of later Roman superiority was reinforced by the experience of Alexander's brother-in-law, Alexander of Molossia, the king of Epirus. He invaded Italy from 334 to 332 BC while Alexander the Great was in Persia. Though he did not fight Rome directly, another Italian people, the Lucani managed to defeat and kill him.[8] Robin Lane Fox has suggested that this Epirote invasion of Italy was conducted at the suggestion of Alexander. Perhaps, as Marta Sordi wrote, it was a part of his overall strategy to rule over both east and west.

Another king of Epirus, a nephew of the great Alexander, named Pyrrhus (319–272 BC), also invaded Italy, 'in order that he might not appear inferior to his uncle…or to have less spirit than Alexander the Great, who had subdued the east'.[9] The Romans were initially afraid of his formidable army and his ties to Alexander. Plutarch would later remark on the Roman regard of Pyrrhus:

> Other kings displayed themselves as Alexander in their purple robes and their bodyguards, in the inclination of their neck and in their exalted speech. Only Pyrrhus did so by his skill in arms.[10]

Plutarch, citing unknown sources, writes of a Roman contemporary of Pyrrhus and Alexander named Appius Claudius Caecus (c. BC 340–273), who in a speech to the senate reminded the Romans of their frequent boasts about defeating Alexander:

> For what becomes of the words that you are forever reiterating to all the world, namely, that if the great Alexander of renown had come to Italy and had come into conflict with us, when we were young men, and with our fathers, when they were in their prime, he would not now be celebrated as invincible, but would either have fled, or, perhaps, have fallen there, and so have left Rome more glorious still?…you tremble at Pyrrhus who used to pass his time following around and flattering one of Alexander's bodyguards.[11]

Plutarch's words are significant in hinting how wide spread the imitation of Alexander had become when he writes, 'Other kings displayed themselves as Alexander'. Seven hundred years later the Emperor Julian ('the Apostate') would write about Roman cowardice in the face of Pyrrhus: 'You know how cowed you were when Pyrrhus crossed (the Adriatic Sea) to invade you'.[12] Such was the respect for the military skills of Pyrrhus that the Roman army copied his tactics and Julian still employed them during his invasion of Persia.[13]

In more recent times, Edward Gibbon, the dean of Roman historians, when comparing Justinian's general Belisarius to Alexander the Great, also mentioned Pyrrhus as their equal.[14]

In the Battle of Asculum in BC 279 the Romans rallied and fought the invader. Pyrrhus managed to defeat the army of Rome but suffered such heavy losses as to make him despair, 'One more victory like that over the Romans will destroy us completely!'[15] This ruinous battle gave rise to the term 'Pyrrhic victory', a battle that is ruinous to the victor.

The wars with Alexander of Molossia and Pyrrhus were significant because they were the first between the Greek east and the Roman west. The fact that

Rome was eventually victorious only bolstered the attitude of Roman superiority over the Greeks and by extension, Alexander.

This contemptuous attitude was reflected in a surviving comedic play by Titus Maccius Plautus (c. 254–184 BC) who wrote in Rome a century after Alexander. In his play *Mostellaria*, he has a slave named Tranto compare himself to Alexander by saying that he had done deeds equal to those of the Macedonian, presumably to comic effect.[16]

Three centuries after the Epirote invasions, Livy would digress from his history of Rome to speculate on the likely outcome if the army of the great Alexander had met that of the Romans of his day: 'I have often pondered in my mind…how the Roman State would have fared in a war with Alexander'.[17] He goes on to say that 'many' of his contemporaries thought that Alexander would have come up second best in a contest with Lucius Papirius Cursor (c. 325 BC) a Roman general who successively defeated the Samnites while Alexander was in Persia. Livy notes:

> Had Alexander the Great, after subjugating Asia, turned his attention to Europe, there are many who maintain that he would have met his match in Papirius.[18]

Papirius was the first Roman in our sources (other than the fictional slave Tranto) to be compared to Alexander. Livy despised the Macedonian conqueror's deeds and if he is correct there were 'many' others who agreed with him. Livy went on to speculate:

> The Roman soldier has averted and will avert a thousand more weighty armies than those of the Macedonians and Alexander, provided that the love of this peace under which we live, and the concern for citizen harmony, be perpetual.[19]

Diana Spencer dismisses Livy by pointing out that he was 'safe' in comparing Alexander to Papirius because by his time all of the Macedonian successor states had been defeated by Rome or Parthia. She concludes by saying, 'still Alexander persists, and Livy's textbook rebuttal of his claims only serves to enshrine his position at the heart of Roman history'.[20]

Philosophers weighed in too. Some writers of both the Peripatetic and Stoic schools ridiculed the Macedonian. The Peripatetics had a bad opinion of Alexander because he had executed Callisthenes, the nephew of Aristotle who was their founder.[21] Yet Spencer sees 'no systematic Stoic hostility to Alexander in antiquity'.[22]

Still, in the first century AD, Seneca the Younger, a leading Stoic of his day, and his nephew Lucan had no trouble calling Alexander a 'madman' and worse.[23] In the middle of the third century AD, Lucian of Samosata wrote a satire in which Alexander's father Philip belittled his son's accomplishments:

> What enemies did you conquer that were worth fighting?
> Your adversaries were always cowards, and armed with nothing better than bows and bucklers and wicker shields.[24]

Long before Livy wrote his history, a Roman army in 197 BC, under the command of a general named Titus Quinctius Flamininus (c. 229-174 BC), defeated the Macedonian army of Philip V at the Battle of Cynoscephalae in Greece. In the process, an agile Roman infantry unit called a *maniple*, developed for fighting on rough ground, got behind the Macedonian infantry formation known as the *phalanx* and destroyed it.[25] The unwieldy *phalanx*, which fought best on level ground, was the same infantry formation that Alexander's army had employed so successfully with his hard-riding cavalry against the Persians of Darius III.

Lucius Annaeus Florus who lived during the time of Trajan and Hadrian took his lead from Livy and wrote of Rome's wars with Macedonia, 'at the time King Philip V (r. 221-179 BC) occupied the throne. The Romans nevertheless felt as if they were fighting against King Alexander'.[26] Philip had tried to portray himself as Alexander. A bust of Philip V in the collection of the Palazzo Massimo alle Terme in Rome shows him with his head inclined to the left and his lips slightly parted in the style of Alexander.

Next the Roman army defeated the powerful Seleucid king, Antiochus III (r.222-187 BC), with apparent ease. At Magnesia a Roman force, which our sources tell us numbered 30,000 men, faced the Seleucid army said to have included 72,000 men backed by elephants and heavy cavalry. The superior mobility of the Romans carried the day and gave rise to the belief in Rome that smaller, more-disciplined Roman armies could defeat the vast numbers of men found in Macedonian and, later, Persian armies.[27]

Before taking on Rome, Antiochus III had led an expedition through mountainous Armenia and Media, through the Parthian heartland and all the way to the Indus River, repeating the success of Alexander. He temporarily suppressed the growing power of Parthia and restored the wavering loyalty of the Iranian kingdoms to his throne.[28] His actions would later inspire Caesar and Antony.

Antiochus even seems to have contemplated invading Italy at the prodding of Hannibal who had sought refuge with him after his defeat in Carthage at the hands of Rome.[29] Antiochus' modern historian John D Grainger calls him the most important ruler of Hellenistic lands between Alexander and Caesar.[30] Yet Rome defeated him with apparent ease.

Marcus Cornelius Fronto (AD 100-170), a court-appointed tutor to a young Marcus Aurelius, dismissed these same Hellenistic successors to Alexander:

> The power of the Macedonians swelling like a torrent with mighty force in a brief day fell away to nothing and their empire was extinguished in the lifetime of a single generation.[31]

Roman attitudes toward the Macedonian Alexander also included contempt for the Greeks. Appian of Alexandria, in the mid-second century AD wrote that the Greek power, 'since the time of Philip… and Alexander…is in my opinion most inglorious and unworthy of them'.[32] These attitudes were not confined to military affairs. There was a very strong Roman affinity for the ancient Trojans of Ilium who were considered to be the founders of Rome and were, as Homer tells it, the enemies of Greece.[33]

The Augustan-era geographer Strabo, possibly using the work of Alexander's court historian Callisthenes, asserts that Alexander himself was of Trojan lineage.[34] That would mean an ancestral kinship between Alexander and the Roman people.

Cultural matters in Rome were just as important as military considerations. While the Romans appropriated Greek rhetoric, literature, philosophy and plundered their art and wealth they had low opinions of contemporary Greeks.[35] The contradictory attitude toward Greece and the Greeks can be seen in the experience of one man – Marcus Tullius Cicero (106-43 BC).

Cicero studied in Greece. He could speak and write the language and had many friends there. As a lawyer, his defence of the Greek poet Archias (BC 62) praised Greek literature. On the other hand, his defence of a Roman named Flaccus in court against his Greek accusers showed a completely different side of him. His biting criticism of the Greek witnesses was designed to play to the sensibilities of the Roman jury:

> When it comes to giving evidence, they [the Greeks] have never shown any concern for scruples or good faith and they are completely ignorant of the meaning, the importance or the value of any of this.[36]

Cicero, like many Romans (as well as the British of the nineteenth century and the Germans of the twenty-first) preferred the Greeks of the past to those of the present. Yet even the Greeks of the mythic past are disparaged by Virgil as he famously wrote for a contemporary Roman audience and is remembered by us today:

> Do not trust the horse, Trojans; whatever it is, I fear Greeks, even when they come with gifts.
>
> —The Aeneid[37]

Three hundred years after the time of Augustus, the Emperor Julian tried his hand at satire and wrote *The Caesars*, a fable in which the gods convened the Roman emperors and Alexander. Julian asked himself rhetorically, 'whether all these Romans [the emperors up till his time] can match this one Greek'.

A contest ensued in which Julius Caesar, Augustus, Trajan, Marcus Aurelius and Julian's uncle Constantine boasted of their accomplishments. Alexander was then permitted a rebuttal and belittled all of them, especially Caesar. He even turned the tables on Roman boasts of being able to defeat him by suggesting that Rome could not have defeated Greece in her prime. Roman attitudes about Alexander (pro and con) persisted for a long time.

Parthia

> Great reputations are only made in the Orient.
> Europe is too small.
>
> —Napoleon[38]

Ever since the Achaemenid Persians first warred on the Greeks, the culture and language of the Hellenes made its way into the Persian Empire. Even before Alexander, Greeks like the philosophers Pythagoras, Heraclitus of Ephesus, the physician Ctesias of Cnidus, the historian Herodotus and briefly the soldier Xenophon lived among Persians. Greeks worked for Persians, wrote about them and influenced them.

Quintus Rufus Curtius, a biographer of Alexander, who wrote sometime between the reign of Claudius and Vespasian (AD 41-79) claims that Alexander's enemy Darius III 'was not unacquainted with the Greek language' and was able to converse with his Greek subjects and soldiers.[39] This suggests that in his youth, Darius may have had a Greek tutor.

The Parthians, like the Romans, were influenced by Alexander or more directly by the successor Macedonian empire of the Seleucids. Little written material of the Parthians survives, so we glean much of our information from their coins and from Greek and Roman sources as well as their Sasanian successors who had little love for them. In Iranian history, the Parthian era is sometimes referred to as 'the dark ages'.

Our sources tell us that the Parthians were related to the Scythians of the Eurasian steppes who migrated from Central Asia to the Iranian plateau during the Achaemenid era.[40] Like their neighbours, they were overcome by Alexander and absorbed into the successor Seleucid Empire. Alexander visited Parthia on more than one occasion and his first appearance in Persian attire was in Parthia.[41]

Later, as the Parthians began to overwhelm the weakening Seleucids, their coins increasingly employed Greek forms as they attempted to portray themselves as the legitimate heirs of Alexander and Seleucus. Greek mythological themes were carved into Parthian drinking cups. Greek gymnasiums were built into early Parthian palaces. Instructions, in Greek, for making tragic masks for the theatre were found in the ruins of one such Parthian palace.[42] Of three Parthian era documents found in modern times at Avroman in Iranian Kurdistan dating from 87 BC to AD 33, two were written in Greek and one in Parthian.[43]

As early as King Artabanus I (211-191 BC) Parthian coins began to bear the inscription 'Philhellene' or 'ΦΙΛΕΛΛΗΝΟΣ' (Greek loving). In a peculiar form of synergy, later kings, starting with Mithradates III (57-54 BC), would assume the Achaemenid title 'King of Kings' (*Shāhanshāh*) but it would be minted on their coins in Greek as 'ΒΑΣΙΛΕΩΣ ΒΑΣΙΛΕΩΝ' (*Basileos Basileon*).

The earliest Parthian coins depicted a beardless king, perhaps in imitation of Alexander. These coins also began to display the king on the obverse wearing a diadem, the white silk head-band denoting authority. The diadem had originated in Assyria and was later favoured by Greek and Seleucid kings and especially Alexander, who was often shown wearing the diadem on his coins.[44] To our knowledge, the Achaemenid kings did not wear it, preferring their own indigenous crowns. The fact that the Parthian kings did wear the diadem suggests at least some imitation of, or identification with, Alexander.

Parthian coins adopted the Attic Greek weight and metal measurements introduced to Persia by Alexander. These coins often supplemented existing types.[45]

Greek lettering would survive on Parthian coins until the end of their dynasty, although the lettering would become indecipherable in the final years and would be augmented or replaced by Aramaic.[46]

Some Parthian kings married Greek women, who became the mothers of other kings. At least some of the Parthian kings spoke Greek. The third-century biographer Philostratus wrote of Apollonius of Tyana's interview with the Parthian King Vardanes I (r. AD 40-47). He noted that the 'king addressed him in the Greek language'.[47]

Other Parthian monarchs enjoyed Greek plays, most notably Orodes II (r. 57–37 BC), who 'was not ignorant of the Greek language and literature'. Orodes was watching Euripides' play *The Bacchæ* when the severed head of Roman general Marcus Crassus was famously brought on stage and used as a prop.[48] A century later, King Gotarzes II (r. 38–51) offered sacrifices to Greek deities.[49]

The Parthians adopted the Seleucid calendar and adapted it to their own use. Rather than begin dating their years with the founding of the Seleucid dynasty (213 BC) they began their calendar era with the founding of their own dynasty by a man named Arsaces around 247 BC.[50] Sometimes both dating systems were used within the Parthian realm.

Yet there were always Persian influences on the Parthians. Percy Sykes argues that Arsaces may not have been a personal name but a throne name meant to connect the Parthians with the greatness of Achaemenid Persia. He points out that Achaemenid king Artaxerxes II (r. 409–359 BC) was also known as Arsaces.[51]

With time the Parthians, like Alexander, found it much more to their advantage and inclination to adopt Persian forms and manners. They came to see themselves as the successors not only of Alexander but the Achaemenids as well. They boldly set forth their claims to the eastern Mediterranean and Egypt that were once ruled by Darius and Alexander.

Tacitus (AD 56-117) tells us, '[Parthian King] Vonones... insisted on the ancient boundaries of Persia and Macedonia, and intimated, with a vainglorious threat, that he meant to seize on the country possessed by Cyrus and afterwards by Alexander'.[52] AJS Spawforth suggests that Parthia may have long nurtured this idea.

> Although we first hear of Parthian ambassadors addressing these claims to a Roman emperor only in AD 35 they probably were a part of Parthian royal ideology long before the late first century BC.[53]

In fact the Parthians had already acted on this belief. In 41–40 BC, Parthian forces overwhelmed and briefly occupied Cilicia, Syria and Judea while threatening Egypt and the interior of Anatolia. Later, in the Sasanian era, Persia would not only claim these lands but regain them, if only briefly. An echo of these attitudes can be seen in modern Iran's support of Shiite factions in Iraq, Syria, Lebanon, Yemen and elsewhere.

The loose yoke of Parthian rule over Persia allowed local people to maintain their ancient traditions from Achaemenid times and earlier. Neilson Debevoise cites the Avroman documents to show that the Parthians had a sophisticated system of land tenure, 'unchanged since Babylonian days'. He goes on to say:

> Parthian occupation entailed no great change in the life of a community; business, science, and society in general continued their course with only such changes as new situations demanded... civilization there [in Babylonia] shows a continuity of development stretching far back into the past.[54]

In other words the Parthians perpetuated the culture and norms of the Achaemenids with an overlay of Hellenism.

Wolfram Grajetzki agrees with Debevoise for the most part but cites two notable examples of change under the Parthians. First, the cumbersome clay-tablet cuneiform writing system was replaced as the administrative language by Greek and Aramaic; and secondly, the Parthians developed their own architecture for the construction of temples and public buildings. Parthian architecture borrowed from Greek and Roman styles but was uniquely adapted to their own use.[55] These developments did not significantly alter daily life for the empire's subjects.

Parthian influence stretched from the Euphrates to the Indus. When Apollonius of Tyana visited the court of Vardanes (as mentioned above), he expressed a wish to see the land of India beyond the Indus River as Alexander had done.

The king, according to Philostratus, wrote a letter of introduction to the Indian satrap who administered the west bank of the far-off river. The satrap, though not subject to Vardanes, was 'honoured' to comply with Vardanes' wishes, host the Greek and help him to cross the Indus River.[56] This incident, whether real or fanciful, demonstrates the influence, if not control, that the Parthian king maintained in the non-Greek east.

While in India, Apollonius entered the scholarly city of Taxila where he visited a temple of the Sun in which, 'were images of Alexander made of gold'. After two days of further travel, Apollonius came upon the field where Alexander had fought King Porus of Paurava at the Battle of the Hydaspes in 326 BC. There Apollonius found another statue of Alexander. In this figure he was poised riding an eight-horse chariot. At length Apollonius reached the Hyphasis River (now the Beas River in India) where Alexander's men mutinied and refused to go further. It marked the eastern limit of his conquests.[57]

Historians may argue over the validity of Philostratus' claims for Apollonius. But true or not his readers and his imperial patrons in the Severan dynasty would have enjoyed the idea that a man of their own age, the Greco-Roman sage Apollonius, the pagan contemporary and posthumous rival of Jesus, had travelled as far as Alexander and was welcomed by all he met.

Chapter 2

First Impressions

One globe is all too little for the youth of Pella [Alexander]; he chafes
uneasily within the narrow limits of the world, as though he were
cooped up within the rocks of Gyara or the diminutive Seriphos; but yet
when once he shall have entered the city fortified by the potter's art [the
mud brick walls of Babylon], a sarcophagus will suffice him!

–Juvenal[1]

Long before Rome came into contact with Parthia, her legions won a series
of victories over Macedonian successor states whose armies fought in the
style of Alexander. Macedonia itself was conquered in 168 BC by a Roman
general named Aemilius Paulus, who reveled in his triumph through the streets
of Rome with 2,000 carts of loot going before him and the last Macedonian King
Perseus (c. BC 212-166) and his family walking behind his royal chariot.[2]

Later, in the wars against Mithradates of Pontus and Tigran of Armenia, Roman
armies won significant victories over much larger 'Eastern' armies. The expectation of victory against Asiatic peoples set the stage for conflict with Rome's new
adversary, Parthia.

By 100 BC, Rome had usurped a good deal of Alexander's legacy. His kingdom
of Macedonia was a Roman province, as was Greece. Across the 'wine-dark' Aegean
Sea Rome was also in possession of western Anatolia. The Roman province of
Asia contained the riverbank battlefield of Granicus, where Alexander first bested
a Persian army in 334 BC. Rome also occupied Cilicia in the south of Anatolia,
through which Alexander had marched and near where he fought the Battle of Issus.

However, the Romans and Parthians weren't the only ones influenced by
Alexander. Aside from the several Macedonian successor kings who modelled
themselves on their founder's glory, there were rulers of Greek-influenced kingdoms who sought to attach themselves to the Alexander mystique, such as the
Epirote kings mentioned above. Among others there was Hannibal of Carthage.

Hannibal, who came near to conquering Rome, was said to have written books
in Greek.[3] Like Alexander, he enlisted scholars and scientists to accompany him on
campaign. Both men preferred battle on the open plains where their wide-ranging
cavalry could be most effective.[4] Hannibal had studied his hero and tried to learn
by his example.

Scipio Africanus, the Roman general who crushed Carthage and vanquished Hannibal was himself likened to Alexander by grateful Romans. Sextus Julius Frontinus was a Roman Senator and governor of Britain in AD 70. He wrote of Scipio:

> The story goes that Scipio Aemilianus used to eat bread offered him as he walked along on the march in the company of his friends.[5]

The same story was told about Alexander III of Macedon.

A mythology developed around Scipio's person just as it did around the Macedonian. In the mid-second century AD, Lucian would write a tract (*The Dialogues*) comparing Hannibal, Scipio and Alexander:

> Alexander of Macedon and Hannibal, quarrelling for precedence, submit the arbitration of their cause to Minos. Each recounts his exploits. Scipio, the conqueror of Carthage, intervenes, and pronounces in favour of Alexander, claiming the second place for himself, and assigning the third place to Hannibal.[6]

Another second-century writer, Aulus Gellius directly compared Scipio and Alexander by the virtuous treatment they each afforded to captive noble women.[7] Gellius also tells the story of a serpent (an attribute of Zeus/Jupiter) that found its way into the bedroom of Scipio's mother and the linking of this to his god-conceived birth. The story is similar to that of the god-serpent that visited Olympias, mother of Alexander.[8] This same 'son of god' story would later be told about Augustus. Some later Roman emperors would tell the same foundation story about themselves.

As late as the fourth century, writers would compare Scipio, Hannibal and Alexander to the current emperor, whoever that might be.[9] Scipio's modern biographer, HH Scullard recognized the importance of the *imitatio* and discusses ways in which the Romans made comparisons, real or imagined, between Scipio and Alexander:

> Parallels abounded: Alexander's siege of Tyre, Scipio's of New Carthage; Alexander's visit to Zeus Ammon and Scipio's relations with Jupiter; Alexander's magnanimity towards the mother and wife of the defeated Darius, and Scipio's towards the wife and children of the Spanish Indibilis (a pre-Roman chieftain). Other parallels were invented. The birth stories…leaping into the enemy's town, Alexander at Malli and Scipio at New Carthage; single combat between Alexander and Darius at Issus, and between Scipio and Hannibal at Zama.[10]

None of our surviving sources tell us that Scipio attempted to compare himself to Alexander or even sought the comparison. There were many others who gladly did that for him. He was the stuff of legend.

There was another foreign king even more obsessed with Alexander than Hannibal. King Mithridates VI (r. BC 135–63) was the ruler of Pontus, a partially Hellenized kingdom on the southeast coast of the Black Sea. Named for the Zoroastrian sun god, he was the fruit of Alexander's policy of mixing Greek and Persian blood and traditions.

On his father's side he claimed to be a descendant of the Achaemenid kings of Persia, while on his mother's side he boasted descent from Alexander and his Persian mistress Barsiné. He would be Rome's bitter enemy for forty years. Cicero himself called Mithridates 'the greatest monarch since Alexander'.[11]

Mithridates liked to remind his people of his connection to Alexander. Even the murder of his father when he was a boy of thirteen was compared to the murder of Philip II when Alexander was young.[12] Mithridates commissioned statues and minted coins depicting himself with his hero's long flowing hair, diadem, and slightly parted lips.[13]

Like Alexander with his horse Bucephalus, an apocryphal story grew around his taming a wild stallion when no one else could. As king, Mithridates adopted a style of dress that combined both Persian and Greek features, just as Alexander tried to do. He had among his treasures a purple cloak that Alexander was said to have owned and worn. The Graeco/Persian affectations that he used in imitation of his hero were meant to suggest to the Greeks, who were unhappy with Roman rule, an alliance of Persian and Greek cultures that would stand together against the western barbarians from far-off Italy.

In 99 BC, the powerful Roman warlord Gaius Marius (157-86 BC) travelled to Asia for a meeting with Mithridates and famously insulted him. Marius bluntly told him: 'King, either try to be stronger than the Romans or else keep quiet and do what you are told'.[14] It is a blunt and even rude comment that we should not take out of context. The Spanish historian Luis Pastor cites the first-century AD Greek writer Memnon of Heraclea (or Heracleia) Pontica who wrote that Alexander the Great sent a similarly worded message to the senate in Rome before he set off to Asia Minor in 334 BC:

> Then he describes how Alexander wrote to them (the Romans), when he crossed over to Asia, that they should either conquer others, if they were capable of ruling over them, or yield to those who were stronger than them; and the Roman sent him a crown, containing many talents of gold.[15]

Memnon's lost work comes to us 'second-hand' from the ninth-century Byzantine Patriarch, Photius. In a slightly different telling of the story, a version of the *Alexander Romance* has Alexander delivering such a message to the Carthaginians.[16]

The phrase has even older roots. In Thucydides work, the *History of the Peloponnesian War* the 'Melian Dialogue' explains Athens' posture toward a weaker city called Melos. Athenian ambassadors tell the Melians that 'the strong do as they can and the weak suffer what they must'.[17] Alexander, Marius, Memnon and Photius would all have known of Thucydides' phrase and its meaning.

Sulla: To the East

However it would be Marius' rival and enemy, Lucius Cornelius Sulla (138-78 BC), who would first fight the forces of Mithridates. In 96 BC, the Senate dispatched him to the kingdom of Cappadocia, which bordered Pontus, to put a pro-Roman claimant on the throne.[18] Sulla, with a single Roman legion and local allied conscripts defeated the Pontic army in Cappadocia the next year.

The easy victory of a single Roman legion over an Asian horde reinforced the belief that a smaller, more-disciplined Roman force could defeat larger oriental armies as Alexander had done. Later in 86 BC he would win two more victories against larger Pontic armies at the Battles of Chaeronea and Orchomenus.[19]

When Alexander was faced with an enormous host of enemies at the Battle of Issus, he 'contemplated the smallness of his own army; but he called to mind, at the same time, how much he had already done, and how powerful the people he had overthrown, with that very moderate force'.[20] The Romans, like Alexander, came to expect swift victories over the superior numbers that Eastern kingdoms could bring against them. They often achieved victory against long odds.

In the course of his campaign in Cappadocia, Sulla reached the eastern border of that kingdom at the Euphrates River. On the eastern bank lay the Persian kingdom of Parthia which was itself growing in power and influence. There he was amicably met by Parthian envoys who sought a peace treaty with Rome. It was the first official communication between the two growing states. Sulla met with a man named Orobazus, the envoy of the Parthian king, Mithradates II.

> During his stay on the banks of the Euphrates, there came to him Orobazus, a Parthian, ambassador from king Arsaces, as yet there having been no correspondence between the two nations. And this also we may lay to the account of Sulla's felicity, that he should be the first Roman, to whom the Parthians made address for alliance and friendship.[21]

Mithradates II (r. 123–87 BC) was one of the greatest Parthian kings. During his reign he expanded Parthian authority into northern Afghanistan in the east and into parts of Armenia in the west.[22] He received ambassadors from the Chinese Han dynasty and negotiated long-lasting and profitable trade pacts with them that led to commerce along the famous 'Silk Road'. Toward the end of his reign however, he began to lose territory to the powerful king of Armenia, Tigran the Great (r. 96–60 BC).

According to Plutarch, Sulla set up three chairs for this first-ever meeting with the Parthians. The first chair was for the Cappadocian king, the second chair for the Parthian ambassador and the third, the one in the middle, for himself. We are reminded of the Camp David accords. A picture of that event shows American President Jimmy Carter standing between Israeli Prime Minister Menachem Begin and Egyptian President Anwar Sadat.

Sulla arranged the chairs to signify that the other two were acknowledging the supremacy of Rome. This arrangement did not sit well with the Parthian king when he heard about it and poor Orobazus was said to have been executed upon his return home.

Sulla, during his time the most powerful man in Rome, appears consciously to have invited comparisons of himself and Alexander. A bust of him now in the Glyptothek Museum in Munich depicts him with his head tilted to the right, his lips slightly parted and an unruly shock of wavy hair, all signs of the imitation of Alexander.

Returning to Rome from the east in 83 BC, Sulla brought with him a number of Macedonian soldiers who would help him to take power as dictator. The power of Macedonia was not yet spent.[23]

The next Roman general with Alexandrian ambitions was Lucius Licinius Lucullus (118–78 BC). When Sulla retired from public life he handpicked his lieutenant Lucullus to be his successor. Lucullus took up the Roman standard in the war against Mithridates of Pontus and became the new Roman heir to Alexander. Lucullus was the first Roman general to reach the Danube, just as Alexander was the first Macedonian general to do so.[24]

Beginning in 74 BC, his disciplined but disaffected legions defeated much larger armies fielded first by Mithridates and then Tigran of Armenia. Lucullus occupied most of Pontus and Armenia by BC 69 but the two kings were able to elude him. He feared they might seek the backing of a new Parthian king who at this time was either Phraates II or III (r. 68–57 BC).[25]

Lucullus courted Phraates as an ally but the Parthian had no intention of joining the war on either side. Perhaps because he had been on the throne for less than a year, Phraates was more concerned with internal issues than with foreign wars. Lucullus was furious at Parthian neutrality. Plutarch wrote that he resolved to invade Parthia. But when he summoned two of his unruly legions, which were on garrison duty in Pontus, to join him for the new campaign season, they refused to come. Many of them were near the end of their very long enlistment period in the army and just wanted to go home.[26]

Distant, aloof and imperious, Lucullus had lost touch with his army. Their mutiny put an end to his plans of Parthian conquest. Like Alexander in India, his troops refused to follow him any further to the east. British historian Arthur Keaveney, second guessing Plutarch, doesn't believe that Lucullus ever seriously considered invading Parthia. With the Mithridatic wars still unfinished and public opinion in Rome running against him, he would have stretched himself too thin with a new war even if he commanded the confidence of his army.[27]

By 67 BC the Senate had relieved Lucullus of his command and appointed Pompey to prosecute the war to its conclusion. Lucullus grudgingly retired to practice his epicurean fancies. He returned to Rome a fabulously wealthy man from the plunder he extracted from his conquests. He spent his money, living and eating well, while building gardens, estates and libraries. He shared much of it with the Roman public.

Plutarch accused him of setting a table like a Persian and reported that he was sometimes called 'Xerxes in a Toga'.[28] This could be a hint that Lucullus may have been influenced by the same Eastern practices that beguiled Alexander.

Julian, in *The Caesars*, has Alexander belittling Caesar's defeat of Pompey by pointing out that it was Lucullus who had won the victories that Pompey claimed: 'Armenia and the neighbouring provinces were conquered by Lucullus, yet for those also Pompey triumphed'.[29] Plutarch also credits Lucullus with victories over Mithridates and Tigran for which Pompey would reap the harvest.[30]

Pompey: The New Alexander

> As concerning all the titles and victorious triumphs of Pompey the Great, wherein he was equal in renown and glory, not only to the acts of Alexander the Great, but also of Hercules in a manner, and god Bacchus: if I should make mention thereof in this place, it would credit not to the honour only of that one man, but also to the grandeur and majesty of the Roman Empire.
>
> –Pliny the Elder[31]

No Roman was more smitten with the idea of Alexander and his conquests than Gnaeus Pompeius, known to us through Shakespeare's pen as 'Pompey'. Even as a child, Pompey was said to resemble Alexander. His boyish good looks and the hair sprouting from the forehead into leonine curls which flowed from a cowlick at the forehead, or what the Greeks called an *anastole*, were said to be just like Alexander.[32]

There was also the way his hair lifted from the forehead and the graceful contours of his face around the eyes that produced a resemblance to portraits of Alexander the Great.[33]

Professor Sarolta Takács of Rutgers, suggests that Mithridates of Pontus may have 'spurred' Pompey's imitation of Alexander, but this is unlikely as the comparisons from his childhood would have already informed his emulation of the Macedonian hero.[34]

Pompey's father, Gnaeus Pompeius Strabo, was, like Alexander's father Philip, if not a king then certainly a leader of men. A wealthy and powerful general, he held his command independent of the Roman Senate. Also like Philip, Strabo died (87 BC) when his son was only eighteen years old. Both the young Alexander and Pompey assumed command of their father's lands, army and legacy. Both men far outshone their father in their accomplishments.

Operating from his inherited estates in Picenum along the eastern coast of Italy, Pompey raised a new army from his father's clients and prepared it for the Roman civil war between the followers of Marius and Sulla. Pompey backed Sulla.

The Marians, who controlled the city of Rome at that time, sent three separate armies against him. Pompey did not wait for them to combine but attacked the one closest to him. Leading the cavalry charge personally, Pompey went directly for the leader of the Marian army and killed him.[35] The enemy force was routed and Pompey had his first victory. He then took on the other two Marian armies and defeated them as well.

This battle with no name is significant because the strategy of personally attacking straight at the enemy commander was the same that Alexander had used to defeat Darius III.[36] Pompey demonstrated not only sound military judgment in fighting his enemies before they could combine but also that he had studied the battles of Alexander. Before the end of the civil war in Italy he would command eight legions for Sulla. He was no more than twenty-three years old.

Sulla was victorious and Rome was his. To keep his young protégé busy he tasked Pompey with snuffing out the last vestiges of the Marian cause, first in Sicily in 82 BC and then in Carthage in 81. His brilliant victories earned him a triumph that not even a resentful Sulla could prevent.

Pompey was thought too young for the uniquely Roman victory parade and a jealous Sulla at first denied his request. Pompey then uttered a defiant reply to the older man: 'More people worship the rising than the setting sun'. Sulla got the point and Pompey got his triumph.[37] It also earned him the name 'Magnus' (the Great) which Sulla sarcastically bestowed on him, mocking his young protégé for his pretensions to Alexandrian greatness.[38] Pompey liked the comparison to Alexander and later encouraged the use of the honorific.

After the death of Sulla in 78 BC, Pompey would win further victories for Rome in Spain. Later he conducted mopping up operations against the slave rebellion of Spartacus. Pompey then took credit for putting down the rebellion which had already been mostly extinguished by the wealthy Senator Marcus Crassus.[39]

Early in 67 BC, Pompey was given command of the war against the pirates that infested the Mediterranean Sea. He replaced the previous commander who had mishandled the campaign and died in battle. That man was Marcus Antonius Creticus, the father of Mark Antony.

His commission extended from the Atlantic Ocean to Phoenicia. In just three months he systematically planned and executed a coordinated military operation that ranged over the length and breadth of the Mediterranean Sea and into the Black Sea.

By a combination of overwhelming power and generous leniency (*clementia*) toward the captured pirates and their families, Pompey was able to pacify them and befriend them at the same time. It was not the way his mentor Sulla or his rival Crassus would have gone about it. Both of them preferred brute force.[40] However, it is the way that Alexander often treated a defeated enemy.[41] This imitation of Alexander was purposeful and his contemporaries understood it that way as in this fragment from the Roman historian Sallust:

> From his earliest youth, Pompeius had been persuaded by the flattery of his supporters to believe that he was the equal of King Alexander. Therefore he tried to rival Alexander's achievements and plans.[42]

Meanwhile, Lucullus was being sacked by the Senate. With the Roman army in the east paralyzed by mutiny, Mithradates and Tigran of Armenia went on the offensive, reclaiming Pontus and Cappodocia which had been laboriously won by Lucullus. The conscript fathers of the Senate turned to Pompey who then began a new campaign in the east.

While the ancient sources are not explicit, Professor David F Graf makes the case that Pompey, like Alexander (and Hannibal), took scholars and scientists on campaign with him including the Greek intellectual Theophanes of Mytilene, who wrote a book (now lost) about Pompey's exploits on campaign in the manner of Callisthenes, a writer at the court of Alexander.[43] That Pompey would surround himself with learned men while on campaign is not surprising in a man who strove to imitate Alexander.

As Pompey advanced on King Mithradates his well-advertised policy of clemency toward the pirates began to pay dividends in the form of deserters who fled the king's cause.[44] By forced marches, Pompey was able to surprise and crush Mithradates' army with an unexpected night attack.

Neither Sulla nor Lucullus had fought at night and the king did not expect it. Alexander did not like to fight at night but often led night marches.[45] Fear of a night attack caused Darius III to keep his men standing on their arms on high alert throughout the night before the Battle of Gaugamela in BC 331 to guard against it.[46]

His army crushed, Mithridates fled first to Armenia and then to the Kingdom of Bosporus in the Crimea where he was still the nominal ruler. After fighting his way through a Roman line with 800 horsemen, Mithridates was left with but three companions. One of these was Hypsicrateia, one of the king's mistresses, who 'always displayed a right manly spirit'. According to Plutarch she was 'mounted and accoutered like a Persian'.[47]

Pompey turned his attention to Armenia. He made common cause with Parthia in an alliance that allowed the Parthians, in return for their support, a slice of Armenian territory known as Gordyene that had once been theirs. Tigran, overwhelmed by enemies, submitted to the Roman. Pompey graciously restored his throne to him but not without cost.

It was standard imperial policy in the ancient world to leave defeated native rulers in power as long as they were loyal, paid their taxes and provided soldiers. Alexander certainly practised this policy.[48] Just so, Pompey left old King Tigran on his throne to rule over a much-diminished Armenia. He was in effect now a Roman client king. Pompey also required of him six thousand talents of silver as war reparations.[49]

Without going after Mithridates directly, Pompey went after the three little Caucasus kingdoms of Albania (today's Azerbaijan), Iberia (eastern Georgia) and Colchis (western Georgia) which had supported him.

When he had defeated the final and eastern-most kingdom, Pompey was anxious to see the Caspian Sea, which was thought by some to have been a part of the great outer Ocean that surrounded the earth. Alexander had reached the Ocean when he was in India and the pull to do the same must have been strong. Pompey was only a three-day march from the Caspian shores before deciding against it. Pliny the Elder however, informs us that at least some of Pompey's men did make the journey to that sea and returned to tell Pompey of it:

> Alexander the Great has left it stated that the water of this sea is fresh, and M Varro informs us that some of it, of a similar character, was brought to Pompey, when holding the chief command in the Mithridatic war in its vicinity.[50]

At the same time that M Varro wrote of Pompey and the water in the Caspian Sea, Pliny suggests that Pompey was informed that India was but a short journey further on through Bactria and that the products of that country might be easily transported to Pontus, presumably bypassing the Parthians.[51]

While Pompey was in winter camp, Phraates of Parthia sent ambassadors to meet with him. The Parthian king did not like Pompey's aggressive activities beyond Armenia and sent a list of grievances against his erstwhile ally. But the Roman no longer needed Phraates. With Mithridates de-fanged and Armenia a client kingdom, the new enemy was looking more and more like Parthia itself.

As it was, Pompey had his own demands. He insisted that Parthia give up its newly won kingdom of Gordyene and return it to Armenia. Rubbing salt in the wounds, Pompey sent the king a short letter that omitted his favourite title 'King of Kings':

> When he [Pompey] wrote to the King of Parthia, he would not conde-
> scend, as others used to do, in the superscription of his letter, to give him
> his title of king of kings.[52]

Pompey then sent his legate L Afranius with a force sufficient to retrieve Gordyene by force if necessary. After securing Gordyene without a fight, Afranius insulted the Parthians further by marching through their territory in the northern Mesopotamian plains to reach the Mediterranean coast of Syria.

But Pompey stepped back from war with Parthia. Cassius Dio tells us that 'he feared the forces of the Parthian and dreaded the uncertain issue of events, and so did not undertake this war [against Parthia], though many urged him to do so.'[53] It is not likely that the confident Pompey feared the Parthians. It is more likely that Dio, who was a court favorite of the Persian-fighting Severan dynasty, thought less of Pompey for not fighting them. Writing thus would please his masters.

Instead of seeking a new enemy, Pompey reduced the remaining Anatolian strongholds of Mithridates. One of these was a fortress city which was surrendered by a woman named Stratonice, one of the king's favourite mistresses. The fortresses of the king held many concubines (not to mention treasure). Pompey treated the women kindly and did not molest them. They received the same consideration and respect that Alexander bestowed on Darius' harem.[54]

In the spring of 64 BC, Pompey left his winter headquarters on the Black Sea and marched to Syria, the last semi-independent vestige of the once-mighty Seleucid Empire, and a sorry remnant of Alexander's conquests. On his way to the Syrian city of Antioch, Pompey probably passed over the battlefield at Issus where Alexander defeated Darius 270 years before. It must have been a memorable scene. Unfortunately, his thoughts about crossing the famous field have not survived.

Pompey marched further south, through Palestine, to invade the territory of the Nabatean Arabs whose kingdom adjoined the Red Sea, another opening to the outer Ocean. While in camp near Petra, he received news that Mithridates of Pontus was dead.[55] His hosts in the Crimea had tired of their former king and sought favour with the Romans. His assassination was assured.

When the body of the king was sent to Pompey he treated it with the same respect that Alexander had shown the body of Darius III. Of all Rome's enemies, Mithridates was the only one who was accorded a regal burial near the tombs of his ancestors. Pompey was consciously making the comparison between himself and Alexander and between the dead king of Pontus and Darius III.[56]

In 61 BC, all of Rome turned out for the most magnificent triumph that the city had ever seen. The procession of riches, loot, captured soldiers, princes and dignitaries took two days to wind through the city.[57] It included wagons loaded with captured weapons and treasure, defeated enemy soldiers, and exotic plants and animals; 'after them all came one huge one, decked out in costly fashion and bearing an inscription stating that it was a trophy of the inhabited world'.[58] In the harbour, two hundred captured pirate ships swayed at anchor. It was another reminder that the whole world belonged to Rome.

Pompey rode in a captured, jewel-encrusted chariot and wore a most unique treasure captured from Mithridates; the purple cloak that was said to have belonged to Alexander the Great. However with a cloak of such age, some, such as Appian, were sceptical:

> These were the facts recorded on the inscription. Pompey himself was borne in a chariot studded with gems, wearing, it was said, a cloak of Alexander the Great, if anyone can believe that.[59]

The historian Diodorus Siculus, a contemporary and friend of Pompey, gushed that he had 'extended the frontiers of empire to the frontiers of the earth'.[60] Florus, echoing Roman sentiment in the second century, wrote that:

> with the exception of the Parthians, who preferred to make a treaty, and the Indians, who as yet knew nothing of us, all Asia between the Red and Caspian Seas and the Ocean was in our power, conquered or overawed by the arms of Pompeius.[61]

The magnificent triumph was the highpoint of Pompey's career. For the next thirteen years of his life he would be visited by bitter disappointment or empty victories. Plutarch speculated that he would have been much better off had he died at the height of his powers as Alexander did:

> How happy it would have been for Pompey to have ended his life at this point, up to which he had enjoyed the good fortune of Alexander; for the future brought him only success that made him hateful and failure that was irreparable.[62]

Pompey had won victories for Rome on three continents. His army and navy were victorious from the Atlantic Ocean to the Caspian Sea. He had crossed the Alps in imitation of Hannibal and cleared the entire Mediterranean Sea of pirates. He had travelled a greater distance than Alexander in his conquests and deserves the comparison. To make sure that everyone knew of his accomplishments, Pompey set up a tablet with an inscription of his deeds. It read:

> Pompey the Great…, *Imperator*, having liberated the seacoast of the inhabited world and all islands this side of the Ocean from the war with the pirates—being likewise the man who delivered from the siege the kingdom of [Cappadocia], Galatia, and the lands and provinces lying beyond, Asia, and Bithynia; who gave protection to Paphlagonia and Pontus, Armenia and Achaia, as well as Iberia, Colchis, Mesopotamia, Sophene, and Gordyene; brought into submission Darius king of the Medes, Artoles king of the Iberians, Aristobulus king of the Jews, Aretas king of the Nabataean Arabs, Syria bordering on Cilicia, Judaea, Arabia, the province of Cyrene, the Achaeans, the Iozygi, the Soani, the Heniochi, and the other tribes along the seacoast between Colchis and the Maeotic Sea, with their kings, nine in number, and all the nations that dwell between the [Black Sea and the Red Sea]; extended the frontiers of the Empire to the limits of the earth; and secured and in some cases increased the revenues of the Roman people—he, by confiscation of the statues and the images set up to the gods, as well as other valuables taken from the enemy, has dedicated to the goddess twelve thousand and sixty pieces of gold and three hundred and seven talents of silver.[63]

Though the tablet was redundant in places and inaccurate in others, the scale of his accomplishments is astounding. Yet, as mentioned above, some saw Pompey's deeds as having been the work of others. In the fourth century, Julian, in his satire *The Caesars*, had Alexander himself belittle the accomplishments of Pompey: 'Pompeius [Pompey] who though he was the idol of his countrymen was in fact wholly insignificant'.[64]

In Spain, Pompey was said to be dependent upon the work of another general. In Italy he took credit for ending the slave revolt of Spartacus which Crassus had already crushed and in the east he reaped the harvest that was sown by Lucullus.[65] When Cato the Younger wanted to denigrate the victories of Pompey in his war against Mithridates he said that Pompey's battles had been fought against *muliercu-lae* (mere women).

Peter Green notes that Cato knew his history. For that statement was origi-nally made by Alexander of Epirus, while fighting in Italy, about his brother-in-law Alexander the Great, who was fighting Persian armies of 'mere women'.[66]

Pompey's contemporary, the poet Catullus, went further. He accused Pompey of plundering the lands he conquered.[67] Catullus was quite naive. Pompey was not the first nor the last Roman general to plunder the lands that he subdued.

While Pompey was obsessed by comparison to Alexander, one of his legates, who was a minor republican general, also had Alexandrian pretensions. His name was Aulus Gabinius (d. 49/8 BC). During the war with Mithridates he was dispatched to the Tigris River. Though we don't know the route of his march or his purpose, if it was not a diplomatic mission then, as far as the Parthians were concerned, this was a provocative act. Later, as Pompey's appointed governor of Syria (BC 57-55), Gabinius took the legions under his command briefly across the Euphrates River into Parthian territory with the goal of backing one Parthian prince against a brother in a dynastic dispute. He did not get far before being recalled and ordered to march to Egypt instead, to deal with dynastic matters there.[68]

This was two years before Crassus led his doomed expedition into Parthia for the same purpose. It was the first time that Rome would attempt to interfere in Parthian (and later Sasanian) succession. Incidentally, in Gabinius' command was a young cavalry captain named Marcus Antonius, who is known to us (again through Shakespeare) as Mark Antony.[69]

There is a bust of Gabinius in the *Museo Archeologico Nazionale* of Naples, which was recovered from the volcanic ash of Herculaneum, which depicts him with a most unusual hairstyle for a Roman. He is sporting dreadlocks which he probably acquired in Egypt. His lips are set slightly apart in the Alexandrian fashion.

Alexander was famed for his curly hair that flowed from the cowlick on his forehead. Most of his coins and statues prominently feature his distinctive hair style. It is likely that Gabinius wanted to distinguish himself by his own unique look. By governing Syria, crossing the Euphrates and then imposing his will upon Egypt, even this minor general could claim the mantle of Alexander.

Summary

In this first phase of the Roman-Parthian relationship the two sides came into contact for the first time. As Rome expanded to the east and Parthia to the west the meeting was inevitable. As long as they had mutual Seleucid and Armenian enemies between them they could be allies working together against common foes.

However, once they were neighbours there was inevitable friction. Parthia tried to impose its will upon Armenia and Seleucid Syria while Pompey in turn would send his legates into Parthian territory without asking permission of their king.

The ease with which Rome trespassed on Parthian land and their lack of response would lead the Romans to think that they, like the Macedonians of old, would have no trouble in subduing the land of the Persians as Alexander had done.

Alexander was both an inspiration for Romans as they moved eastward and a convenient foil for patriots like Livy who believed that Roman arms were superior to that of the Macedonian. While Roman opinion favoured the idea that they could have defeated Alexander and his army, that same belief informed them of the ease which Eastern enemies, once conquered by Alexander, could in turn be defeated by Rome. Both the Roman people and their army grossly underestimated the power of Parthia, to their peril.

Chapter 3

Parthia Triumphant: Crassus and Antony

Crassus: In the footsteps of Alexander

> Those who praise Alexander's enterprise and blame that of Crassus,
> judge of the beginning unfairly by the results.
>
> –Plutarch[1]

R ome had proven herself the master of the Mediterranean Sea and all the people round about. There was only one enemy of note that threatened Roman borders: Parthia. Rome's generals had every reason to believe that they would be the masters of the Parthians also.

Their conviction stemmed from their own victories over Macedonian armies whose ancestors had overrun Achaemenid Persia with Alexander. Roman opinion was also informed by victories over Eastern armies of vastly superior size, giving them an unwarranted confidence that they could do no less than the Macedonian conqueror. Because of Alexander's success, a Roman war with Parthia was inevitable.

Plutarch alerts us (above) that there were those in Rome who compared the campaign of Marcus Licinius Crassus (115-53 BC) to that of Alexander. As we shall see, Crassus had reason to think that he was following in the Macedonian's footsteps.

While Pompey, Caesar and Crassus allied themselves in the senate dominating First Triumvirate, there was a time of civil unrest in Parthia. King Phraates was assassinated by his own sons, Orodes II (r. 57–37 BC) and Mithradates III (r. 57–54 BC). The brothers then fought each other for control of the Parthian realm. The chaotic situation was not unlike the civil strife in Persia when Darius III came to the Persian throne in 336 BC.[2] Darius had not fully consolidated his power by the time that Alexander attacked.

Orodes was still trying to consolidate his own power. In the ensuing civil chaos, in which Gabinius was momentarily embroiled, only a weak response could be made to any Roman threat. Orodes was wary of Rome's increasing insults to his territory, especially the incursions of Afranius and Gabinius.

In Rome, meanwhile, Crassus was named proconsul governor of Syria to replace Gabinius in 54 BC. He would have seven legions (approximately 35,000 infantry) under his command as well as 4,000 cavalry and 4,000 auxiliaries, roughly the same number of men that Alexander commanded when he began his invasion of Persia.[3]

The Byzantine writer Zosimus implausibly hints at a Parthian threat, with Rome merely making a defensive response: 'when the Parthians bestirred themselves the senate selected Crassus general with supreme power'.[4] Clearly, however, Crassus would be the aggressor.

Plutarch gives us a hint about what was on the mind of Crassus as he took up his new post in Syria:

> he would not consider Syria nor even Parthia as the boundaries of his success, but thought to make the campaigns of Lucullus against Tigranes and those of Pompey against Mithradates seem mere child's play, and flew on the wings of his hopes as far as Bactria and India and the Outer Sea.[5]

Plutarch, in hindsight, painted a picture of Crassus wanting to be the new Alexander. He hoped to surpass all of the other great Roman generals of the republic especially his rival and fellow triumvir, Pompey. Up until that time, it was Pompey who was regarded as the Roman heir to Alexander's glory.

For Crassus the strategic picture was bright. In addition to his own force, he counted on support from allied Armenia and local Arab tribes. The chaos in Parthia boded well too, with Mithradates III still fighting his brother Orodes for the Parthian throne. Mithradates held southern Mesopotamia and was impatiently waiting for Crassus to reinforce him.

On reaching Syria, Crassus at once crossed the Euphrates and captured some small towns in northern Mesopotamia. These towns, Ichnae, Nicephorium and Carrhae, were largely populated by Greeks. Founded by Alexander or his successors, the towns' Graeco-Macedonian inhabitants, for the most part, welcomed Crassus. But it was late in the season. Rather than continue his march to support Mithradates in the major cities of Seleucia, Ctesiphon and Babylon, Crassus returned to Syria for the winter.[6]

While Orodes prepared for a war, Crassus set about funding his by confiscating the wealth of Syria including all the gold he could find in the Temple of Jerusalem.[7] While amassing a significant treasury, he was visited by the new client king of Armenia, King Artavasdes II (53–34 BC), a son of Tigran the Great. Artavasdes insisted that Crassus march through the hills of Armenia which would allow him relative safety against Parthian cavalry while protecting Armenia. Crassus rebuffed him so he returned to his own country to await events.[8]

From Syria there were three routes that Crassus could take to invade Parthia. He had already rejected the route through Armenia that the Seleucid king, Antiochus

III, had used successfully to subdue Parthia. The second was the southern route along the eastern bank of the Euphrates River into southern Mesopotamia or Babylonia. This would allow him to be resupplied and enjoy protected communications by boats on the river. The river would also protect his right flank. This route had been used by the famed 'Ten Thousand' Greek mercenaries in 401 BC.[9]

Babylon seems to have been Crassus' first destination. While still in Antioch a Parthian ambassador named Vagises asked him his intentions; Crassus replied that he would give him an answer in Seleucia, the major city in Babylonia and the place where Mithradates III awaited him.[10]

The third route was across northern Mesopotamia and then across the Tigris River before turning southward to Babylon and Seleucia as Alexander had done. That is what Crassus decided to do. He would follow in the footsteps of his hero.

His immediate goal was to engage in a climactic battle with the Parthians in imitation of Alexander. In many ways Crassus was already in a better position than Alexander had been. The Macedonians, starting from Greece, had to overcome Anatolia, the Levant and Egypt before turning their attention to Mesopotamia.

For Crassus, all of that territory, including the battlefields of Granicus and Issus, was already in Roman hands (Egypt being a compliant client kingdom deeply in debt to Roman bankers). Crassus had approximately the same size army as Alexander and was fortified by the prevailing attitudes that Roman legionaries were superior to Asiatic warriors.

Despite Plutarch's insistence on a duplicitous Arab who lulled him into this course of action, Crassus' modern biographer, Gareth Sampson, sees this route as his best option.[11] Yet Sampson does not notice that this was the course that Alexander had taken.[12] Alexander's ancient biographer, Arrian, explains why he chose to invade Persia through northern Mesopotamia. It probably influenced Crassus' own decision:

> When he [Alexander] started from the Euphrates he did not march to Babylon by the direct road; because by going the other route he found all things easier for the march of his army, and it was also possible to obtain fodder for the horses and provisions for the men from the country. Besides this, the heat was not so scorching on the indirect route.[13]

Crassus crossed the Euphrates at Zeugma where Dio and Florus say that Alexander had crossed.[14] He then headed into the interior of Mesopotamia following the lead of Alexander.

To meet the Macedonians, King Darius III had sent between 3,000 and 6,000 cavalrymen under his able general, Mazaeus, to harass Alexander when he crossed the Euphrates but they fled at his approach and did not challenge him to battle.[15]

Crassus now faced just such a cavalry detachment which, like Mazaeus, fled before him. Perhaps he felt that he too had brushed them aside. For Crassus the victory of Alexander was playing out for him in the same way.

Arrian, Curtius and Frontinus agree that Alexander rushed across Mesopotamia, 'for fear that Darius might make for the interior of his kingdom and that it might be necessary to follow him through places altogether deserted and without supplies'.[16] Yet modern historians like Richard Stoneman and Robin Lane Fox want to second guess them. They write that some ancient dating methods suggest that Alexander did not hurry but took several weeks to cross Mesopotamia from the Euphrates to the Tigris River.[17]

Yet Alexander had every reason to bring Darius to an early battle.[18] Perhaps NGL Hammond and AB Bosworth are more accurate when they suggest a slow march across Mesopotamia until Alexander learned (erroneously) that Darius planned to hold the banks of the Tigris against him. At that point he advanced with all deliberate speed.[19]

Like Alexander, Crassus hurried his soldiers along into Mesopotamia. Rather than camp at the Belikh River (more of a stream) to rest his men and horses, he rushed them forward in order to come to grips with the enemy. He was following the Macedonian's strategy and expected the same results.

Crassus might have thought that the Parthians would not face him until he crossed the Tigris River. But the Parthians did not behave or fight as Darius' Persians did. They were setting a trap.[20] Worse, even as Crassus marched, the strategic situation was changing. The Parthian pretender Mithradates had been defeated and killed by forces loyal to Orodes in southern Mesopotamia. Arab allies were proving untrustworthy and Orodes himself was over-running hapless Armenia. Crassus had run out of friends.

We have two major sources for Crassus and the battle at Carrhae: Dio and Plutarch. Sampson dismisses Dio out of hand and prefers to lean on Plutarch's more even-handed telling of the tale.[21] Near Carrhae the Parthian commander, Surenas (more likely his title than his name), unleashed a force of 9,000 light and 1,000 heavy cavalry on Crassus' much larger Roman infantry force. Surenas' horsemen were armed with the powerful reflex composite bow which had a longer lethal range than the bows used by the Romans.[22]

The Parthians galloped in, out of range of Roman arrows and loosed their own which easily pierced Roman shields and armour. Even worse, in retreat the Parthian bowmen would turn on their mounts and fire backwards. This tactic was known as 'the Parthian shot' and would strike fear into Roman hearts for generations. The term would enter the English language as 'the parting shot'. In addition they had a reliable supply of extra arrows packed into the battle by camel caravan, proof of at least a rudimentary logistics organization. The Parthians refused close combat, the very strength of the Romans.

Crassus ordered his cavalry, commanded by his son Publius, to sally against them. This force, including Publius, was led into a trap, surrounded and slaughtered. His severed head was galloped up to the Roman lines and thrown in to their midst. His father lost heart. That night, while the Parthians slept, the Romans fled in disordered haste.[23]

Of the 40,000 Romans who marched into Mesopotamia, only 10,000 made it back to Syria. All the rest were killed or taken prisoner. Crassus was among the dead. He was captured during negotiations and stabbed to death. His attempted imitation of Alexander failed him utterly.

The fate of the 10,000 Roman prisoners has been discussed by ancient and modern historians. According to Pliny, some of these Romans may have been used by the Parthians to guard their northeastern frontier at Margiana in Sogdiana (a culturally Iranian kingdom north of Bactria). He wrote that Margiana was 'the place to which the Roman prisoners taken in the disaster of Crassus were brought'.[24] Significantly, Sogdiana had once been conquered by Alexander the Great.

While Crassus was being overrun, King Orodes took a second Parthian army into Armenia to deal with King Artavasdes who greeted the invader with forced hospitality. The two were watching the Euripides play *The Bacchae* (mentioned above) when Crassus' severed head was delivered on stage and used as a prop in the play.[25] Orodes and Artavasdes sealed their alliance with marriage and Rome lost not only an army but an allied kingdom. The first Roman military encounter with Parthia was a resounding Parthian victory that would be remembered for centuries. According to Zosimus who lived in the late fifth and early sixth centuries:

> He [Crassus] came to blows with the Persians and, having been captured
> in the battle and killed by them, bequeathed the Romans ignominy that
> has lasted to this day.[26]

Following their victory at Carrhae, the vengeful Parthian warriors raided deep into Syria and even Cilicia (50 BC). In Cilicia they were met by the proconsul governor of the province, Marcus Tullius Cicero. More famous for talking than fighting, Cicero nonetheless won some victories against the bands of Parthian marauders. He was even acclaimed *imperator* by his army. One night he found himself camped near the battlefield of Issus and, writing to his friend Atticus, obliquely compared himself to Alexander:

> For a few days we encamped near Issus in the very spot where Alexander,
> a considerably better general than either you or I, pitched his camp
> against Darius. There we stayed five days.[27]

In Rome, Pompey thought that he would have to be the one to avenge Crassus and wrote to Cicero to say so, temporarily reviving his hopes of foreign conquest in the East.[28] Instead Pompey's attention turned to the growing rivalry with Julius Caesar. Their conflict was all consuming and at length it consumed Pompey.

Julius Caesar: Persian Dreams

> In the military field he [Caesar] planned…an attack on Parthia by way of Lesser Armenia; but decided not to risk a pitched battle until he had familiarized himself with Parthian tactics. All these schemes were cancelled by his assassination.
>
> —Suetonius[29]

The humiliation that Rome felt at the defeat and death of Crassus weighed heavily on the collective consciousness of the people. The captured men and their legionary standards were a public humiliation. Unfortunately revenge had to wait. With the death of Crassus and the recent death of Caesar's daughter, who had been married to Pompey, there existed no more reason for Caesar and Pompey to abide one another. Rome convulsed with a new civil war.

Caesar, too, would have his turn of wanting to be the new Alexander. At the beginning of his career, when he was about the same age as Alexander when he died, Caesar served his quaestorship in Gades (Cadiz), Spain. Here, in 69 BC, our sources tell us he saw a statue of Alexander (or read an account of him) and lamented, 'it is a matter for sorrow that while Alexander, at my age, was already king of so many peoples, I have as yet achieved no brilliant success'.[30]

Peter Green recounts the claims of Suetonius and Dio that this event was tied in with an Oedipal dream that Caesar had.[31] But there is another possible explanation as to Caesar's feelings. Gades was an auspicious place for Caesar to have this sad revelation. The city fronts not the Mediterranean but the Atlantic, the outer Ocean that, it was believed, surrounded all land. Curtius referred to the city as 'Gades on the Ocean'.[32] Alexander had traveled the enormous distance to India and the outer Ocean on the other side of the world. That to Caesar was 'a brilliant success'. The fact that Caesar was a minor administrator, and not the conqueror, of Gades would have added to his 'lament'.

The Ocean continued to be a theme for Caesar during his Gallic campaign. He may have thought (and wanted Romans to think) that reaching the Ocean (the French Atlantic coast) equalled the feats of Alexander. Only a generation or two after Caesar, Nicolaus of Damascus, who was a tutor to the children of Antony and Cleopatra before befriending Herod the Great and then Augustus, likened Caesar's conquests to Alexander in that both men pushed their conquests as far as the Ocean.[33] The modern Dutch historian Jona Lendering, examining Caesar's words, notes that 'Caesar never ceases to remind his audience of the country he was fighting in. The Ocean shores are often mentioned, even when there is no need to'.[34]

Yet Caesar aspired to be greater than Alexander. This may have been part of the reason he decided to sail into the unknown Ocean and invade Britain. When he made his twin raids on Britain he surpassed Alexander by venturing out upon the Ocean. Plutarch said of him: 'he was the first to launch a fleet upon the western Ocean and to sail through the Atlantic sea carrying an army to wage war'.[35] Ovid exults, inaccurately, that he 'conquered the sea-going Britons'.[36]

British historian Edward Conybeare notes that while Cicero belittled this achievement, 'this was far from being the view taken by the Roman in the street. To the people Caesar's exploit was like those of the gods and heroes of old; Hercules and Bacchus had done less, for neither had passed the Ocean'.[37] Though Conybeare does not include Alexander, the association of these two gods would have made it clear to the people that Caesar had exceeded him as well.

The contemporary poet Catullus, who focused the attention of his pen mostly on his lady love, also belittles Caesar's achievements yet still admits that he set foot on 'that farthest island of the west', Britain.[38]

Gaul, however, was Caesar's Persia, the source of his wealth, power and fame. For control of the empire though, he would have to defeat Pompey and the republicans that he reluctantly championed.

When Pompey lost crucial battles to Caesar he was desperate. In a last-ditch bid for victory he sent representatives to the court of King Orodes, the man who had held Crassus' head in his hands, to ask for Parthian help against Caesar. The Roman poet Marcus Lucannus, or Lucan (AD 39-65), speculated on Pompey's tortured state of mind:

> Would that my lot forced me not thus to trust that savage race of Arsaces! Yet now their emulous fate contends with Roman destinies: the gods smile favouring on their nation.
>
> Parthian hosts shall fight the civil wars of Rome, and share her ills, and fall enfeebled. When the arms of Caesar meet with Parthian in the fray, Then must kind Fortune vindicate my lot or Crassus be avenged.[39]

A little further in the text, Lucan reveals himself to be at least sympathetic to Pompey and his cause: 'If the Parthians conquer for Pompey's sake, Rome will welcome her conqueror'.[40]

When Orodes demanded Syria in return for his assistance, Pompey, to his credit, declined. His integrity sealed his fate. He was forced to flee to Egypt.

Curiously, during Caesar's war with Pompey we have hints that he adopted at least some Parthian battle tactics. Cicero snidely remarked to his friend Atticus, 'Caesar retreats like the Parthians'.[41]

At the end of the civil war in 48 BC, after Caesar defeated Pompey at Pharsalus, he crossed to Asia Minor and, according to Lucan writing a century later, visited the ruins of ancient Troy as Alexander had once done.[42] Strabo tells us of a Caesar who was:

> filled with youthful enthusiasm to help the Ilians [people of Troy] both because he admired Alexander and because he possessed clearer evidence of his kinship with the Ilians.[43]

From there he chased his rival, the doomed Pompey, to Alexandria, only to find him already dead. One of Pompey's assassins was Lucius Septimius who had served with him in the war against the pirates and probably against Mithradates too. He then served under Gabinius and probably crossed the Euphrates with him before moving on to Egypt, where he served the Egyptian king.[44]

After attending to the disposition of Pompey's body, Caesar had very definite priorities when he arrived in Alexandria. According to Lucan:

> No thing of beauty attracted him, neither the gold nor the ornaments of the gods, nor the city walls; but in eager haste he went down into the vault hewn out for a tomb. There lies the mad son of Macedonian Philip.

In the *Pharsalia*, Lucan juxtaposes Caesar's single-minded desire to view the body of Alexander with his (Lucan's) own contempt for the 'mad' Macedonian. There follows in his text a litany of Alexander's crimes against humanity.[45]

Later generations saw the comparison of Alexander and Caesar as well. Velleius Paterculus, writing during the reign of Tiberius (r. AD 14-37) noted:

> In the magnitude of his ambitions, in the rapidity of his military oper-ations, and in his endurance of danger, he [Caesar] closely resembled Alexander the Great, but only when Alexander was free from the influ-ence of wine and master of his passions.[46]

Velleius, a court favourite of Tiberius, noted Caesar's temperance and even tem-per, and compared him favourably with Alexander. The Macedonian may have done great deeds but he had serious character flaws that virtuous Roman com-manders, he argued, did not have.

Julian, writing four centuries later, favoured Alexander over Caesar.[47] Diodorus (f. late first century BC) writes favourably of both Alexander and Caesar in the same paragraph of the introduction to his *Library of History*.[48] Sextus Aurelius Victor, who was a contemporary of Julian, also compared Alexander and Caesar when he noted the time it took for each to achieve their fame.[49]

Upon his return to Rome, Caesar began to exhibit signs of imitating Alexander. Gruen argues that he not only sought to emulate Alexander but to surpass him. He cites Statius who tells us that Caesar replaced the image of Alexander on Lysippus' equestrian statue in the forum with his own.[50] But Statius' account is sketchy and we have no other corroboration. What we do have is a sense of Caesar's rivalry with Alexander and a centuries-long comparison of the two.

Caesar minted coins bearing his own portrait. While Alexander did that extensively and other and earlier famous Romans minted coins with their portraits, Caesar was the first Roman to do so systematically.[51] He also solicited support from influential senators for a campaign against Parthia to avenge Crassus. One of these was Cicero.

Cicero also remarked on the similarities between Alexander and Caesar. In a letter to his friend Atticus he likened himself to the 'men of eloquence and learning' who advised Alexander while he himself was an advisor to Caesar (in his vanity, Cicero probably means to compare himself to Aristotle).

This letter was sent to explain a letter that Cicero had earlier written to Caesar supporting him in his decision to wage war on Parthia. Cicero confides in Atticus that he only wished to flatter Caesar by telling him what he wanted to hear: 'what view ought I to have taken of the Parthian war except what I thought he wanted?'[52] In another letter to Atticus sent the next day, Cicero called Alexander a 'cruel and intemperate tyrant' and feared that Caesar might become one as well.[53]

Caesar had fixed his mind on an invasion of Parthia. To avoid being caught in the open by Parthian cavalry as Crassus had been he proposed to march through the hilly and even mountainous countryside of Armenia to neutralize the advantage of active Parthian cavalry. In 209 BC, the Seleucid king, Antiochus III, had marched by this route through Armenia and Media to get at the Parthians. He had met with admirable success.[54]

Antiochus was able to temporarily restore Parthia to Seleucid control before he himself was defeated by Rome. Even though Grainger, writing about Antiochus' war with Rome, does not make the connection, it is very probable that Caesar knew of the success of this Seleucid king and the direction of his march, and sought to copy his methods.[55]

There could be another reason for Caesar's choosing to take his army through Armenia. If Pliny knew that Roman troops, captured at Carrhae, were posted in Sogdiana to protect Parthia's eastern frontier, then Caesar would have known it too. By travelling through Armenia he would be on a path to rescue them, though this is mere speculation.

Caesar planned to attack with an overwhelming force of 16 legions and 10,000 cavalry.[56] According to Fox, some Romans suggested that when Caesar entered upon his Parthian campaign that he imitated Alexander by dressing as he did when among the Persians:

> when Julius Caesar planned to invade the Parthian empire in Alexander's footsteps, there were those who wished him, as a fit precaution, to be attired in the diadem and Persian costume before he even entered Asia.[57]

Caesar, however, disdained the wearing of the diadem, a silk headband that denoted kingship. It had been made popular by Alexander and every Hellenistic king had worn one. As Plutarch notes however this symbol of kingship was highly unpopular with the people because of its association with monarchy, 'when Caesar refused it there was universal applause'.[58] If he planned to wear Persian garb and the diadem when he reached Parthian territory, we can only guess.

In any event the diadem would not be worn in public by a Roman emperor until the mid-third century AD, by which time emperors no longer resided in Rome and the Roman people were not the same vehement anti-monarchal crowd they had been in Caesar's time.

By March of 44 BC Caesar was ready to move against Parthia. He stockpiled weapons at armouries along his line of march, including a supply dump at Demetrias (modern Volos) in central Greece. (This armoury would later be looted by Caesar's assassins for their war with Antony and Octavian).[59] He sent his legions on the march from Rome ahead of him. His great nephew and adopted son Octavian was waiting for him en route. Caesar planned to catch up with the army after wrapping up business in Rome.

His plans were brought to ruin by his assassination just two or three days before his scheduled departure. Even on the day of his death he ruminated on the coming war. Despite the warnings of danger, 'he came into the senate house thinking of his campaign against Parthia'.[60] Revenge for the defeat of Crassus had to await the conclusion of a new Roman civil war.

Appian, in the mid-second century, like Plutarch saw clearly the similarities between Caesar and Alexander. He noted that both men were 'well-formed and handsome in person'.[61] Caesar he said was:

> fit to be compared with Alexander. Both were men of the greatest ambition, both were most skilled in the art of war, most rapid in executing their decisions, most reckless of danger, least sparing of themselves, and relying as much on audacity and luck as on military skill.[62]

In fact Appian took several paragraphs to compare the two great men.

The Russian historian Michael Rostovtzeff suggests that the situation in Rome following the death of Caesar 'was approximately the same as after the death of Alexander the Great in that there were several leaders contending for power'.[63] Of these one stood out.

Mark Antony: Persian nightmares

There are few more romantic characters in Roman history than Mark Antony. He is the tragic figure, the doomed Romeo, the fallen hero. He is a man who had it all and lost it for the love of a woman. At least that is the popular perception. However, Cleopatra was not the only factor that played on his mind and informed his decisions. There were others, not the least of these was the towering figure of Alexander the Great.

Antony imitated Alexander in diverse ways, starting with his early Greek education in Athens where he gained a love for all things Greek. Even Antony's relationship with Cleopatra had Alexandrian overtones. She was a direct descendant of Alexander's general, Ptolemy, and as such was the very last vestige of the era of Alexander.

When Alexander set out for the East he was nearly bankrupt. When he defeated Persia his coffers were filled with immense wealth. For Antony, defeating Parthia would bring him wealth beyond the dreams of avarice and demonstrate to Rome that he, and not Octavian, was the true heir of Caesar and Alexander.

First, there was another Roman civil war to fight. This time the war was between Caesar loyalists led by Antony and Octavian on the one side, and Caesar's assassins, including Cassius (who had been a cavalry commander with Crassus at Carrhae) and Brutus, on the other side. After the Battle at Philippi in 42 BC, the climactic battle of the civil war, Brutus committed suicide. Soon after, Antony came across his body. Plutarch explains, 'When Antony found Brutus lying dead, he ordered the body to be wrapped in the most costly of his own robes'.[64]

It is very likely that this act was a deliberate imitation of Alexander because when the Macedonian encountered the murdered body of Darius III, he respectfully covered his dead enemy with his own cloak.[65]

Perhaps because of his affinity for the Greeks, when Antony divided the empire with his young rival, Octavian, he took the wealthier Greek East for himself. Antony then began a tour of Asia Minor, summoning client kings who had recently sided with Cassius and Brutus to explain their actions as well as to help finance his upcoming war with Parthia.

As he made his progress through Asia he began to be identified by the people of Ephesus, and elsewhere, as the New Dionysus. Dionysus was thought to have originated in the East and according to Michael Grant was 'the deity who stood for Eastern conquest'.[66]

Alexander had also eagerly associated himself with Dionysus and had an affinity for the god. He was said to have spared the city of Nysa in the Indus Valley because the inhabitants convinced him that their town had been founded by Dionysus who, it was said, had once ridden from the town in a cart pulled by tigers. 'Accordingly', by Arrian's account, 'he granted to the people of Nysa the continuance of their freedom and autonomy'.[67]

Alexander used the event to assert that he had travelled further than the globe-trotting Dionysus. He also claimed to have reached the limits of the god's travels when in 327 BC he captured the distant kingdom of Sogdiana (which was located immediately north of today's Afghanistan).[68]

Antony welcomed the comparison to both the god and the man. The Romans had adopted Dionysus and called him Bacchus and Antony had every intention of living up to the comparison to Alexander with his own invasion of Persia. It was during his sojourn in Asia that he summoned Cleopatra to meet him at Tarsus in Cilicia. Their meeting was a public spectacle, 'and the word spread on every side that Venus [Greek Aphrodite] had come to revel with Bacchus [Dionysus] for the happiness of Asia.'[69]

There was another Greek demigod of legend in whom both men felt a great affinity. That was Heracles (Hercules). Alexander claimed to be a descendant of Heracles on both his father's and mother's side.[70] His side journey to Siwa was taken because Heracles had also visited the same Egyptian oasis.

> Caranus, a man of royal race, eleventh in descent from Hercules, set out from Argos and seized the kingship of Macedonia. From him Alexander the Great was descended in the seventeenth generation, and could boast that, on his mother's side, he was descended from Achilles, and, on his father's side, from Hercules.[71]

Antony also claimed to be Heracles' descendant: 'there was an ancient tradition that the Antonii were Heracleidae, being descendants of Anton, a son of Heracles'.[72] He made the most of the connection to this god and sometimes imitated him in dress and actions in public. It was another way of associating himself with Alexander. Plutarch tells us:

> Now, Antony associated himself with Heracles in lineage and with Dionysus in the mode of life which he adopted, as I have said, and he was called the New Dionysus.[73]

Having met Cleopatra, Antony was soon distracted by her charms or, more likely, the charms of a fabulously wealthy Egypt. He accepted an invitation to winter at her palace in Alexandria (41–40 BC). It was his first mistake in his relations with Parthia. Alexander had several liaisons with foreign women but never left his army to do so. Antony on the other hand was now easily parted from his men. According to Plutarch,

> ...at the very moment when...a Parthian army was hovering threateningly on the frontier of Mesopotamia and was about to invade Syria, he allowed the queen to carry him off to Alexandria.[74]

Apparently Antony loved Alexandria. The city had been founded by his hero Alexander. The great man's tomb was there, a symbol of his legacy and a place of pilgrimage. During an endless round of parties and games hosted by Cleopatra, he began to abandon his Roman toga and military kit in favour of the local linen robe worn by the Greeks. It was after all more suited to the climate. Perhaps he had in mind the Persian dress that Alexander began to wear as he became more familiar with the land that he had conquered.[75] As with Alexander, Antony's aping the dress of foreigners did not sit well with his countrymen.

Antony wanted to use the wealth of Egypt to finance his campaign against Parthia. He could then bring all of Alexander's former empire under the authority of Rome. Cleopatra knew and approved of his plans. Once, when she found him fishing along the Nile unsuccessfully, she gently reproached him: 'Imperator, hand over your fishing-rod to the fishermen of Pharos and Canopus; your sport is the hunting of cities, realms, and continents'.[76]

During that pleasant winter, while Antony luxuriated in Egypt his plans for invading Parthia were subverted. The Parthians knew that Antony planned to attack them in the spring. Therefore they made a pre-emptive strike early in 40 BC.

One army of swift Parthian riders soon overran Syria, Phoenicia and Judea while another force of Parthians raided deep into Anatolia as far as Lydia and Ionia. With his provinces in turmoil Antony sailed to Rome to shore up his position at home, raise money and troops and reconcile with his young rival Octavian.

Antony entrusted the war with Parthia to his lieutenant, Publius Ventidius Bassus (f. 41–38 BC), who defeated Parthian armies in a series of stunning battles. First was the Battle of the Cilician Gates in 39 BC, in which he defeated Quintus Labienus, a former general under Brutus and Cassius who had defected to Parthia.

In that battle he ordered his men to occupy a hill commanding the pass and hold it against the Parthians. By doing so he neutralized the advantage of the Parthian cavalry. Their charge was slowed by their climb. Then Ventidius ordered his men to charge down on the milling horses and caused panic and flight in the Parthian ranks.

In the second fight, the Battle of Amanus Pass in 39 BC, the Parthians sent a small force to hold the southern end of the Syrian Gates against the Romans. Before they could reach their objective they were met by a Roman force with the same purpose. A battle was forced with the Parthians getting the best of it until Ventidius brought his army up in time to sweep the field. As a result the Parthians abandoned Syria. Alexander had forced this same pass after his victory at Issus.

Finally, at the Battle of Mount Gindarus in 38 BC, the Parthian crown prince, Pakores (or Pacorus), led an army back into Syria. Ventidius once again placed his forces on a hill side and waited for the attack of Parthian cavalry. When it came, he charged down on them, won the victory and killed Pakores, the oldest and favourite son of King Orodes, along with a reported 20,000 of his men.[77]

Pakores died on the fifteenth anniversary of Crassus' death. Ventidius, acting on Antony's authority, had at last avenged the death of Crassus and proven that the Parthians could be defeated.

Antony was in Athens when he heard of the victories of Ventidius. He celebrated with games and feasts demonstrating the extent to which he loved and favoured the Greeks:

> To celebrate this victory Antony feasted the Greeks, and acted as gymna-siarch [financial patron] for the Athenians. He left at home the insignia of his command, and went forth carrying the wands of a gymnasiarch, in a Greek robe and white shoes, and he would take the young combatants by the neck and part them.[78]

However, Antony could not let his general have all the glory. Arriving in Syria, he showered Ventidius with faint praise, relieved him of duty and sent him home to enjoy a well-deserved 'triumph de Parthis', the first ever victory parade celebrated for defeating the Parthians.[79] Thereafter Ventidius disappears from history. Yet history remembers him through Shakespeare who caused him to say:

> Now, darting Parthia, art thou struck; and now
> Pleased fortune does of Marcus Crassus' death
> Make me revenger.
> Bear the king's son's body before our army.
> Thy Pacorus, Orodes,
> Pays this for Marcus Crassus.[80]

Antony chose the spring of 36 BC to launch his invasion of Parthia. By then he had amassed a Roman and allied army, which according to Plutarch consisted of 100,000 men.

> The Romans themselves numbered sixty thousand, together with the cavalry…, ten thousand Spaniards and Celts. The other nations a total of about thirty thousand.[81]

Rumors of this powerful force travelled to distant India at the far ends of the Parthian realm.

During his preparations he summoned Cleopatra to meet him. She brought with her the twin babies (b. 40 BC) whom their father had never met. She had named the boy Alexander and the girl Cleopatra. Antony now gave them additional names. Alexander he called Helios (sun) and Cleopatra he called Selene (moon). Perhaps he had a devious reason for this. One of the titles of the Parthian king was 'brother of the sun and moon'. Antony was co-opting this title by implying that he was the father of the sun and moon.

As Antony was preparing his assault, word came of a crisis in the Parthian royal house. Orodes II had become king when he and his brother murdered their father. His son now murdered him. A ruthless Phraates IV (38 BC – AD 2) emerged as the new king after killing all of his brothers and their families. As mentioned above (see Crassus), there was similar unrest in Achaemenid Persia following the assassination of a king when Alexander prepared his invasion. Antony saw the coincidence between the two events of chaos in the royal court of Persia. He hoped to capitalize on it as Alexander had done.

Flush with confidence, Antony began his invasion. Following the route of Antiochus III and the plans of Caesar, Antony marched his army into Armenia. Artavasdes II, the Armenian king who had once allied himself with and then abandoned Crassus, now allied himself with Antony and journeyed with him into neighbouring Media.

In his haste, Antony rushed ahead, leaving his baggage train to catch up over the rough roads. It was not unusual for a commander to leave his baggage while sending a strike force forward. Alexander did it often, such as his attack on the Mardi in Hyrcania, not that distant from where Antony would fight.[82] But Alexander had excellent intelligence from disaffected Persian satraps and knew where his enemy was at; Antony did not.

While he rushed ahead, the highly mobile Parthians learned of his folly and attacked his supply train. At first sight of them, the 6,000 Armenian horsemen charged with guarding the slow-moving wagons abandoned their Roman counterparts. The Parthians then killed the Roman guard before looting and burning the wagons. When King Artavasdes heard of it, he too abandoned Antony.

Without his supplies and siege engines Antony could not take the fortress town of Phraaspa which housed the Median treasury. Antony dallied there, laying siege to the city while fighting off the incessant raids of the Parthian cavalry.[83] In October he found himself, as Napoleon would at Moscow, deep in enemy territory, lacking supplies, with winter coming on. He began a long, tortured retreat through cold and snowy mountain passes back to Armenia and safety in Syria. Fear of the Parthian cavalry kept him on the high ground. Still his progress was constantly threatened by Parthian attacks.

Like Crassus before him, Antony lost his battle with Parthia. As many as 30,000 men died in his attempt to become the new Alexander. Most of them perished from the winter conditions and sickness.[84]

Even after this bitter defeat, Antony still dreamed of Eastern conquest. In 34 BC, two years after his defeat in Media, the king of that country had a change of heart. Conflict with the Parthian king caused him to invite Antony to send his army there once more.

Antony accepted the invitation but got no further than Armenia. While there, he took its duplicitous King Artavasdes prisoner and packed him off to Alexandria. After the Battle of Actium, a vengeful Cleopatra ordered him to be executed.

Armenia was made into a Roman province. Antony left a strong garrison in Armenia for the winter to hold the country and perhaps to be ready for further Eastern conquest, while he returned to Cleopatra in Egypt.

Here again we see the difference between Alexander and Antony. Alexander stayed in the field with his army for over eleven years in his war with Persia but Antony could not. It was said that the charms of Alexandria and its bewitching queen made him hasten to be near her. It is more likely that he felt increasingly threatened by Octavian, who was building his power base in Rome. Octavian's position improved after Antony's defeat in Media.

Before Alexander set out for the East he had quelled or killed his rivals and dealt with the nearby kingdoms of Thrace, Illyria, the Getae and the Greek city states.[85] He had secured his position at home before his foreign conquests.

Antony failed to do the same. He had left a hostile Octavian in control of the Roman West. Antony needed to win over public opinion at home. He tried to do this by sponsoring a celebration of his victory over Armenia.

Unfortunately his celebration did not take place in Rome but in Alexandria. The four-day extravaganza began with a traditional Roman triumphal parade, with Artavasdes bound in chains as the main attraction:

> He made them [his prisoners] walk at the head of a kind of triumphal advent into Alexandria, together with the other captives, while he himself entered the city upon a chariot. And he presented to Cleopatra not only all the spoils that he had won, but even led the Armenian together with his wife and children before her, bound in chains of gold. She herself was seated upon a golden throne on a stage plated with silver, amidst a great multitude.[86]

Antony himself was not dressed in his Roman uniform or even a toga. He dressed as the god Dionysus:

his head bound with the ivy wreath, his person enveloped in the saffron robe of gold, holding in his hand the *thyrsus* [a fennel staff associated with Dionysus], wearing the buskins [an actor's boots], and riding in the Bacchic chariot.[87]

Writing at the end of the Antonine era, Athenaeus, quoting the lost work of Ephippus, describes Alexander dressing in similar fashion at banquets.[88] Antony was acting in the tradition of Alexander and victorious Hellenistic kings.

In Rome, however, it was not seen that way. If Antony was a Roman general, the heir to Caesar's greatness, why wasn't his triumph celebrated in Rome? Why weren't the spoils of war shared with the Roman people instead of Greeks and Egyptians? Octavian exploited the popular discontent to his advantage.

Following the triumph there were three days of feasts and games centred on what have been called 'The Alexandrian Donations'. Antony and Cleopatra sat together on golden thrones and bequeathed kingdoms to their children.

Ptolemy Philopator Philometor Caesar, nicknamed Caesarion, Cleopatra's son by Caesar, was named her co-ruler of Egypt. He was given the title 'King of Kings', a title borrowed from the Persians. Cleopatra was now called the 'Queen of Kings'. The couple's youngest son, Ptolemy Philadelphus (b. 36 BC), was made king over most of what is now eastern Turkey and Syria, lands formerly under the control of the Seleucids. Their young girl, Cleopatra Selene, was to have Libya. Her twin brother Alexander Helios was to have Armenia, Media and Parthia and 'all of the other lands east of the Euphrates as far as India; and he bestowed these regions as if they were already in his possession'.[89] In this 'donation' the young boy was to inherit realms once occupied by his namesake, Alexander, as soon as Antony was able to conquer them.

The children were dressed in the costumes of the lands they would one day rule. Young Alexander wore the robes of a Persian king and received an honorary bodyguard of Armenian mercenaries. All of these 'donations' were given without even a nod to the Roman Senate. After the fact, Antony would write to the Senate asking them to ratify his actions. No senatorial action was ever taken.

The next year (33 BC), young Alexander Helios was betrothed to Iotape, herself a child, the daughter of King Artavasdes I of Media.[90] The deal offered the hope that the boy might one day inherit that kingdom. Antony sought by alliance what he could not gain by conquest.

However, fate intervened. The growing power of Octavian at Rome forced the issue of who controlled the Roman world. As part of his propaganda campaign against Antony, Octavian illegally took Antony's will from the Temple of Vesta. He then announced that Antony wanted to be buried in Alexandria instead of Rome.[91]

Perhaps Antony dreamed of being laid to rest near (or in) the tomb of Alexander. In Rome it was considered to be a form of treason. Antony's obsession with Greek and Eastern forms lost him the propaganda battle at home, the ultimate source of his power.

At last, Octavian and Antony moved their armies to face one another. In hindsight, the propagandist Velleius Paterculus, writing during the reign of Tiberius, saw the battle as a forgone conclusion. After discussing Antony's debilitating losses in Parthia he wrote: 'The victory of the Caesarian party was a certainty long before the battle'.[92]

At Actium in 31 BC, Antony's troops slightly outnumbered those of Octavian but many of them were hastily conscripted foreign auxiliaries of dubious value. They were about even in the number of Roman legionaries they each fielded. Each had about 70–75,000 men, both infantry and naval personnel.[93] As it happened the ensuing battle was a naval affair.

Octavian bottled up Antony's fleet in the Adriatic Sea and forced a naval battle at Actium when Antony would have preferred to fight on land. Octavian's naval forces were victorious and Antony was forced to flee. Antony and Cleopatra made it safely back to Egypt with their treasury intact. In taking command of the naval fight, Antony once again separated himself from his all-important army.

After a few days without his personal leadership his men did not have the stomach to continue the fight and surrendered *en masse* to Octavian. If Antony could have had with him a significant portion of the 30,000 men he had lost to Parthia, he might very likely have challenged Octavian on land and had the best of it.

It was the end of Antony's dreams. Without the instrument of conquest and with no one to protect him from a vengeful rival, he and Cleopatra both ended their lives rather than be Octavian's captives. Cleopatra was the last of Alexander's successors. Her death marked the end of the age of Alexander. The age of the Caesars had dawned.

Antony had tried his best to walk in the footsteps of Alexander. He respected his fallen rival, Brutus, with the shroud of his own cloak. He tried to create a melding of civilizations as Alexander had done. He attempted to recreate the empire of Alexander and named his son Alexander. Gruen suggested that none of our ancient sources have Antony claiming Alexander 'as a precedent, a model or symbol'.[94] Antony didn't have to. His actions spoke louder than Gruen's words.

If he had been successful, Roman authority might have stretched from Spain to India. As it was Antony would be romantically identified as the willing captive of Cleopatra's charms. Writers like Shakespeare, historians and film makers would remember him thus.

Octavian, now calling himself Augustus Caesar, inherited the Eastern lands that Antony and the other late-Republican generals had so meticulously and painfully collected for Rome. His relationship to Parthia would be much different.

Summary

The study of the *Imitatio Alexandri* is largely focussed on the Roman Republican era. Gruen is correct when he states that none of the Republican generals made a claim to be the 'new Alexander'. But their armed conquests spoke for them and the Roman public, as well as foreigners, understood this. By imitating the actions of Alexander, the successful (and unsuccessful) generals invited the comparison.

Scipio Africanus, Gaius Marius, Sulla, Lucullus, Pompey, Gabinius, Crassus, Caesar and Antony all adopted some forms of Alexander's behaviour without actually claiming to do so (in our surviving sources). It is possible that Roman cultural norms of the age forbade this type of hero worship or more likely during the Republic it was not wise to affect too close an association with a monarch. It is very unlikely that any of these ego-driven conquerors could have suffered from false modesty.

Crassus, trying to outdo Pompey, attempted to re-enact Alexander's Eastern success. He had with him about the same number of soldiers as Alexander and he followed the same route. When confronted by enemy cavalry that fled from him, as had happened to Alexander in a similar situation, he hurried forward against an elusive foe.

The Parthians however had evolved different battle tactics from those of the Persians of Darius III. They were able to play to their strengths while denying the Romans theirs. They defeated Crassus' army and in the process took his head.

Antony, while assuming many of the personal attributes of Alexander, sought to neutralize Parthian advantages by marching through Armenia to lessen the effectiveness of cavalry, as Caesar had planned it. Further he brought forward a much larger army than Crassus had employed. Yet he did not have the advantage of fortune or the intelligence system that allowed Alexander to pinpoint the location of his enemies.

Without this knowledge Antony could not bring his forces to bear in the right place at the right time. He was defeated in Media because he was bereft of supplies and siege equipment, with winter coming on and an active enemy harassing his every movement. His loss to the Parthians assured his loss to Octavian.

Chapter 4

The Empire Strikes Back

Augustus Caesar: The Diplomat

The Parthians also were ready to grant Augustus' claims on Armenia and
when he demanded the surrender of the Eagles captured from Crassus
and Antony not only returned them but offered hostages into the bargain;
and once, because several rival princes were claiming the Parthian throne,
announced that they would elect whichever candidate he chose.
—Suetonius[1]

After the humiliating defeats of Crassus and Antony, the early Caesars
would adopt diplomacy when it came to relations with Parthia. Begun
by Augustus and perfected by Nero, negotiations and workable treaties
served the two sides reasonably well for over a century.

During this time the imitation of Alexander took on new forms. It became fashionable for an emperor, rather than rely on military conquest, to copy Alexander with some of his personal affectations. The era of Augustan diplomacy would be brought to an end by Trajan's Persian conquests when military action more closely emulated Alexander. As Michael Grant noted, 'there was always a militaristic party urging emperors to behave like Alexander the Great'.[2]

Augustus, the empire's new ruler, was careful in the way that he compared himself to Alexander. When Octavian entered Alexandria to 'conquer' Egypt from Cleopatra, the last of the Macedonian successors, he could have pillaged the city. Instead he displayed clemency, partially out of respect for the city's founder. To announce his mercy he delivered a speech to the citizens in his halting Greek.[3] His mercy however, did not extend to the royal treasury, which he confiscated.

While wrapping up his affairs after the defeat of Antony, Augustus visited Alexander's tomb and gazed upon him for a long moment. He expressed proper veneration by placing a golden diadem upon the mummified head and placed flowers on the body, perhaps inadvertently breaking off his hero's nose in the process. For the Ptolemaic kings, ancestors of Cleopatra, he expressed nothing but contempt: 'I came to see a king, not a row of corpses'.[4]

Octavian's contempt for lesser men echoed that of Alexander in his veneration of Achilles. While visiting Troy, Alexander sacrificed at Achilles' tomb. When he was there asked if he would like to see Paris's lyre, he 'said he thought it not worth looking on, but he should be glad to see that of Achilles'. Art historian Andrew Stewart points out that comparisons of Alexander and Achilles are omnipresent in Plutarch's *Life of Alexander*.[5]

Perhaps, in his contempt for the Ptolemies, Octavian was remembering Alexander. For a time Octavian (now Augustus) wore a signet-ring with the image of Alexander on it before switching it for an image of himself.[6]

When Alexander fought an important battle, such as at Issus and in India on the banks of the Hydaspes River, he would found a 'victory city' on the site. Augustus would copy him. He founded a 'victory city' or *Nicopolis* on the site where his army had camped before the Battle of Actium. He founded a second such city where his cavalry had bested the feeble remnants of Antony's loyalists in Egypt and then, like Alexander, sponsored games in commemoration of the event. Pompey had also established cities on the sites of his victories.[7]

Back in Rome, Augustus was more circumspect in his association with Alexander, though he did display images of the Macedonian by the Greek artist Apelles (f. 332–339 BC), stolen or purchased from Greece. Then, too, statues that had once graced Alexander's own tent were placed conspicuously in the forum.[8]

Others however liked to see comparisons between the founders of two empires. Suetonius reports that a god-serpent visited Octavian's mother Atia one night and ten months later the boy was born. As we have seen the story is similar to those told about Alexander and Scipio.

Andrew Stewart writes of fragments of an Augustan-era red glazed terracotta pot in a style called '*arretine*' that includes a partial male figure, thought to be either Alexander or Augustus, facing a woman dressed as a Persian. Not enough of the pot is left to us to pinpoint the exact meaning or identification.[9]

Suetonius tells the story of Octavian's father Octavius when he visited a temple in the grove of Father Liber (whom the Romans associated with the Greek Dionysus) in Thrace. When inquiring about his young son Octavian, a pillar of flame shot into the air. The phenomenon had happened only once before, when Alexander had sacrificed at the same altar.[10]

Augustus was only thirty-three years old when he began to rule over a united empire that was far more populous than that of Alexander. At about the age when Alexander died, Augustus had to assume a task that neither the great Macedonian nor any of the Roman generals of the past had been required to do. Now that the conquering was done he had to administer an empire:

> He [Octavian] learned that Alexander, having completed nearly all his conquests by the time he was thirty-two years old, was at an utter loss to know what he should do during the rest of his life, whereas Augustus

expressed his surprise that Alexander did not regard it as a greater task to set in order the empire which he had won than to win it.

–Plutarch[11]

Edward N Luttwak argues that Alexander left his empire in better shape for his Macedonian successors than the republican generals had for Augustus. The Roman conquest of empire, he says, had been a product of 'undirected expansionism', while Alexander at least had left 'the workings of a rational administrative policy'.[12]

Augustus saw to it that his great uncle, Julius Caesar, was the first Roman to be deified, *divus Julius*. Just as the respectable early emperors could not adopt the trappings of a king, they, modestly, could not be enrolled among the gods until they died.

This action allowed Augustus, the adopted son and heir of Caesar, to portray himself as 'the son of a god' just as Alexander had portrayed himself as the son of god (Zeus-Ammon) when he went to Egypt.[13] These claims came long before those of the followers of Jesus to his divine birth.

The deification of Caesar also set the stage for Augustus himself to be deified upon his own death and for the divine cult of the emperors which spread throughout the empire. Through his mother, Atia, a Julii and niece of Caesar, he could assert the Julii family claim to be a descendant of the goddess Venus through Aeneas.

His father and namesake, Gaius Octavius, had once served as the Roman governor of Alexander's home land, Macedonia.[14] The people knew this and he would not have had to point it out to them.

Coinage had a political use in the ancient world. Much like a portable bulletin board it could announce victories, associate leaders with deities or show the people a robust portrait of their leader. Alexander had retained control of his mints and relied on coinage to portray himself as the 'King of Asia' and perpetuate the imperial and divine cult throughout his empire. Even more coinage of him was produced by the Macedonian successor kingdoms after his death.

Augustus would be the first Roman to perpetuate an imperial cult with coins. Christopher Howgego, a numismatic authority, observed that 'from the reign of Augustus imperial themes dominated the coinage'.[15]

Alexander often retained the services of Achaemenid Persian and non-Persian satraps to continue to rule their provinces in his name. The continuity of administration eased the path of control. Augustus also retained local elites to govern their territories as client kings. The most memorable of these was Herod the Great of Judea. Herod had been loyal to his friend Mark Antony, but Augustus kept him on as a client king anyway.[16] It was a gesture that Alexander would have understood.

Professor Ernst Badian notes that Alexander had made use of native peoples to collect his taxes for him in Egypt.[17] Just so, the Roman tax-farmers, who bought contracts from the government, made use of local people called *publicani* to collect taxes from their fellow citizens. We know of their Augustan-era activity most notably from the bible (eg Luke 18:9-14).

The outer Ocean had been an obsession with Alexander and, as we have seen, with Caesar as well. During the reign of Augustus, Seneca the Elder (and later his son, the younger Seneca, tutor of Nero) would write about Alexander and his obsession with the Ocean. In one of the elder Seneca's exercises for students of rhetoric, called *The Suasoriae*, he poses the theme 'Alexander debates whether to sail the Ocean'. This debate was also taken up by Arrian.[18]

By the time of Augustus there was no more debate. He dispatched at least three expeditions to the northern Ocean (North Sea) from the mouth of the Rhine River. Each of these expeditions was led by a member of the imperial family. The first voyage into the unknown was commanded by his son-in-law Drusus in 12 BC. The second, in AD 5, was led by Drusus' brother, the future emperor Tiberius, and the last by Germanicus, the son of Drusus and father of Caligula, in AD 16. They explored as far as the Frisian Islands and maybe beyond, around the northern tip of Denmark to the mouth of the Elbe River, where they would have sought sources of amber and lumber.[19]

In other ways Augustus was careful in the way he imitated Alexander, especially in his personal life. For a man who claimed to be restoring the republic and claimed only to be the first among equals in the Senate, it would not do to mimic a king. As Alaric Watson notes, 'Augustus (was) careful to avoid presenting too monarchial a self-image'.[20]

The Augustan policy toward Parthia began magnanimously. King Phraates of Parthia, who had bested Antony, was threatened by an Arsacid rival named Tiridates. Tiridates was forced to flee to Roman territory, taking with him a most-important hostage, a son of the king. After some negotiations and events in Armenia (below), Augustus returned the boy to his father in exchange for the standards of Crassus and Anthony.[21]

Since the Armenian king, Artavasdes II, had been kidnapped by Antony and killed by Cleopatra, Armenia had aligned itself with Parthia.[22] When Artaxias II, son of the pro-Parthian Artavasdes, became unpopular at home, a pro-Roman delegation approached Augustus and asked that he be deposed and replaced by his brother, Tigranes, who had lived in Rome for ten years.

Augustus dispatched an army commanded by his son-in-law, the future emperor Tiberius, to accomplish the task. Artazias was conveniently assassinated (in 20 BC) before they arrived. Tigranes III (r. 20-10 BC), with the help of Tiberius, was unopposed for the crown of Armenia.

Meanwhile Augustus himself moved to Syria to personally command the legions there. Justin suggests that the Parthian King Phraates feared renewed opposition from Tiridates and the presence of Roman field armies on two of his borders. He therefore negotiated for the return of the standards or 'eagles' taken from Crassus and Antony as well as their surviving prisoners. Florus suggests that they were returned 'voluntarily'.[23]

Back in Rome the return of the lost standards signified a great 'victory' over Parthia. When the standards were brought back to Rome the event was celebrated as a great military deed. A victory arch was commissioned and built near the Temple of Vesta in the Forum. A triumph was offered to Augustus by the senate, which he politely declined.

The event was also commemorated on the breastplate of the famous Prima Porta statue of Augustus now in the Museo Chiaramonti at the Vatican and recorded by the contemporary writers and poets friendly to Augustus. Among these were Propertius, Horace, Virgil and Ovid. These Augustan propagandists envisioned bringing not just Parthia but India too under the rule of Rome. They contributed to a body of literature which could be called 'Laudes Romae' (In praise of Rome).[24]

Sextus Aurelius Propertius waxes patriotic as he glories in the prospect of the conquest of Parthia and India:

> [Augustus] Caesar, our god, plots war against rich India, cutting the straits, in his fleet, across the pearl-bearing ocean. Men, the rewards are great: far lands prepare triumphs; Tigris and Euphrates will flow to your tune. Too late, but that province will come under Ausonian (Italian) wands, Parthia's trophies will get to know Latin Jupiter. Go, get going, prows expert in battle. Set sail and armoured horses do your accustomed duty! I sing you auspicious omens. And avenge that disaster of Crassus! Go and take care of Roman history.[25]

Quintus Horatius Flaccus, better known as Horace, saw a new era of peace in the Roman world ushered in by Augustus and the closing of the doors of the Temple of Janus as he relates in *The Odes*:

> Caesar, this age has restored rich crops
> to the fields, and brought back the standards, at last,
> to Jupiter, those that we've now recovered
> from insolent Parthian pillars,
> and closed the gates of Romulus' temple [the temple of Janus],
> freed at last from all war.[26]

Publius Vergilius Maro, known to us as Virgil (70-19 BC), saw the return of the standards as a bit of revenge in *The Aeneid*:

> from the boasting Parthians would regain
> their eagles, lost in Carrhae's bloody plain.[27]

With this diplomatic victory over the Parthians, Virgil, like Propertius, saw an ever-expanding Rome under the leadership of Augustus:

> he shall extend our dominion beyond the Garamantians [a people in North Africa] and the Indians into a region which lies outside the path of the constellations, outside the track of the year and of the sun, where Atlas the Heaven–Bearer holds on his shoulders the turning sphere, inset with blazing stars.[28]

For Virgil, Parthia was already conquered and absorbed into the empire, the fruit of Augustan diplomacy. From there the sky was the limit. Ronald Syme sees Virgil's language as following a precedent when he tells us that the 'motive and language owe much to panegyrics of the world conqueror Alexander the Macedonian'.[29]

Brian Bosworth credits Virgil with even more praise for Augustus. He demonstrates how Virgil uses the forms of Hellenistic hero worship to liken Augustus to Jupiter (Zeus), Hercules and Dionysus just as the Macedonians likened Alexander to these same gods. In both Virgil and the Alexandrian propagandists, their hero was even greater than the gods.

The diplomatic 'victory' of Augustus over the Parthians was the product of the propagandist's imagination and gave him at least literary (if not factual) domination from Spain to the Indus, far exceeding anything that Alexander had done.[30] All he had to do was to send his armies to the east to fulfill their prophecy.

Publius Ovidius Naso, who we know as Ovid, also saw Rome on the verge of ruling as far as India. In his *Ars Armatoria*, he digresses from his theme on the art of love (an otherwise-ribald tract of which the prudish Augustus disapproved) to predict Rome's future conquests:

> Behold, now Caesar's [Augustus] planning to add to our rule
> what's left of earth: now the Far East will be ours.
> Parthia, we'll have vengeance: Crassus's bust will cheer,
> and those standards wickedly laid low by barbarians.[31]

The reduction of Parthia, according to Ovid, would be accomplished by the grandson (and adopted son) of Augustus, Gaius Caesar (20 BC – AD 4). The passage above is followed by references to both Hercules and Bacchus (Dionysus), both 'super-heroes' associated, as we have seen, with Alexander.

Ovid reminds us that Bacchus had conquered India. Gaius thus is painted in the mould of Alexander, who inherited from his father Philip as Gaius would inherit from Augustus. 'Your father's years and powers arm you, boy, and with your father's powers and years you'll win.'[32] But Gaius didn't win. He was wounded and died in AD 4 while fighting in Armenia. Another promising 'new Alexander' was laid low and at a young age.

The Roman interest in India could have been fuelled by real events. Once Augustus had secured Egypt to the empire, Greek and Roman traders moved out from Red Sea ports to catch the monsoonal trade winds to India. During Augustus' lifetime as many as 120 ships a year plied the India trade from the Egyptian Red Sea port of Myos Hormos.[33]

This was only one port. There were likely hundreds of other ships that sailed to India from other Red Sea ports. In doing so they had by-passed Parthia as a middleman for trade and cut them out of lucrative commissions. This in itself was a victory for Rome.

India, the fabled land of riches became tangible, accessible and inspirational to the Augustan poets. Romans (merchants at least) had reached the Indian Ocean, just as Alexander had done. Propertius seemed to be alluding to this in his quote above. People living along the west coast of India to this day will display Roman coins their ancestors earned from this trade.

Not all Augustan-era literature was positive toward Rome. There was a body of anti-Roman material, most of which has not survived. Livy suggests that there were Greek writers who favoured Parthia over Rome. These were 'the most frivolous of the Greeks, who actually extol the Parthians at the expense of the Romans'. Livy identifies two of these writers as Timagenes and Metrodorus of Scepsis.[34]

There was more than literature to remind Romans of their victory. In his work *Bunte Barbaren*, Rolf Schneider reconstructed an imperial monument of the Augustan era from fragments now in Naples and Copenhagen museums. He suggests that this 'lost' monument was commissioned by Augustus to proclaim his 'victory' over the Parthians.[35]

In another project, Augustus had his engineers construct a large reservoir of water diverted from the Tiber. There he hosted a *naumachia*, a mock naval battle that told the story of a Greek victory over Achaemenid Persia in a not-so-subtle reference to his own diplomatic victories. Perhaps Rome now viewed itself as the successor to Athenian resistance to the Eastern foe.[36]

Blissfully unaware of Roman gloating, the Parthians continued to improve their relations with Rome. Ten years after the return of the standards, Parthian King

Phraates entrusted four of his sons to Augustus as 'hostages'. In the *Res Gestae* the emperor would boast:

> Phraates, son of Orodes, King of Parthia, sent all his sons and grandsons to me in Italy, not that he had been overcome in war, but because he sought our friendship by pledging his children.[37]

In reality this meant that the boys were to be taken into the imperial family and educated alongside Roman boys of noble birth. Augustus introduced the boys to the cheers of the Roman public, 'by leading them down the middle of the arena and seating them two rows behind himself'.[38] Alexander too had taken noble Persian youths into his household but the experiment did not last long enough to see results.

In 2 BC, Phraates died, perhaps at the hand of a younger son named Phraataces, born to him of an Italian slave girl named Musa. She had been a gift to the king by Augustus in 20 BC in the same exchange that returned the standards of Crassus and Antony to Rome. She must have caught his fancy for she became his queen while his older sons were enjoying Roman hospitality.[39]

With rivals out of the way, she was able to advance her own son to be the new king of Parthia. With a half-Roman king on the Parthian throne the Roman public had every expectation that Parthia would soon become (or had become) a new client kingdom. Augustus, unlike Alexander, had conquered Persia without a fight, or so it seemed.

Of course Parthia had no intention of becoming subservient to Rome. Phraataces and his mother were assassinated in AD 4. Even then Parthian nobility had to rely on Rome. A Parthian delegation dutifully visited the eternal city and asked for one of the hostaged sons of Phraates to be their new king. This was the Roman-educated Vonones I (r. AD 7–12).[40] Once again it seemed to Rome as if they had a client king in Parthia, for which Augustus took credit:

> The Parthian and Median peoples sent to me [Augustus] ambassadors of their nobility who sought and received kings from me, for the Parthians Vonones, son of King Phraates, grandson of King Orodes.[41]

Unfortunately Vonones was not raised to the horse or the hunt and kept company with Greek friends and advisors. Whatever good qualities he might have possessed, his lack of manly skills and his effete Western ways were an affront to Parthian independence. He was at length overthrown by an acceptably virile and anti-Western relative. Arsacid Persia was not to become a Roman province.

Instead, as Neilson Debevoise argues and Wolfram Grajetzki concedes, Parthia continued to support the culture of the Persian past. Their style of organized feudalism did little to promote social change but rather encouraged continuity of existing societies. Parthian claims on the Achaemenid legacy were deeper than just territorial similarities. Cultural and institutional continuity would have daily reminded the Parthians and the people they governed of their Achaemenid roots:

> Parthian occupation entailed no great change in the life of a community, business, science, and society in general continued their course with only such changes as new situations demanded... civilization there [in Babylonia] shows a continuity of development stretching far back into the past.[42]

Perhaps a little cynical about the accomplishments of Augustus, the first century writer Lucan expressed a ready contempt for Alexander, but he also accords him some grudging admiration for his accomplishments, while subtly deprecating those of Rome. He writes that Alexander 'died in Babylon, and with the Parthians in fear of him', and later that Parthia 'was a peaceful province of Pella [the Macedonian capital]'.

Writing at a time after Parthia had defeated Crassus and Antony, Lucan points out to his readers that, while Parthia feared Alexander and was a province of little Pella, mighty Rome and her greatest generals were powerless against the Eastern enemy.[43]

Augustus could not escape, and probably didn't want to, from comparison to Alexander. Alaric Watson wrote:

> The theology of victory by which his [Augustus'] position of power was expressed and legitimated was inevitably influenced by... the image of the archetypal divinely inspired victor, Alexander the Great.[44]

Tiberius: The Hated Enemy

An aging Tiberius (he was 56) succeeded Augustus in AD 14. Thirty-four years earlier he had personally received the captured standards from the Parthians, presided over the coronation of an Armenian king and later sailed upon the outer Ocean (the North Sea). He had done his bit to imitate Alexander.

Rostovtzeff believed he was 'a competent general of the old Roman type. He was strict, methodical, and sincerely devoted to his country.'[45] Yet we have a hint from Suetonius that he may not have been popular with his troops. His last command was in Germany between AD 7 and 9. When Augustus died in AD 14, 'the legions there were unanimously opposed to Tiberius' succession'.[46]

During his reign he sought once again to dominate Parthia. He sent Tiridates, a Roman-educated grandson of the late Parthian King Phraates to contest the Parthian throne. Tiridates III (AD 36) defeated Artabanus III (AD 12-38) and chased him from the kingdom. With his Greek education at Rome he was popular with the Greek community in Babylonia and was crowned in Seleucia. Unfortunately, his Western ways made him unpopular with the native population of the rest of the Parthian realm. Artabanus was able to collect an army among the eastern satraps and soundly defeated Tiridates, who then fled back to Roman territory to be the cause of future troubles.[47] The incident left Artabanus with an intense hatred for Tiberius:

> Artabanus, king of the Parthians, who always expressed outspoken hatred and contempt for Tiberius, made unsolicited overtures of friendship to Gaius (Caligula), attended a conference with the Governor of Syria and, before returning across the river Euphrates, paid homage to the Roman eagles and standards, and to the statues of Caesar.[48]

So convoluted were the royal relationships of antiquity that the father of Artabanus, Darius II of Media, was the brother of Iotapa, who as a child had been betrothed to Alexander Helios, the son of Antony and Cleopatra.

Tiberius may have felt threatened by his popular nephew called 'Germanicus', an *agnomen* or 'victory name' earned by his defeat of Germanic tribes. Germanicus had the bluest blood in Rome. He was the great-nephew of Augustus (Augustus was the great-nephew of Caesar), the grandson of Antony and Octavia and the nephew of Tiberius. Like his father Drusus and his uncle Tiberius, he had explored the outer Ocean along the Frisian Islands. Many saw him as the heir to the Principate.

According to Tacitus, Tiberius was jealous of his popularity in Germany, where he had won victories and was more admired by the legions than the emperor, so Germanicus was sent to Syria. On his journey to the east he made significant stops in the footsteps of Alexander, including Troy, where he probably visited the tomb of Achilles.[49] He then travelled to Egypt where he dressed like the local Greeks in imitation of his grandfather, Mark Antony. He visited a mouth of the Nile sacred to the Egyptian Heracles, a god revered by Alexander.[50] Tacitus does not tell us if Germanicus visited the tomb of Alexander but this too is probable.

At length Germanicus reached Syria and the banks of the Euphrates River where he met amicably with Parthian King Artabanus, 'a young man of distinguished presence', and even helped him against a rival. This was the above-mentioned Vonones, who, while in exile in Syria, stirred up rebellion against Artabanus. Germanicus removed him to Cilicia at a distance from the frontier.[51] Parthia and Rome enjoyed good relations while Germanicus lived and kept the border at peace. His sudden and mysterious death in AD 19 changed that.

Germanicus was greatly mourned in Rome. Some, including Tacitus, saw his short life and 'manner of death' as similar to that of Alexander:

> Both were handsome, both died soon after thirty, both succumbed to the treachery of compatriots in a foreign land [Tacitus seems to have believed the story that Alexander had been poisoned]....If he [Germanicus] had been in sole control, with royal power and title, he would have equalled Alexander in military renown as easily as he outdid him in clemency, self-control, and every other good quality.[52]

Dutch historian GJD Aalders argues that Tacitus is looking at the life of Germanicus posthumously and that we have no evidence that Germanicus himself thought that he was imitating Alexander. Aalders cites EG Turner's reading of the *Oxythnchus Papyri* to suggest that while in Alexandria, Germanicus made allusions to Alexander but left 'a deliberate ambiguity as to whether he is associating only himself, or the whole populace of Alexandria, with the aspirations of Alexander'.[53] The coy nature of his association with the Macedonian hero mimics the caution of his Julio-Claudian predecessors.

Artabanus of Parthia was especially bitter toward Tiberius after Germanicus' death. The antipathy increased when the king of Armenia died. Artabanus was quick to place his eldest son Arsaces on the often-contested Armenian throne, to the great displeasure of Tiberius, who had once personally crowned an Armenian king.

Arsaces was soon poisoned and killed but replaced by his younger brother Orodes. Tiberius backed the brother of the king of Iberia to rule Armenia and Orodes was exiled. Furious at the treatment of his sons in Armenia, the Parthian king let it be known that he considered himself to be both the heir of the Achaemenid Persia and the Macedonian empires, with a claim to all the territory that they once ruled over. That would include Egypt, the Levant and Anatolian peninsula clear up to the Hellespont. According to Tacitus, 'Artabanus added menacing boasts about the old frontiers of the Persian and Macedonian empires, promising to seize the lands that Cyrus and Alexander had ruled'.[54]

Flavius Josephus suggests another reason for Artabanus' antipathy for Tiberius. The emperor, through Lucius Vitellius his governor in Syria, secured the Euphrates against a threatened Parthian invasion. Dio explains:

> He [Vitellius] terrified the Parthian by coming upon him suddenly when he was already close to the Euphrates, and then induced him to come to a conference, compelled him to sacrifice to the images of Augustus and Gaius, and made a peace with him that was advantageous to the Romans.[55]

Vitellius bribed the kings of Iberia and Albania to allow Alani (or Scythian) invaders through the Caucasian passes to pillage Parthia, 'and the country of Parthia was filled with war and the principal of their men were slain and all things were in disorder among them'.[56] Artabanus had good reason to despise Tiberius and Rome.

Incidentally, another act of Vitellius while governor of Syria was to relieve Pontius Pilate from his office as Procurator in Judea. His nephew, also named Vitellius, would be a short-lived emperor of Rome in AD 69.

When Tiberius died in AD 37 he was followed by his great-nephew, Gaius (Caligula), the youngest son of Germanicus.[57] Initially popular for the sake of his father, this bizarre ruler had a strange attachment to Alexander. He plundered Alexander's tomb and took the Macedonian's breast plate, which he was fond of wearing in public when he displayed himself as Alexander.[58]

Dio mentions Caligula's usurpation of the breastplate in the context of the building of a two-lane pontoon bridge across the Bay of Naples from Puteoli to Baiae. With great pomp, Caligula rode across the bridge in both directions. On the first trip across the bay he wore the breastplate and a purple silk robe, called in Greek a *chamys*, adorned significantly with gems from India. Caligula boasted that his bridge was longer than the one built by Xerxes to cross the Hellespont.[59]

However, there is an interesting modern view of this event. Professor Simon Malloch makes the case that Caligula acted in imitation of Alexander's bridging of the Indus River.[60] It is in this context that the wearing of the breastplate and the Greek and Indian influenced *chamys* makes sense.

Caligula's return trip across the bridge led to a drunken free-for-all among the people who followed the procession, more or less instigated by the emperor. Malloch sees this as a deliberate imitation of Alexander's Bacchic procession through Carmania in southern Persia. He further adds that Caligula was 26 or 27 years old at the time, approximating the age of Alexander in India.[61]

In his retinue on the bridge that day Caligula had with him a young Persian man named Darius, a son of Parthian King Artabanus, who was a hostage in Rome. The identification with the Achaemenid Darius III would have been obvious to the onlookers.

The boy's name, which was also his grandfather's name, could suggest Parthia's claim to be the successors of the Achaemenid Empire. Caligula no doubt enjoyed having a Persian 'Darius' as his 'hostage', as it served to promote his own comparison to Alexander. Whatever Caligula's other failings; his foreign policy with Parthia seems to have been successful.

Early in the year 40, Caligula led a military expedition to the North Sea. According to Dio Cassius, who doesn't seem to know for sure, he might have been preparing for an invasion of Britain.[62] While on the shore in front of his legions he boarded a trireme and was rowed a short distance out to sea. Then he put about and landed again. Back on shore he reviewed his troops and then made the curious order that they collect sea shells from the beach, some of which were displayed in temples at Rome as 'spoils of war' in his 'victory over the Ocean'.

As a member of the Julio-Claudian dynasty, Caligula had to go to the North Sea as a matter of honour. It was expected of him. The key to understanding his short voyage on the North Sea is embedded in two themes that recur throughout first-century Rome. First, as we have seen, was the lure and mystery of the Outer Ocean and second was the direct connection between the Julio-Claudians and the North Sea which was considered to be a part of the outer Ocean.

As far as the Romans were concerned, the gold standard of association with the Outer Ocean was Alexander the Great. The reason that Caligula ventured out on the ocean in a Roman warship was because his father Germanicus, great-uncle Tiberius, grandfather Drusus and the great Caesar, the founder of his dynasty, had all done it. Just as important, Alexander, for all his conquering, ventured only briefly upon the Ocean. Caligula placed importance upon symbolism and by venturing upon the Ocean he had equalled his predecessors and Alexander.

As for the collection of sea shells, this was done for a very Roman purpose. In Holland, near the mouth of a branch of the Rhine River, Caligula built a fortress that year (AD 40) and named it Praetorium Agrippinae, after his mother Agrippina. Nearby has been found an old Roman road. Significantly, this road was paved in part with crushed sea shells.[63]

There is another comparison or *imitatio* that modern historians have missed. Suetonius reported that Caligula had wished to make his horse, Incitatus, a consul of Rome. This incident is often used as an example of the emperor's growing madness. Whatever his state of sanity he could very well have been thinking about Alexander who named a city in India after his beloved horse, Bucephalus.[64]

Another sign that is often cited by modern historians as proof of Caligula's madness was the proclaiming of himself to be a god.[65] Even in this there is Alexandrian precedent, for in his final years Alexander too sought to be worshipped as a god and sent messengers to Greece to demand their acquiescence to his godhead. The response of Damis the Spartan still gives us a chuckle.

> Damis, with reference to the instructions sent from Alexander that they should pass a formal vote deifying him, said, 'We concede to Alexander that, if he so wishes, he may be called a god'.[66]

Caligula's pretention to godhood was treated in much the same way in Rome but with a bit more care as the tyrant was near at hand rather than half a world away.

Still, in Rome his erratic and dangerous behaviour led British historian Diana Spencer to rightly suggest that the use of Alexander as a positive comparison for emperors was badly compromised by Caligula's distorted devotion to him. He was followed to the throne by his disabled uncle, Claudius.

During the reign of Claudius (r. 41–54) there was little if any 'Alexander-style personal excess'. Claudius went so far as to replace the face of Alexander with that of Augustus on the statues and images once owned by Alexander that were then in the forum.[67]

There was, however, turmoil in Parthia following the death of Artabanus in 38. Two of his sons, Vardanes (r. circa 39-47) and Gotarzes (r. circa 38-51) carved up the empire and plotted against each other. Into the middle of this squabble, supposedly, wandered, in 42, the Greek sage Apollonius of Tyana, who enjoyed the hospitality of Vardanes, as recorded by Philostratus.

A few years later, Gotarzes masterminded the assassination of his brother while he was on a hunting expedition. Gotarzes then took up the Parthian throne and a united Parthian realm around July of 46. He was the sole ruler of Parthia for the next four years. All of Vardanes male relations, their children and even their pregnant wives were slaughtered. He ruled with such cruelty that soon another delegation of disaffected Parthian nobility reached Rome in 49, asking for one of the growing stock of Romanized royal Arsacids to contest the throne once again.[68]

Claudius was happy to oblige. So too was the royal hostage in question, a young prince named Meherdates, another grandson of Phraates IV. A squadron of Roman cavalry accompanied him and his Parthian followers into Mesopotamia, but Gotarzes defeated and captured Meherdates in battle, ending another Roman attempt at influence in Persia.

Within a year of the death of Gotarzes, Vologeses I (r. 51–80) would succeed to the Parthian throne. Once again, Rome had an adversary worthy of the name. Vologeses' mother was a Greek courtesan, making him illegitimate, with all that implied in an age when such things still mattered. He presumably learned his Greek at his mother's knee but it was of little value at court. Vologeses grew up with the disposition of a brooding and bitter outsider, a dangerous personality trait in an absolute monarch.

Perhaps to forestall public resentment of the Greek half of his nature, he began to pursue the use of Persian forms.[69] Aramaic began to be used on coins, alongside or replacing Greek (depending on the mint) as well as depictions of the Zoroastrian fire temple. He founded new non-Greek cities and allowed the names of existing Seleucid-era Greek-named cities to revert to their native names. We are reminded of the renaming of Russian cities at the end of the Soviet era. The aura of Alexander was beginning to lose its grip on the Parthians. Richard Frye, the dean of Persian historians, wrote that 'the "orientalisation" of the Parthian state can be connected especially with the reign of Vologeses I'.[70]

Meanwhile, in Rome during the reign of Claudius, in at least one incident we have a hint of Alexander's influence. The emperor assumed command of the army during the conquest of Britain (in the Ocean) and even employed elephants during the campaign. Though we have little information about this campaign that completed what Julius Caesar began, it is an action which suggests the memory of the great Macedonian.[71]

Nero: The Great Compromise

Seneca the Younger was the tutor of the young Nero. It was an echo of Aristotle's tutoring of Alexander and perhaps a model for their relationship. Seneca's criticism of Alexander may well be a cautionary tale written for Nero's benefit.[72] Like Alexander, Nero would come to disregard his tutor.

The influence of Alexander on the young Nero can be clearly seen. When he first became emperor, early portraits of him in statuary, such as the bust at the Glyptothek Museum in Munich, and in coins issued during his reign, depicted him with features in common with Alexander, like the slight tilt of the head and curly hair.

A first-century bronze weight used for measuring, now at the University of Delaware, gives us a portrait of Nero with Alexandrian features including the turn of the head, slightly open mouth and the *anastole*.[73] A statue of a young Nero found at Suffolk in Great Britain suggests that he is like Alexander in that he is dressed in armour with Greek designs, while coins minted at Ephesus show him with curly hair and his lips slightly parted.[74]

On the east architrave of the Parthenon in Athens, an inscription paid tribute to Nero. The inscription is located alongside Greek heroes, including Alexander, who were victorious over Eastern enemies, especially Persia. It was dedicated during the time of Nero's war with Parthia over Armenia.[75]

That war began in 58 when the pro-Roman king of Armenia died. King Vologeses I of Parthia was able to place his own half-brother Tiridates, or Trdat (r. 52–58 and 62–88), on the Armenian throne. This was unacceptable to Rome. A savage series of battles was fought between Parthia and Rome over the kingdom and the succession of its king.

The Italian writer Carlo Maria Franzero argues that the war had more to do with the Roman desire for silk.[76] It is also likely that the wars over Armenia were fought to secure the gold, silver and iron found in Armenian mines which the Persians needed and the Romans wished to deny them.

Nero dispatched one of his most competent generals, Cnaeus Domitius Corbulo to right the situation. There followed five years of war which ravaged Armenian cities, countryside and populace until a compromise was agreed to. Tiridates might keep his throne if he would accept the crown from Nero's own hand. In 63, all parties agreed that this suggestion would be the best course.[77]

Tiridates set out for Rome to receive his crown from Nero. He arrived in 66 after a magnificent progress of nine months. There, in a pre-planned public ceremony, he laid down his crown at Nero's feet, only to have it graciously returned to him by the emperor. Nero then delivered a speech designed to demonstrate to Tiridates and Rome that he, like Alexander, could dispose of oriental despots at a whim:

> You have done well in coming here in person to enjoy my presence your-self. Your father did not leave you this kingdom; your brothers, though they gave it to you, could not guard it for you; but that is my gracious grant to you, and I make you King of Armenia, in order that both you and they may learn that I have the power both to take away kingdoms and bestow them.[78]

Nero may have even accepted initiation into the Parthian religion of Mithraism at this time, though we know little about it and at any rate he would soon have abandoned it.[79]

After the departure of Tiridates, Nero seemed to conceive Alexander-like schemes of expansion in the east. One likely goal was the territory of the restless Alani north of the Caucasus Mountains.[80] They were an ongoing threat to both Roman and Parthian territory.

Nero began recruiting soldiers throughout the empire. Included in the conscription was a legion of men from Italy, all of whom were over six feet tall. They were named 'The Phalanx of Alexander the Great' and he may or may not have planned to lead them himself.[81] Unfortunately we know nothing more about them.

Nero had other schemes as well. He dispatched an expedition of exploration, led by military men, up the Nile River to explore its source and possibly chart the way for an invasion of Kush, a territory and people just to the south of Egypt. Halted by an immense and impenetrable swamp (the Sudd in southern Sudan), the expedition turned about and returned home. Seneca spoke with two of the centurions of the party about their experiences.[82]

Alexander, always curious about what lay over the horizon, was supposed to have also sent an expedition up river to try to discover the Nile's source. Nero's efforts could be seen as an imitation of that event.[83] As it was, the source of the Nile would not be discovered until 1858.

Perhaps to follow up on the findings of the expedition, Nero planned to visit Alexandria.[84] He spent time 'dwelling in his secret imaginations on the provinces of the east, especially Egypt'.[85] However, he cancelled his Egyptian trip on the very day of his intended departure. He might have travelled later but events overtook him before any of his plans reached fruition.

Nero's wars with Parthia over Armenia and his subsequent actions do not appear to bear the stamp of Alexander but our principal source for his times is the work of Tacitus. His book, *Histories*, which is partially lost, breaks off before the end of Nero's reign, leaving us uninformed about his intentions.

Late in the year 68, Nero committed suicide rather than be taken by his domestic enemies. He was the last of the Julio-Claudians. One of the greatest accomplishments of his abbreviated reign was the establishment of fifty years of peace between Rome and Parthia, the longest period of *concordia* the two rivals would ever know.

The Flavians: Roman Revenge

In 69, following the death of Nero, Vologeses viewed the Roman general Vespasian as the likely winner of the struggle for the Roman throne. He offered to send him a troop of light cavalry to augment his forces. Vespasian politely declined. Later, in 72, when the Alani again crossed the Caucasus Mountains to ravage Armenia and Media Atropatene, it would be Vologeses' turn to ask Vespasian for help. The emperor turned him down even though his own son, the future emperor Domitian, perhaps dreaming of Alexander, was keen to lead the expedition.[86]

Vespasian used the truce with Vologeses to shore up the eastern frontier right up to the banks of the Euphrates River. He annexed the kingdom of Commagene, which included the important town of Zeugma with its strategic pontoon bridge across the river (today most of the city lies beneath the waters of Birecik Dam in southern Turkey). He gained control of the important caravan trading city of Palmyra, improved roads to and from the Black Sea across Anatolia and fortified distant Marmozica (in modern Georgia) in 75.[87] The fortifications at Marmozica were meant to guard against the Alani and so served both Rome and Parthia. He was able to do all this without leading to a breach with the Parthians. At the same time Vologeses was busy extending his control to Babylon and Nippur in southern Iraq without complaint from Rome.

Around 79 or 80 Vologeses died, leaving the Parthian throne to his young son Pakores (r. 79-105). His early (and rare) coins depict him without a beard. Too old for the guiding hand of a regent, Pakores had to sort out the complexities of kingship as best he could. A contemporary Roman writer, Publius Papinius Statius (c. 40/45-96), while writing an epic poem of Greek mythology, included a simile of a young Parthian king, thought to be Pakores. It is surprisingly sympathetic of the problems faced by the young king:

As may happen if a Persian boy (safer were his father still alive) has taken over the throne and the ancestral tribes; he balances joy with ill-defined dread – whether the noble will prove loyal, lest the common people resist his governance, to whom he should entrust the flank of the Euphrates? To whom the Caspian Gates? At that time he shrinks from taking up his father's bow and setting himself upon his father's horse, in his own judgment his hand is not broad enough to hold up the sceptre, nor yet can he fill out the tiara.[88]

The reference to the 'flank of the Euphrates' is the Parthian border with Roman Syria and lesser Armenia. Though Parthia and Rome were at peace, the note here suggests tensions between the two. The reference to the 'Caspian Gates' refers to a pass through the Caucasus Mountains and the dangerous Alani to the north, who had twice breached the pass to despoil Armenia and Media, both Roman and Parthian territory.[89]

Though specific to this monarch, the passage illustrates the concerns of all Parthian kings and the Sasanian kings after them. Still, the Flavian era was one of cooperation and at least a limited friendship between Rome and Parthia.

Trajan: In Alexander's Footsteps

The praises of Alexander, transmitted by a succession of poets and historians, had kindled a dangerous emulation in the mind of Trajan.

–Gibbon[90]

Trajan is difficult for the historian. He was considered by much of the Roman public, even long after his death, to be the *Optimus Princeps* or 'best of emperors' yet much of the documentation of his reign is lost to us. Modern scholars like Anthony Birley, Theodor Mommsen and FA Lepper have tried to piece together the little we know about him from the fragmentary sources available to create a coherent history. What follows, benefits from their work.

We know that Trajan's father, Marcus Ulpius Traianus, was for a time the governor of Syria. The father had commanded the Tenth Legion in support of Vespasian's bid to be emperor and was a favourite of his dynasty.

The younger Trajan served his father as his military tribune in Syria. He would have visited the eastern defences along the west bank of the Euphrates. His route took him through Issus where he could have, and probably did, visit Alexander's battlefield. These experiences would serve him when he became emperor in 98.

Lepper analyzed the causes of Trajan's war with Parthia. Earlier historians and ancient sources suggested such varied reasons for the war as frontier adjustment, economic factors, the desire for glory and a continuation of imperial policy. Lepper concludes that these all may have been contributing factors, but the trigger for war was Parthian neglect in the matter of sending the Arsacid candidate for king of Armenia to Rome for coronation.[91]

This occurred during what Richard Frye calls 'a time of decentralization' in Parthia. The cause of this movement away from centralized power was that at least three Arsacid princes vied for the Parthian throne. When one of these, Oroses (r. 109–128), had the opportunity, he replaced the Roman-anointed Armenian king with one more to his liking.[92]

Mommsen initially blamed Trajan for aggression but later placed the responsibility on the Parthians.[93] In the autumn of 113, Trajan departed Rome, resolved to go to war.[94] Once he was on the march, no negotiation or appeasement would be tolerated. Parthian ambassadors met him at Athens to plead for peace but to no avail. It was the same with Alexander who would not negotiate with the representatives of Darius once he was on the march. Crassus had also rejected Parthian pleas for peace but with disastrous results.

The emperor arrived in Antioch in January of 114. From there he set out for Armenia, stopping in Satala (Turkish Sadak) in lesser Armenia. Satala is 474 miles (760 km) from Antioch. Birley estimates it took Trajan seven weeks to march that distance.[95]

There he met with several minor kings and either confirmed or appointed them to their respective kingdoms. This action was in keeping with Alexander, who secured Anatolia before confronting Darius directly. Julian saw Trajan attempting to follow in the footsteps of Alexander and in *The Caesars* makes him say: 'My aims were the same as Alexander's but I acted with more prudence'.[96] In that satire the gods then rebuke Trajan for his boasting.

Parthamasiris, the offending Arsacid king of Armenia, appeared one day in the Roman camp. Copying the ritual begun by Nero, the king laid down his crown at Trajan's feet hoping that it would be restored to him. Trajan had no intention of doing so. Parthamasiris was deposed on the spot. Armenia was to become a Roman province and that was that. The former king was provided with a Roman guard of 'honour' for his return to Parthia but was treacherously killed on the way, probably at Trajan's direction.

At least one Roman writer, Fronto, would see Trajan's later setbacks as divine retribution for this treachery against Parthamasiris.[97] Armenia was then occupied and a Roman provincial governor appointed. With Armenia secured, Trajan returned to Antioch for the winter, where he survived a powerful earthquake that destroyed much of the city.[98]

In the spring of 115, Trajan turned his attention to Parthia. He crossed the Euphrates and then the Tigris. Trajan found himself marching in Alexander's footsteps. He probably crossed the Tigris where Alexander himself had crossed.[99] Cassius Dio explains:

> the Romans crossed over [the Tigris River] and gained possession of the whole of Adiabene. This is a district of Assyria in the vicinity of Ninus [Nineveh]; and Arbela and Gaugamela, near which places Alexander conquered Darius.[100]

Dio's passage is significant because it tells us that Trajan not only sought to imitate Alexander but he took the same route that his hero had taken to defeat the Persians.[101] Gaugamela was the field where Alexander fought the climactic battle with Darius III in 331 BC.[102] But if Trajan was hoping that the Parthian King Oroses would fight him there he was disappointed.

A generation later, Fronto echoed the respect that Romans felt toward Trajan when he wrote that the 'Empire of the Roman people was advanced beyond the hostile rivers [Tigris and Euphrates] by the Emperor Trajan', confirming the deeds of 'the stoutest of emperors'.[103]

Trajan left a garrison in Adiabene and returned to the Euphrates to lead a Roman column southward. The Roman force still east of the Tigris also marched southward in a coordinated pincer movement against the Parthians at Ctesiphon.[104]

As the Romans approached Ctesiphon, the Parthian king fled over the Zagros Mountains into Iran. He deserted the battlefield just as Darius III had done when confronted by Alexander. When the Romans entered the city they found among other booty, the Parthian throne and a daughter of the king.

The capture of the king's daughter and the Parthian throne are significant because of their symbolic importance. Alexander had captured the women of Darius' court and, of course, captured Darius' throne both literally and figuratively. Now Trajan could claim that he had duplicated the same feat. Trajan's expedition was shaping up to be a repeat of Alexander's triumphs.

From Ctesiphon, Trajan resolved to visit the Persian Gulf, whence ships sailed for India and where half of Alexander's army had made landfall after their visit to that country. Again Cassius Dio:

> Then he came to the Ocean itself, and when he had learned its nature and had seen a ship sailing to India, he said: 'I should certainly have crossed over to the Indi, too, if I were still young'. For he began to think about the Indi and was curious about their affairs, and he counted Alexander

a lucky man. Yet he would declare that he himself had advanced farther than Alexander.[105]

Of course he had not advanced further than Alexander. Perhaps Trajan was including his campaigns in Dacia and Armenia in this calculation. It is just as likely that Trajan also considered that by viewing the Persian Gulf he had reached the outer Ocean and therefore had duplicated the Macedonian's achievements.

The reports of his exploits made thrilling news in Rome. Circus games were held in his honour and the imperial mint issued coins announcing the defeat of Parthia with the inscription *Parthia capta*. One such coin was a part of the Sanpex collection which was auctioned off in 2011.[106]

Professor Touraj Daryaee writes that the campaign of Trajan signalled a 'major shift in Roman imperial policy toward the East.'[107] Lepper on the other hand argues that Trajan's actions were a continuation of Flavian policy. Vespasian had, Lepper tells us, 'annexed Commagene and Armenia Minor in 72 AD'. He then quotes French historian F Cumont:

> There is no doubt that the purpose of annexing these two buffer states was to allow the realization of a work that was to ensure the supremacy of Rome on Greater Armenia… This conquest prepared by the engineers of the Flavians was obtained without effort by the legions of Trajan.[108]

They are both right. Trajan certainly did reverse Julio-Claudian diplomacy and revive the expansionist policy of the rapacious generals of the late republic. Vespasian had laid the groundwork for him, though he remained within a framework of cooperation with Parthia.

Next Trajan wanted to visit the ancient city of Babylon to pay tribute to Alexander. The mud-brick city had fallen into ruin. Most likely the river had changed its course, bypassing the city. Seleucid rulers had depopulated Babylon by moving residents to their new capital of Seleucia. The Parthians continued the population shift when they built the competing city of Ctesiphon. But at least one structure in Babylon still stood, it was the house where Alexander had died. Dio tells us of Trajan's entry into Babylon:

> for he had gone there both because of its fame — though he saw nothing but mounds and stones and ruins to justify this — and because of Alexander, to whose spirit he offered sacrifice in the room where he had died.[109]

Once Trajan had occupied southern Iraq, resistance came in the form of guerrilla warfare. Squabbling among Parthian princes was suspended because of the Roman threat. Parthian warriors infiltrated Roman-occupied towns in Mesopotamia and picked away at Roman garrisons and small detachments. They were even victorious against larger Roman units. At the same time, several Jewish communities within the Eastern Roman world rose up in revolt, perhaps at the instigation of the Parthians.[110]

With tough fighting, Trajan was able to recapture much of what he lost to the guerrillas but he was in danger of being trapped in Babylonia, cut off from supplies and communications. Perhaps the strain of the uprising caused his health to deteriorate and he was forced to retreat to Syria. He died soon after.

In his war on Parthia, Trajan had been a sound tactician. He had protected his flanks and kept his supply lines open but he could not effectively counter Parthian guerilla tactics in the small urban settings of the day without recourse to massive retaliation and what we would call 'collateral damage'.

Even though Trajan had won most of the conflicts, he was compelled to withdraw from Babylonia because of his suddenly declining health. The Parthians would soon regain control of most of their former territories. Like the Tet Offensive during the Vietnam War, the insurgents lost the battles but won the war.

Yet the comparison to the work of Alexander was obvious. If it occurs to us that Trajan's campaigns had similiarities to that of Alexander the Great, it certainly occurred to the Greeks of his day.[111] Contemporary artists may also have promoted the comparison to Alexander. An equestrian frieze on Trajan's Column is remarkably similar in appearance to the equestrian mosaic of Alexander in the House of the Fawn mosaic at Pompeii. In our own time, Graham Webster delivered an appropriate eulogy:

> Trajan might have intervened with diplomacy and a show of force, but lured by the vision of Alexander, chose to mount a vast expedition with a view to settling the Parthian problem once and for all.[112]

In perhaps a last attempt to imitate Alexander, Trajan was said by some to have purposely not announced his choice of successor.[113] He gave his ring to Hadrian, just as Alexander had given his to Perdiccas but that was all. Hadrian soon saw to it that that the world knew that he was the chosen one.

Hadrian's first official act, within hours of his accession, was to abandon the provinces of Mesopotamia, Assyria and Greater Armenia. The army in the East was loyal to Hadrian but he needed it to challenge potential rivals elsewhere. He could not have the legions bogged down in war with Parthia.

Hadrian tried to make the best of a bad situation. Perhaps it was his propagandists that informed the author of the *Historia Augusta*:

The Parthians always regarded him as a friend because he took away the king whom Trajan had set over them. The Armenians were permitted to have their own king whereas under Trajan they had had a governor, and the Mesopotamians were relieved of the tribute which Trajan had imposed.[114]

Hadrian was much more in the mould of Augustus, the administrator of empire and negotiator rather than Alexander and Trajan, the conquerors. He would spend much of his time binding the provinces of the empire into a single imperial unit. Like Augustus, he favoured negotiations with the Parthians rather than war. He returned the king's daughter (captured by Trajan) to him but refused to return the Arsacid throne. Nevertheless he was able to restore peace by personal diplomacy.

This did not mean that the influences of Alexander were not all around him. When the army was putting down a rebellion in Britain a large Roman force sailed to the mouth of the Tyne River. There they sacrificed to the gods Neptune and Oceanus, the deities of the Ocean. Alexander had sacrificed to these same two gods when he reached the Ocean at the mouth of the Indus.[115]

There were other reminders of Alexander that Hadrian very well may have witnessed. When he was in Asia in 124, he had occasion to cross the Granicus River near Alexander's battlefield. In 130, he had an extended stay in Alexandria while visiting Egypt. No surviving sources tell us that Hadrian visited the battlefield at Granicus or Alexander's tomb in Alexandria but it is most likely that he did both.[116]

Then too there was the death of his friend and lover Antinous in Egypt. In his grief, Hadrian had statues, 'or rather sacred images' (as Dio writes), dedicated to him set up all over the empire.[117] His actions mirror those of Alexander when he lost his friend and lover Hephaestion. Alexander's grief was profound. This dead youth was worshipped as a 'hero', just short of a god.[118] Alexander also lost his beloved horse Bucephalus. Alexander founded a city in India naming it Bucephalus. Hadrian would found a city in Egypt and name it after Antinous.[119]

Another nod to Alexander was the portraiture of Alexander on coins minted in Alexandria during the reign of Hadrian 'in the guise of the Genius of Alexandria.'[120]

A favourite of both Trajan and Hadrian was the contemporary Greek writer Plutarch. We are familiar with his *Parallel Lives* which link men of the Roman world with the Greek past. Alexander is famously paired with Julius Caesar. Plutarch also wrote two admiring essays known as *The Fortune of Alexander*. Plutarch's glowing accounts of Alexander most certainly had imperial approval.

Hadrian was succeeded by Antoninus Pius (r. 138–161). We know less about the reign of Pius than any of the other Antonines. This is because the surviving work of the principal historian of the age, Cassius Dio, is incomplete. While he is our most trusted source about the Antonines, his writings on Pius have not come down to us. We have to rely on the sketchy outline of the *Historia Augusta*. We are less able to trace an Alexander connection without more information. However, a series of coins minted in Alexandria during his reign depict Heracles performing his different labours. Depicted on the coin, Heracles is killing the Nemean lion. The god then wore the skin on his head as copied by Alexander on some of his coins. It is probable that Pius wished to associate himself with Alexander for the benefit of his Greco/Egyptian subjects.

Summary

The defeats of Crassus and Antony by the Parthians had a profound and sobering effect on early imperial policy. The era of the Julio-Claudians represented the most hopeful and cooperative time in the relations between Rome and Parthia. The diplomacy of Augustus led to a Roman client king in Armenia, royal Parthian hostages in Rome, the return of the standards of Crassus and Antony as well as the hope and expectation on the part of his contemporaries that Rome would absorb both Parthia and India into the empire as Alexander had done.

Relations deteriorated briefly during the reign of Tiberius but were restored by Gaius (Caligula) and Claudius. The control of Armenia however was disputed during the reign of Nero. Fighting was confined to that country and no hint comes down to us that the Romans contemplated expanding the war to Parthia itself.[121] Conflict ended when an ingenious compromise was found that kept the peace for the next fifty years.

The imitation of Alexander continued but in style and not function. When Nero offered the crown of Armenia to a Parthian prince he was making a rather flamboyant show of associating himself with Alexandrian (and Roman) control, but without substance.

Alexander's martial influence of expanding to the east, practised in the late republic, revived with Trajan. He imitated the Macedonian hero by crossing the Tigris River and then southward into the heart of Persia as Alexander had done. He then lamented that, because of his age (and deteriorating health), he could go no further in his footsteps.

Peace would be restored by Hadrian who surrendered most of the territorial gains made by Trajan, resumed the Augustan model of administrating the empire and relied on diplomacy to achieve foreign aims.

Chapter 5

Marcus Aurelius: Unintended Consequences

Alexander the Great, and his groom, when dead,
were both upon the same level, and ran the same chance
of being scattered into atoms or absorbed into the soul of
the universe.

–Marcus Aurelius[1]

In the mid-second century interest in Alexander apparently waned. The leading Roman figure of that time was Marcus Aurelius who was one of the most popular and beloved rulers in Roman history. Unfortunately, our surviving sources are minimal, sketchy and in some cases questionable.

Aurelius mentions Alexander twice in his *Meditations* (above) but in a detached, philosophical way. Nothing he writes speaks of admiration or imitation of the Macedonian. Surviving art and coins also tell us little. From what we know the model for the *imitatio* in official art had changed to one of imitating Roman heroes such as the venerated Augustus and Trajan.

The lack of primary sources is reflected in the dearth of secondary sources. Angela Kühnen's otherwise-comprehensive dissertation on the imitation of Alexander contains less than a page about the entire Antonine dynasty. The present chapter will deal with at least the peripheral ways in which the Antonines may be compared to Alexander.

In 148, a strong king rose up to reinvigorate the Parthian realm. Vologeses III (r. 148–192) became the sole ruler of Parthia. A long period of civil war was over and the new king could focus his attention on the Roman enemy. Vologeses enjoyed, or endured, a reign of over forty years.[2] He is credited with beginning the process of gathering in one place all of the holy books of the Zoroastrian religion so important to the Achaemenids and later Sasanians. Under his leadership the now-united Parthian army grew in size and strength. He would augment his powerful cavalry with conscription of light and even some heavy infantry.

One of his first acts as far as Rome was concerned was to write to Antoninus Pius and request, perhaps demand, the return of the Parthian throne that had been stolen by Trajan. Antoninus turned him down cold. The Parthian throne would remain a trophy in Rome.[3] The insult rankled. This throne then fades from history as it is not mentioned again by our surviving sources.

In 155, Vologeses threatened to invade Armenia which at the time was friendly with, if not dependent upon, Rome. However, such was the power and authority of Antoninus Pius that he was able to curtail the Parthian's plans by merely writing the Parthian king a letter advising him not to do so. The timely letter was backed up when additional Roman troops were sent to garrison Syria.[4]

In 161, Antoninus Pius lay dying after a short illness. The end came calmly. In delirium, he famously cursed the conduct of certain foreign kings, including most assuredly, Vologeses of Parthia. He then slipped away in his sleep at the age of 75.[5] His successor was Marcus Aurelius.

The godly aura of Alexander waned somewhat after Trajan. We do not see the influence of Alexander on Marcus that we see with Trajan, even though Marcus assumed a pan-Hellenic role in the Greek-speaking world of his time that was once undertaken by Alexander.

In his study of the famous equestrian statue of Aurelius at the Capitoline Museum in Rome, weapons authority Helmut Nickel sees Parthian-inspired designs in his horse blanket but no Alexandrian touches.[6]

Aurelius himself seems to disparage any links with Alexander. In his *Meditations*, he condemns Alexander, Pompey and Caesar for 'completely destroying whole cities' and 'cutting to pieces many tens of thousands of cavalry and infantry'.[7] Julian would later echo this theme in *The Caesars*.

Unlike Alexander and the Roman heroes of the past Marcus fought, for the most part, defensive rather than offensive wars. His wars were aimed at conserving cities, cavalry and infantry. In fact there is little in the few surviving sources or the literature to link Marcus Aurelius with Alexander. His statuary and coins are uniquely Roman and there is a dearth of surviving images of Alexander produced during the later Antonine years.[8]

Aurelius was not a warrior. Instead, before his rise to power, he had pursued the life of the mind as a philosopher of the Stoic school. He was his own man, not swayed by pretensions to grandeur or greatness. While WW Tarn and MH Fisch may argue over the association between the Stoics and Alexander, Aurelius, a Stoic himself, does not make the connection.[9]

Ironically, while Aurelius did not invite comparisons between himself and Alexander, he may have been closer to the Macedonian in spirit than any of his imperial predecessors. Though physically weak and constantly ailing, during Aurelius' nineteen-year reign he spent over half of his time with his army in the field, a time span that rivals Alexander.

Verus: Victory and Death

Aurelius and another noble youth, Lucius Verus, were the adopted sons of Antoninus Pius. Aurelius unselfishly asked the senate to give Verus the same powers and honours that he had, creating two emperors for the first time.[10] It was Verus who would face Parthia.

Trouble in the East erupted with the death of Pius. Expanding Roman influence with Armenia by a growing and mutually beneficial commerce had been chaffing at Parthian King Vologeses III. Without an internal rival to distract him, he began assembling his forces even before the passing of Pius. That emperor's death and the ensuing transition of government in far-off Italy was the trigger to turn them loose.

In Parthia it was expected that brothers would fight each other to the death to control the government and the kingdom. Vologeses thought the Romans would do the same. He miscalculated, for Verus and Aurelius worked in harmony to share power.

Expecting Rome to be preoccupied, Parthian cavalry swept unexpectedly through Armenia capturing the capital in 161. The Roman-backed King Sohaemus was lucky to escape with his life while the Parthians swept on toward Syria.[11]

A royal Arsacid relative of the Parthian king named Pacorus (or Bakur) was put on the Armenian throne. He was thought to be a choice that would please the Romans as he had lived in the eternal city and may have even been a Roman citizen.[12] Parthia had not demonstrated this much aggression since the time of Mark Antony. Though Armenia was far from Rome, the neighbouring provinces of Cappodocia and Syria were threatened.

The first Roman reaction was a provincial one. Marcus Sedatius Severianus, the governor of Cappadocia, prompted by a soothsayer or oracle named Alexander of Abonoteichus, led a single legion into Armenia to confront the invader. At the town of Elegeia, the provincials were surrounded and crushed after a three-day siege. Among the dead was the hapless governor who apparently killed himself.[13]

The contemporary writer Lucian mentions this Roman defeat in the context of one of his satires. In the piece, a bogus oracle living in Cappadocia advises a client to take part in the Armenian campaign promising victory and glory:

Lo! The Parthians and Armenians
Bow beneath thy conquering spearhead
Back to Rome and Tiber's waters
Thou shall come, a crown of triumph
Flashing splendour on thy temple.

When the fake oracle's client was killed in that disaster he is said to have deleted his rosy prediction from the records and replaced it with one more prophetic:

> Wage not war with Armenia
> Such a war is best avoided
> Lest a man in female clothing
> Shoot from bowstring fate disastrous
> Stop thy breath and quench the sunlight.[14]

The Romans, feeling more threatened than ever, organized a second provincial expedition into Armenia. This time it was the notoriously unprepared troops of Syria who marched into the foothills of Armenia. They too were repulsed.[15] Aurelius then dispatched Verus to Syria to right the situation. For Verus it was the perfect opportunity to imitate Alexander by military success against a Persian enemy. For reasons of his own he did not do so.

The joint emperors had shared the same tutor in their youth at court, the learned Fronto. His relationship with the young princes was similar to that of Seneca to Nero and Aristotle to Alexander. In his *Meditations*, Marcus acknowledged his former teacher who taught him about the dangers of tyranny: 'From Fronto I learned to observe what envy, duplicity and hypocrisy are in a tyrant'. Fronto had plenty of Romans to show as examples but he may also have included Alexander. Unlike his predecessors, Marcus seems to have learned the lessons his tutor taught him.[16]

When it came to practical matters Fronto was well aware of the Parthian menace. He wrote to the boys while he was their teacher:

> The Parthians alone of mankind have sustained against the Roman people the role of enemy in a fashion never to be despised, as is sufficiently shown, not only by the disaster of Crassus and the shameful flight of Antonius [Mark Antony], but by the slaughter of a general [Maximus] with his army, under the leadership even of Trajan, the stoutest of emperors, and by the retreat, by no means unharassed or without loss, of that emperor as he retired to celebrate his triumphs.[17]

There was no mention of Alexander in his exhortation.

Verus, who may or may not have absorbed the lessons of his tutor, established himself in the pleasant grove at Daphne in the hills above Antioch. Here the clear flowing springs had, according to Libanius, once reminded Alexander the Great of his mother's milk.[18] But Alexander had moved on with his army, whereas Verus remained and dispatched his troops, under the command of others, against the

Parthians, while relaxing in luxury. In what may have been a small gesture to imitate Alexander, Verus shaved off his beard at the request of his mistress Panthea.[19]

According to the *Historia Augusta,* rather than having philosophers and scientists with him at court as Alexander did, Verus was partial to actors, jugglers, gamblers and charioteers. Flavius Eutropius, who would accompany Julian on his Persian invasion, agreed, writing that Verus 'was a man who had little control over his passions, but who never ventured to do anything outrageous, from respect for his brother [Marcus Aurelius]'.[20] This was not the picture of a man from whom martial success was likely to be forthcoming.

Some modern historians don't believe that Verus could have been as depraved as the *Historia Augusta* and Eutropius make him out to be.[21] We must keep in mind that Eutropius and the authors of the *Historia Augusta* wrote in the fourth century and probably give us a glimpse into what was expected of imitators of Alexander in late antiquity. In the minds of the later writers, Verus could not meet the Olympian standard set by Alexander or, for that matter, his own adoptive brother, Marcus.

Just as in Trajan's time, Armenia was the cause of the war with Parthia and in both cases it was dealt with first. Following the early setbacks of the hapless Severianus and the lacklustre Syrian troops, Roman soldiers led by Statius Priscus poured across the border in 163 and quickly restored Sohaemus to the Armenian throne.

In 165, having secured Armenia, another Roman army, commanded by Verus but led by his general C. Avidius Cassius, marched down the east bank of the Euphrates River to Babylon, supported by supply ships and meeting little resistance. Cassius entered Seleucia and, according to Eutropius, captured 'forty thousand prisoners' and 'brought off materials for a triumph over the Parthians'.[22] It was a triumph that Verus, not Cassius, would enjoy.

While the Parthians retreated before the advance of Roman arms as they had before Trajan, they had an inadvertent ally, disease. Roman soldiers contracted the plague which they took with them back to Roman territory. According to some accounts, hundreds of thousands of people throughout the empire died of the Iraqi-borne disease, seriously weakening the fabric of Roman society and the army. The Romans of this age encountered obstacles that Alexander never dreamed of. Eutropius remarked that Marcus Aurelius was greatly hampered in the war he later conducted against the Marcomanni because:

> after the victory over the Parthians, there occurred so destructive a pestilence, that at Rome, and throughout Italy and the provinces, the greater part of the inhabitants, and almost all the troops, sunk under the disease.[23]

Modern scholar Peter Christensen, studying Mesopotamian diseases, does not believe this outbreak of the plague could have been as virulent as ancient observers like Eutropius would claim.[24] The most extensive modern survey of the ancient sources is probably that of JF Gilliam, who looked at tax records and military enlistments and discharges as well as the scant surviving literary sources. He concluded that there was indeed a plague during the time of Aurelius but drew the same conclusion as Christensen, that it was probably not as devastating as later Roman historians suggest.[25]

In any event, while the war against Parthia raged, Verus remained behind in Daphne content to let his generals win the victories, a dangerous precedent for a monarch. Only his old tutor, Fronto, depicts him as a man of action and even compares him favourably to Trajan.[26] His is a lone voice.

Verus knew the value of having Fronto on his side and wrote to him that he was willing to follow his suggestions so long as 'my exploits are set in a bright light by you'.[27] Yet no one, not even Fronto, would compare Verus to Alexander. The extant works of Fronto tell us little about Alexander or any comparison of the Macedonian hero to his royal students. However, C R Haines believes that he has found a reference to Alexander in a fragment attributed to Fronto. His observation gives rise to the possibility that Fronto might have written more about the Macedonian king but, without more to go on, we just don't know.[28]

After Verus' death in 169, possibly due to the same plague that ravaged the Roman world, Marcus would have to deal with a rebellious general himself. Avidius Cassius, who was a descendant of Seleucid kings, was emboldened by victory and soured by ambition.[29] At first Avidius maintained the confidence of Aurelius, who appointed him governor of Syria.

Then in 175, upon the false rumour that Aurelius had died, Avidius proclaimed himself to be the new emperor of Rome. The armies of Syria and Egypt, perhaps because of his Seleucid blood, sided with him until it was learned that Aurelius still lived. The rebellion then collapsed.

It is tempting to suppose that Avidius was influenced by Alexander.[30] He had, after all, commanded a successful war against the Parthians and occupied their capital at Ctesiphon. His blood line reached back to Alexander's generals and successors. In any event his enterprise failed and he died in the attempted usurpation of the throne at the hands of an assassin who sought favour with Aurelius.[31]

Marcus graciously pardoned the family of Avidius as well as the provinces and legions who had backed him when they thought Marcus was dead. There would be no blood bath against the rebels. Aurelius was as renowned as Pompey, Caesar or Alexander for his *clementia*. Though he was a complete original himself, Marcus succeeded in an almost unconscious imitation of Alexander by devoting himself to his duty, his soldiers and the empire while avoiding the pitfalls of the tyrant.

When Marcus died on 17 March 180, he was beloved by the army, the Senate and the people. 'Even now,' the author of the *Historia Augusta* later remarked,

'Marcus is called a god and worshipped'.[32] He was venerated for protecting Rome and defending its borders rather than for expanding the empire. Julian considered him the wisest of the emperors and worthy of imitation himself. He would directly compare Marcus to Alexander as a worthy role model. Julian commented in *The Caesars* that there 'was a time when I believed that I ought to try to rival men who have been most distinguished for excellence, Alexander for instance or Marcus [Aurelius]'.[33] When his time came, Julian was bound to the attempt.

Commodus: The Comforts of Home

The benevolent Marcus Aurelius was followed by his cruel and depraved son, Commodus (r. 177-192). A child during the Parthian war of Verus, he played no part in the conflict. Once he assumed the purple, Commodus showed himself to be no Marcus or Alexander by abandoning the unfinished war against the invading peoples in Dacia and hastening to the comforts and diversions of the palace, leaving government and war to underlings.

Surviving statues and coins typically portray him with a beard, though a few of them, depicting him in his youth, show him clean shaven. He was compared by his flatterers to Hercules (Herakles) and was depicted in some statues in the dress of that hero.[34] The most obvious sign of Hercules in these statues is the wearing of a lion's skin with the fanged head atop his own head. In this we see an obvious imitation of Alexander who also was sometimes depicted in his coins and statues as Heracles, wearing the lion's head.

We also have literary reminders of Commodus' affectation of Alexander. A contemporary Greek writer, Athenaeus, paraphrasing the now-lost work of Ephippus, a historian contemporary with Alexander the Great, wrote of the two men:

> What wonder then is it, if in our time the Emperor Commodus, when he drove abroad in his chariot, had the club of Heracles lying beside him, with a lion's skin spread at his feet, and liked to be called Heracles, when even Alexander, the pupil of Aristotle, represented himself as like so many gods, and even like Artemis?[35]

At some point in his life, Commodus was devoted to the Egyptian cult of Isis, even shaving his head as the priests of Isis did.[36] It was not his only religious experiment. In a bronze bust dredged from the Tiber in the early twentieth century, Commodus is shown wearing a Phrygian cap dotted with stars. In that bust Commodus imitates another god, the Parthian god Mithras. It could have been produced around the time that Commodus took initiation into Mithraism.[37] He was also initiated into the Eleusinian mysteries in 176, along with his father.[38] Commodus, like Alexander and Mark Antony, enjoyed dressing up as gods.

Commodus dabbled in several different religions before deciding to be a god himself. In this he probably had Alexander's precedent in mind. He reigned for thirteen years until he was assassinated. His death in 192 ended the dynasty of the Antonines and unleashed a long season of anarchy.

Summary

Edward Gibbon considered the era of the Antonines the happiest time in the Roman experience, if not in human history. The empire was at the height of its power, wealth and peace. With Trajan, the Romans believed, they had surpassed the accomplishments of Alexander and found little reason to imitate him. Our lack of reliable sources limits the conclusions we can draw about the need for the Antonines to imitate Alexander.

What little we know about Antoninus Pius suggests that he, too, preferred peace, though he was not above going to war if he had to. Aurelius and Verus were compelled to fight the aggressive Parthians but did not do so in imitation of Alexander's conquests but as a defensive measure. Verus was not interested in army life, while Aurelius was a reluctant but successful warrior and a true original, venerated by later generations and, in that sense, comparisons were made between him and the Macedonian hero.

His son Commodus copied some of the forms of Alexander but was much too self-absorbed and a lover of luxury to imitate his military prowess. Yet the memory of Alexander never faded and would await a season to reawaken.

Chapter 6

The Severans: Father and Son Invade Iraq

Septimius Severus: Parthia laid low

> He [Severus] used to declare that he had added a vast territory to the
> empire [Mesopotamia and Assyria] and had made it a bulwark of Syria.
> On the contrary, it is shown by the facts themselves that this conquest
> has been a source of constant wars and great expense to us. For it
> yields very little and uses up vast sums; and now that we have reached
> out to peoples who are neighbours of the Medes and the Parthians
> rather than of ourselves, we are always, one might say, fighting the
> battles of those peoples.
>
> –Cassius Dio[1]

The influence of Alexander, which had waned during the era of the Antonines, would revive during the dynasty of the Severans. The wars of the Severans against Parthia would bring renewed interest in Alexander's conquests.

The death of Commodus, like that of Nero, was the end of a dynastic era and ushered in a new civil war between multiple contenders. The ephemeral candidates of the Senate and Praetorian Guard were soon undone and the commander of the army on the Danube, Septimius Severus (r. 193-211) faced rivals from Britain and Syria. Pescennius Niger, commanding in Syria, was proclaimed emperor by his troops. After an early victory over forces loyal to Severus, Niger's men, to his obvious delight, began hailing him as the new Alexander:

> At this time he was more puffed up than ever, so that, when men called him
> a new Alexander, he showed his pleasure, and when a man asked, 'Who gave
> you permission to do this?' he pointed to his sword and answered, 'This.'[2]

With his province bordering the Euphrates River, Niger appealed to Parthia for support during the civil war. A troop of horse archers from the Arab-populated city of Hatra (Al-Hadr) answered his call, with the approval of their nominal over-lord the king of Parthia. This suggests at least some Parthian meddling in Roman affairs to the extent of trying to influence the choice of a new emperor, just as Rome had often tried to influence the kingship of Parthia and Armenia. Herodian explains:

> He [Niger] also sent word to the king of the Parthians [Vologeses V], and to the king of the Hatrenians [Hatra], asking for aid. The Parthian king said that he would order his governors to collect troops – the customary practice whenever it was necessary to raise an army, as they have no standing army and do not hire mercenaries. Barsemius, king of the Hatrenians, sent a contingent of native archers to aid Niger.[3]

There is a sense of irony (or pathos) that Niger as 'the new Alexander' felt the need to call upon the Persians for aid in his war upon a countryman. Pompey and Vespasian had turned down similar offers.

Parthian motivation could very well have been their on-going claim to the eastern Mediterranean lands once ruled by the Achaemenids. With civil war raging in Roman territory, there was always a chance for Parthia to expand its influence at Rome's expense.

Parthian support, or sympathy, was not enough. Septimius quickly overcame Niger. Their climactic battle was fought at Issus, on the very field where Alexander had defeated Darius III. Hidden by low-lying clouds Severus' cavalry got behind the enemy and crushed Niger's army in the field.[4] If the significance of the battlefield occurs to us then it most certainly must have occurred to Niger, who had been so 'puffed up' by the comparison of himself to Alexander.

However, it was Severus who adopted the tactics of Alexander at Issus, getting his cavalry behind his enemy.[5] As it was, Niger was defeated and killed at Issus, ending the short lived career of the latest 'new Alexander'.

While Niger had relished the comparison with Alexander, Severus focussed on the deeds of the Macedonian. Severus felt the need to go to war against Parthia for its support of Niger and because they had been raiding into Roman territory while Roman armies were distracted with fighting each other.

Like Alexander, Trajan and Verus before him, he first secured Anatolia and Mesopotamia before marching southward into Babylonia in the autumn of 197. The Romans had learned by now to invade Iraq in the autumn of the year, when the scorching summer weather had abated. Severus took advantage of that knowledge and marched down the east bank of the Euphrates River after the heat of summer had dissipated.

As with Trajan, he was supported by a river flotilla of supply and war ships. Yet the soldiers suffered privations on this campaign. The author of the *Historia Augusta* gives us an idea of the hardships suffered by his soldiers:

When the summer was already ending, he [Severus] invaded Parthia, defeated the king, came to Ctesiphon, and took it. It was almost winter – for in those regions [Iraq] wars are better carried out in winter, although the soldiers live on the roots of grasses and contract diseases and sickness as a result...and the soldiers' bowels were loosened on account of the unfamiliar diet.[6]

In his winter campaign against the Parthians, Severus marched virtually unopposed into the heart of Babylonia, where he captured the cities of Babylon, Seleucia and Ctesiphon. However, when King Vologeses V (r. 207-227?) escaped into the Zagros Mountains of Iran, Severus did not pursue him as Alexander would have.

It is this Vologeses that the ninth-century Islamic historian al-Tabarī mentions briefly, giving us an idea of how a Parthian king without a standing army raised a force among his feudal lords to resist the Romans:

Balāsh [Vologeses] wrote to the regional princes informing them of the campaign planned by the Romans against their lands, and of the Roman forces which he could not confront. He wrote that should he succumb, the Romans would defeat all of them. Then the princes, each according to his ability, sent Balāsh men, arms and money.[7]

It is likely that this is the method that all Parthian and later Sasanian kings used to amass armies to fight the Western enemy. We do not know Tabarī's source for this anecdote. Written records of the Parthian era were scarce even in his time. It is likely that he benefited from some Sasanian chronicles and a strong Iranian tradition of heroic oral story telling.

Rather than strike deeper into Parthian territory, Severus, satisfied with his victory, was ready to leave Babylonia for home. He claimed to be unfamiliar with the countryside and low on supplies. He may also have feared to stay in Babylonia for too long because of the outbreak of disease which had accompanied Verus' army home.

There may have been other factors in his early departure from Ctesiphon. Birley writes of Severus' fear of the 'myth' of Alexander.[8] Wags at Rome must have unfavourably compared Serverus to Alexander who did not let the Persian king escape and who, unlike the emperor, had no trouble crossing the Tigris River to get at his enemy.

Reflective of the public interest in the conquest of Persia is Philostratus, who we have previously mentioned as the author of a work on Apollonius of Tyana. Philostratus was active as a writer during the dynasty of the Severans. In his book,

Apollonius reaches India where he, like Alexander, had conversations with holy men.[9] The interest in far-off India revived with the Severans.

Instead of imitating Alexander's romp through Persia, Severus chose to compare himself with the victorious Roman emperors of the past. He proclaimed Parthia to be conquered on 28 January 198. The significance of the date was that it was the one-hundredth anniversary of the accession to the throne of Trajan, *optimus princeps* (the best of emperors), of whom Severus claimed to be a great-great grandson.[10]

Following his victory against Parthia, Severus journeyed to Egypt, where he continued to distain the memory of Alexander. Approaching Alexandria, he stopped in Pelusium at the tomb of Pompey, which had been restored by Hadrian, to sacrifice and pay his respects. It may seem odd that both Hadrian and Septimius would honour the republican general Pompey, enemy of Caesar, but after the passage of so many years Pompey had been rehabilitated and acknowledged among the pantheon of Roman heroes.

Severus then entered the city and viewed Alexander's tomb briefly before closing it to all others. Perhaps he did not want to be unfavourably compared to the Macedonian hero. Severus, it seems, preferred to revere the Roman past rather than that of Macedonia.

The compliant Senate awarded Severus the title of *Parthicus Maximus* and a triumphal parade for his victory over the Parthians but he refused to accept the honour. As he grew older he suffered from gout and could no longer stand in a chariot or mount a horse. He refused to be seen in public with his disability. The Byzantine historian John Malalas later confirmed that Severus had 'crippled feet'.[11]

Unlike Trajan, Severus was able to hold on to northern Mesopotamia and it would remain a part of the empire for the next 200 years. Yet, as Dio noted (above), the occupation of what is now northern Iraq and south central Turkey was not worth the money or the manpower it cost the Romans to hold it.

At the time though, Severus was flush with victories and these were seemingly significant at the time. He had defeated a rival at Issus. He had subdued a restive Egypt and he had conquered Persia. The comparison to Alexander was not difficult to make.

Caracalla: The Last Battle with Parthia

when he (Caracalla) passed beyond the age of a boy, either by his father's advice or through a natural cunning, or because he thought that he must imitate Alexander of Macedonia, he became more reserved and stern and even somewhat savage in expression, and indeed so much so that many were unable to believe that he was the same person whom they had known as a boy. Alexander the Great and his achievements were ever on his lips.[12]

–Historia Augusta

The last war between Rome and Parthia was occasioned by Severus' son Marcus Aurelius Severus Antoninus (r. 211-217). He is known to us as 'Caracalla', the nickname derived from a type of cloak that he favoured. The young emperor (he was 21 when his father died in 211) disposed of his younger brother Geta before taking sole possession of the throne.

At some point he began to think of himself as the reincarnation of Alexander the Great and wished to duplicate his prowess both personally and militarily. This attitude may even have prompted the murder of his brother, bearing in mind Alexander's actions:

> When he [Alexander] set out to the Persian war, he put to death all his stepmother's relations whom Philip had advanced to any high dignity.... Nor did he spare such of his own kinsmen as seemed qualified to fill the throne, lest any occasion for rebellion should be left in Macedonia during his absence.[13]

Like Pompey and Caligula he used items once owned by Alexander. According to Dio, he 'was so enthusiastic about Alexander that he used certain weapons and cups which he believed had once been his'.[14] He also sought to be associated with Alexander in the form of artwork, as in a medallion found in Egypt and now at the Bode Museum in Berlin, which depicts Caracalla in the Alexander tradition. There is also a statue of Caracalla in the guise of Helios at the North Carolina Museum of Art. The statue was made while Caracalla was a youth and not yet emperor but is designed to make the connection between him and Alexander, who also had been depicted in the form of Helios.[15]

A hoard of twenty gold disks was found at Abukir, Egypt in 1902. Most of these Roman-era medallions date from the Severan dynasty and depict Alexander in a style reminiscent of Hellenistic coinage. Three of these disks depict Caracalla on the obverse. On two of these, Alexander is depicted on the reverse. On the third disk, Olympias, the mother of Alexander, is shown on the reverse. Caracalla's association with Alexander was the clear message.[16] Andrew Stewart said of Caracalla's coinage: 'his portraitists had no compunction in showing him with his neck inclined and head turned either way'.[17] In other words, his artists conspired with him to demonstrate the identification with Alexander.

Caracalla was said to enjoy the distractions of Rome as a boy but soon grew tired of the city's noise, politics and intrigue. He left Rome in 213, never to return. His first destination was the camps of the army along the banks of the Danube River. Like Caligula, he had been raised in the army camps of his father and felt at home there. He made a point of joining in the soldier's life:

> If a ditch had to be dug anywhere, the emperor was the first man to dig; if it were necessary to bridge a stream or pile up a high rampart, it was the same; in every task involving labour of hand or body, the emperor was the first man on the job. He set a frugal table and even went so far as to use wooden dishes at his meals.[18]

Both Herodian and Dio wrote of his sharing the hardships of the troops as well as the generous donatives (money) that endeared him to his men even as it depleted the Roman treasury. It was the same formula that Alexander and the successful generals of the republic had used to bond with their soldiers. The next year these men were ready to follow their emperor to the East.

Caracalla led the army through Thrace into Macedonia and, according to Herodian, 'immediately he became Alexander the Great'.[19] While in his hero's homeland Caracalla ordered statues and paintings of Alexander to be made and displayed in all the cities of the empire. Herodian tells us that Rome was filled with these works that were 'designed to suggest that he [Caracalla] was a second Alexander'.[20] He even wrote to the Senate to tell them that Alexander had come back to life as their emperor.[21]

While in Macedonia, he recruited local youth to form a unit which he called the 'Macedonian phalanx'. These men were uniformed and armed in the style of Alexander's infantry phalanx. According to Dio, their equipment 'consisted of a helmet of raw ox-hide, a three-ply linen breastplate, a bronze shield, long pike, short spear, high boots, and sword'.[22] Their officers were given the names of Alexander's generals.[23] Dio suggests that their number reached 16,000, though this seems excessively high, especially since they are not heard of again.

With Alexander-like ambitions, it is not surprising that Caracalla would want to lead his army against Parthian Persia. In 214 he set out for the East. He crossed over to Asia Minor and landed near Troy. He toured the site and inspected the ruins. He sacrificed at the tomb of Achilles as Alexander had done because, like Octavian, he venerated Achilles' tomb for its association with Alexander. Then Caracalla was said to have spent at least some of the winter months visiting cities that Alexander had passed through.[24]

His next stop was Egypt. In Alexandria he reopened the tomb of Alexander that had been closed by his father. Herodian informs us that, while gazing at his hero:

he [Caracalla] removed his purple robe, his finger rings set with precious gems, together with his belts and anything else of value on his person, and placed them upon his tomb.[25]

The generous gesture would have helped pay for the upkeep of the tomb that was by that time a cultural museum.

Caracalla took other inspiration from Alexander's corpse, as Aurelius Victor explains:

After he viewed the body of Alexander of Macedon, he gave orders for himself to be called 'the Great' and 'Alexander', having been drawn by the intrigues of flatterers to the point that, with fierce expression and neck turned toward his left shoulder (which he had noted in Alexander's face), he reached the point of conviction and persuaded himself that he was of very similar countenance.[26]

That 'fierce expression' is captured in a bust housed at the J Paul Getty Museum (among other places). It was this type of statue which prompted art historian Andrew Stewart to note:

Among the most remarkable portraits of the age are the nervous, scowling Alexander-emulating busts of Caracalla with restless head and wrinkled brow.[27]

Caracalla was initially popular with the people of Alexandria for the honours he paid to their city. But he held a grudge against these people for making him a butt of their jokes. According to Herodian, the Alexandrians 'were mocking him because, in his insignificance, he imitated the bravest and greatest of heroes, Alexander and Achilles'.[28]

The mocking insults, many of which compared him unfavourably to Alexander, stung and Caracalla, like his father, was a vindictive man. He set a trap for the unsuspecting young men of the city. At a signal, his soldiers produced hidden weapons and slaughtered many of them.

Next he turned his attention to Parthia. Dio relates that about this time the Parthian king Vologeses V died and that his sons fought over the throne.[29] Al-Tabarī may have been referring to this interlude when he mentions in passing, 'Persian rule continued to break down until the rise of Ardashir (the first Sasanian king)'.[30] The situation was not dissimilar to the death of the Achaemenid King Arses (Arsha) in 336 BC, which resulted in the civil war that brought Darius III to the throne.

Like Crassus, Caracalla wished to make war on Parthia during a time of peace. He adopted a scheme that he thought would give him control of the kingdom. He offered himself up for marriage to the daughter of the new Parthian king, Artabanus V (r. 207-227). It is very possible that his reasoning stemmed from Alexander, who had married a daughter of Darius III. This union would create a single earth-spanning empire, facilitate trade and combine the strength of both armies to jointly combat the northern barbarians. It would be an empire greater than Alexander's, spanning the globe from Spain to India.

We have two versions of Caracalla's Parthian war, one by Herodian and the other by Dio. Both men were contemporaries of the events. In Herodian's version the Parthian king reluctantly agreed to the marriage. Perhaps he saw it as a way to shore up his own position, which was deteriorating from the defection of some of the satrapies and client kingdoms in the unsettled empire.[31] When Artabanus agreed to these arrangements, Caracalla set out to meet his bride. In this narrative, Herodian tells us that Caracalla led his army into Parthia 'as if it were already his' and approached the palace of Artabanus.[32] He does not tell us where the palace was located. It is possible that the city of Ctesiphon is meant. The king and his court were lured out of the city for the wedding celebration. At a signal from Caracalla his men raised their concealed swords and slaughtered the Parthian dignitaries much as they had done with the youth of Alexandria. The king escaped with wounds but among the dead were some of 'his children and kinsmen'.[33]

In Dio's version, Artabanus declined the wedding proposal while the Roman army swept through northern Mesopotamia and Media, looting and pillaging. In Arbela (near the Gaugamela battle ground) they desecrated tombs said to belong to Parthian kings. Perhaps Caracalla was challenging the Parthians to meet him at Gaugamela for battle as Alexander had done. The Parthians did not oblige.

The *Historia Augusta* is no help. On the one hand the Romans are 'advancing through the lands of …the Babylonians' which would put them at Ctesiphon and supports Herodian's claims. But in the same sentence Caracalla is reported fighting only the satrapies of the king which gives credence to Dio's account.[34] The *Historia Augusta* must be viewed with some scepticism in any event as Herodian has been shown to be one of the sources used by its writers.

It is very unlikely that Artabanus would have allowed Caracalla to approach his capital for the wedding with his army in train. The story of the concealed weapons is too much like the incident in Alexandria. Dio, on the other hand, has Caracalla committing atrocities near the Alexandrian battlefield at Gaugamela, which could have been a ploy to entice the Parthians to battle in that very place. So, in this instance, Dio's version seems to make more sense than that of Herodian.

The emperor, having done so much to identify himself with Alexander, did not follow through in his campaign against Parthia. Instead, having won at least some kind of preliminary victory over the Parthians, he withdrew and wintered in Mesopotamia, where he prepared for the next campaign season.

There he wrote to the Senate, requesting triumphal honours and the victory name of *Parthicus* for the little he had already accomplished. It was during the lull in the fighting that he was assassinated near the memorable town of Carrhae, site of Crassus' defeat and death.

Caracalla died in the sixth year of his reign. He was not able to fulfill his dreams of Persian conquest. Birley observed that 'Caracalla's obsession with Alexander had been pathological'. He is probably right.

Caracalla's incursion into Parthian territory, no matter how ephemeral, set into motion the last war between Rome and Parthia. As the Romans cast about for a new leader, Artabanus had been busy in the winter of his discontent. He collected a large army from his realm in the manner described by Al-Tabarī above, and marched against the Romans in Mesopotamia.

The Romans meanwhile chose a new emperor. We know him by the name Macrinus (r. 217-18). He needed to return to Rome quickly to solidify his right to rule. Artabanus by that time had brought up his army and would not let him leave without a fight. There followed a two or three day battle (the sources differ) that forced Macrinus to pay a large sum of gold as restitution for damages done to Parthian territory.[35] Imperial propagandists called the embarrassing payment a 'gift'.

The last battle between the two enemies was a Parthian tactical victory. They remained in possession of the field and a good deal of gold besides. Strategically, however, both sides were losers. Rome disintegrated into the near-anarchy of the third century, while the Parthian dynasty was overthrown by the powerful Sasanians of Persia in 224.

Summary

It's accepted that our [Roman] power reaches as far as the Artic and the home of the west wind, and that we oppress the lands beyond the burning south wind, yet in the East we yield to the lord of the Parthians.

–Lucan[36]

Septimius Severus, like all new dynasts, had to consolidate his hold on power while protecting his borders. His invasion of Parthia was a response to Parthian moves in support of his rival Niger, as well as their incursions into Armenia and raids into other Roman territory. His son Caracalla, conscious of his father's achievements against the Persians, was instrumental in reviving the memory and imitation of Alexander.

With the death of Caracalla, his successor, Macrinus, was compelled to buy peace with gold. But for the Parthian victor, Artabanus, gold was not enough. His new-found wealth could not save him or the Parthians from the vigorous rebellion of the Sasanians and their allies.

In one of the quirks of history that lead us to remember that history repeats itself, in our own time the father-and-son American Presidents, George Bush the elder and younger, also both invaded Iraq. Septimius Severus, like Bush the elder, was successful, quickly declared victory and got out. Caracalla, like Bush the younger, was not so lucky.

Chapter 7

The Sasanians

Worthy Successors

> The Great King Ardashir orders the Romans to retire from Syria and all
> of Asia opposite Europe and make way for the Persians to govern as far
> as the [Mediterranean] sea.
>
> –Zonaras[1]

The imitation of Alexander by Caracalla was emblematic of a new wave of interest in the Macedonian hero. A certain amount of literary interest in Alexander had begun not long after his death. By the third century AD it had become widespread and influential.

The books of Curtius, Arrian and Plutarch, who all wrote about Alexander, were available, as well as other writings that have not come down to us. Parts of a Greek work called *The Alexander Romance*, a romantic view of Alexander's life, was known in republican Rome in a Greek edition and would eventually be translated into Latin in the fourth century, probably by a man named Julius Valerius.[2]

Another extant work attributed to Valerius was the *Itinerarium Alexandri* or *The Itinerary of Alexander*. It is a short summary of Alexander's conquests based on the work of Arrian. It complemented a twin essay on the conquests of Trajan, now lost. It was written specifically for the Emperor Constantius II (r. 337-361) as he set out for war with Sasanian Persia.[3] It was hoped that his war on Persia would be as successful as Alexander's.

As early as the end of the first century AD, 'Domitian (r. 81-96) wanted to be known as *dominus et deus noster* (our lord and god)', in the style of a Hellenistic monarch.[4] As the centre of power within the empire shifted from the Latin West to the Greek East, the trappings of imperial Hellenism became popular.

Two centuries after Domitian those words would appear on the coinage of Aurelian (r. 270-275).[5] It would become one of the titles of the later emperors. *Dominus* would give its name to an age, the 'Dominate'. Emperors no longer cared about being 'first among equals' with Senators in Rome who were increasingly divorced from the workings of empire.

The wearing of the diadem became popular. The *Historia Augusta* stated that Gallienus (r. 253-268) was the first Roman to wear it.[6] Alaric Watson, the modern biographer of Aurelian, points out that Gallienus posing for his coins [in a diadem] is an 'allusion to Alexander the Great that is unmistakable'.[7] By the time of Constantine, this white silk ribbon would be replaced by gold and bejeweled substitutes. The diadem began to take on its modern definition as a crown.

It is no coincidence that the rise of interest in Alexander among Romans came at a time when Rome faced a resurgent and aggressive Persia. This was a new and virile enemy: the Sasanians. Born of a native people, the Sasanians would value their Persian roots and attempt to distance themselves from Western culture. But this would be difficult.

The Australian historian A D Lee suggests that Sasanian Persia was a Western-oriented empire. He argues that the majority of Sasanian population centres were in the west, especially in Mesopotamia near the Roman/Byzantine border, where there was extensive trade, religious, military and cultural contact.[8] Bordering Greek culture, the Sasanians would still feel this influence.

The last Parthian king, Artabanus, had staved off the advances of the hapless Caracalla, and bludgeoned the desperate and doomed Macrinus. By 220, with the equivalent of millions of dollars of Roman tribute in his purse, the Parthian king was at the height of his fame. No one outside the country could foresee that his dynasty would effectively end with him. Yet dependent kingdoms all over Iran became increasingly disaffected with Parthian rule.

In the south of the Iranian plateau, astride the Persian Gulf, resided the Fars people. In the distant past their mighty kings, Xerxes, Darius I and Cyrus, had ruled over the Persian empire at its height. After the humiliating defeat at the hands of Alexander the Great, Fars was reduced to a client kingdom, subordinated first to Alexander and his Seleucid successors and then, for over four hundred years, to the Parthians, a people not originally from Iran and therefore thought of as occupiers.

The very word 'Fars' became the root of the name 'Persia' as well as that of the modern Iranian language, Farsi. Subjugation sat hard with the Persian people and they nursed their grudges for centuries.

There was a major uprising of the Fars people during the reign of the Parthian king Vologeses IV but it was premature. Parthia was still too strong. In the 220s, the Fars' leader was a man named Ardashir. His grandfather had been named Sasan and the dynasty that Ardashir would found would be known as 'Sasanian'.[9]

In 220 he revolted against his Parthian masters. Other Persian kingdoms joined his cause, especially as they began to see which way the wind was blowing. The Parthians did not present a united front against Ardashir and his allies. The powerful Suren clan, second in the Parthian realm only to the royal Arsacids, allied themselves with the new Sasanians. Suren horse archers would be numbered among the new king's cavalry and be a permanent force in any Sasanian army.

Other Parthian clans followed suit. The dissident Parthians would hold key positions under the Sasanians.[10] As late as the reign of Shapur II, the general who defeated the Roman emperor Julian was from a Parthian clan.[11]

In three hard-fought battles Ardashir was finally (in 224) able to defeat and kill Artabanus on the Plain of Hormuz (east of Ahwaz, Iran) and proceeded over the next several years to bring almost all of Parthian territory under his control. Three hundred years later, Agathias would view this event in the context of Alexander's achievement: 'Artaxares [Ardashir] seized the throne of Persia 538 years after Alexander the Great of Macedon'.[12]

In Armenia, the royal family and aristocracy continued to be members of the Arsacid clan. They found themselves at odds with the new regime of Ardashir who was dedicating himself to overthrowing their kinsmen. Parthian refugees were welcomed to resettle in Armenia. The Arsacid kings of Armenia considered themselves the legitimate heirs to the Persian throne. In an ironic twist of fate, the Armenian Arsacids turned to Rome for protection from the ascendant Sasanians.

Ardashir was an active man. He was an avid horseman and an early advocate and player of the game of polo. (In the *Alexander Romances*, the Macedonian king was also associated with polo.)[13]

Ardashir sprang from a priestly family of Magi, and dedicated himself to the restoration of the old ways. He believed that he was a direct descendant of the Achaemenid rulers of old, and therefore the heir to the glory that was ancient Persia.

Eutropius, writing in the fourth century, and the Christian writer Paulus Orosius in the fifth century, refer to this king as 'Xerxes', the name of a famed and powerful Achaemenid king. Eutropius does not name his source but we do know that the Latinized renderings of Ardashir's name include the name 'Xerxes'.[14]

His coins proclaim him to be of the 'lineage of the gods'. Professor Daryaee views the background of this claim to divinity as being introduced to Persia by Alexander the Great.[15] Even the Sasanians would find themselves at least subtly imitating Alexander.

There is a small body of Sasanian writing that can be called *Imitatio Alexandri*, which alternately vilifies and admires Alexander. Seven of these Middle Persian texts contain references to Alexander.[16] These Sasanian-era texts, like that of the twelfth-century Persian poet Abu Tāher, consistently referred to Alexander as a 'Roman' (*hrōmāyīg*).[17] Daryaee suggests that the Sasanians bought into Roman imperial propaganda that Alexander was the ancestor of the Severan emperors, especially Caracalla and Severus Alexander.

There is another possibility. The Hellenized peoples of the eastern Roman (later Byzantine) Empire consistently referred to themselves as 'Roman' (*Romaioi)* because, even though they were culturally Greek, they considered themselves a part of the Roman Empire. This identity would persist until the end of the Byzantine Empire in 1453. It may have been this self-description that informed Sasanian and later Islamic opinion.

The new Persian regime would, from the outset, portray Alexander as a villain. In an ancient Pahlavi work, *Karnamak-e Ardeshir* or *The Records of Ardashir*, the second paragraph tells us of the Sasanian point of view, 'During the evil reign of Alexander…'.[18] Some historians see the demonization of Alexander as part of Sasanian political and religious propaganda.[19]

In at least one Zoroastrian text, the *Ardā Wīrāz Nāma*, there are references to Alexander destroying Zoroastrian documents, persecuting the Magi and suppressing their religion.[20] It is likely that these Middle Persian condemnations were written at a time when Christianity was threatening the state religion of the Sasanians and used by them as a defence of their beliefs. Alexander then is updated and brought into the middle of the contemporary religious conflicts.

There is at least one late Sasanian document in which the prior Arsacid (Parthian) dynasty is linked to the wickedness of Alexander:

And the third brazen branch that you saw, which is the rulership of Arsacids, who are manifest in the way and manner of evil, and in the manner of Alexander of the seed of wrath, they rule over Ērānšahr (Iran or Persia), and they destroy the Good Religion, and then themselves will fall inverted into hell from the material world.[21]

With the Sasanians, Zoroastrianism (The Good Religion) once again became the official religion of the realm, supported by a fervently devout monarch and the power of the state. It is in this context that we have some reference to Alexander. According to the Zoroastrian establishment, Alexander and the Macedonians were wicked and of the demon seed of Wrath who savaged the earth, slaying the Magi and destroying the true religion.[22]

Like the Romans, the Persians were of two minds about this man who had become a myth. A sympathetic view of Alexander was taken by the Persian poet Abu Tāher Mohammad al-Tarsusi, who, in the twelfth century, long after the Sasanian era, wrote an Iranian version of the Alexander Romance, the *Dārāb Nāma*, in which Alexander is viewed (improbably) as a champion of Islam.[23] Another work attributed to the 1200s was *Sikandar Nāma, e Barà* (*The Book of Alexander*) by Abu Mohammad Bin Yusuf, which also refers to Alexander as a champion of Islam.[24]

The Persian epic poem *Shahnameh* refers to Alexander as a powerful Persian king while calling him a 'Caesar' who travelled widely, including a visit to Mecca.[25] If the Zoroastrian Persians vilified him for his opposition to their religion than at least some of the Islamic Persians favoured him for those same actions.

Even Persian Romances that were not about Alexander include obvious allusions to him. The Iranian court poet Asadi Tusi, who may have been the teacher of Ferdowsi, wrote a romance called *Garshāsp Nāma* in 1058. His hero, Garshāsp, travels to India and converses with the Brahmans.[26] This was not a coincidence. The Islamic-era Persian poets were influenced by the Alexander Romances and several, including Ferdowsi, had their heroes take long journeys. Greco-Roman writers such as Charion, Apuleius and Longus were also influenced by the long journeys taken by Alexander in the Romances.[27]

In the field of religion, the Parthians had adopted Zoroastrianism from the Achaemenid Persians but they did not embrace it. During their reign, religions of all kinds were treated with alternating favour and benign neglect. All religions were tolerated because the Parthian rulers were not passionate about any one religion.[28] Christianity and Judaism were even encouraged when these faiths were persecuted in the Roman world (the enemy of my enemy is my friend).

That changed with the Sasanian revival of Zoroastrianism as the state religion of Persia. The priests of that faith, called Mobads or Magi, gradually regained their ancient status and privileges. With power sprang intolerance. Now that they were influential again at the court of Ardashir, the Magi would in time suffer no other faith within their realm. Within a few generations, the Christians and Jews would begin their age-long decline into second-class citizenship that would continue under Islam. Other religions such as Manichaeism and Mithraism would disappear altogether.[29]

The Magi grew in power and influence. In a very real way they were the spiritual ancestors of today's ayatollahs. They were guardians of the official Iranian state religion and their power derived from the people who revered or feared them.

The very model of Magian intolerance was a priest named Kartir. He came to power as a pillar of the Sasanian rulers during the reign of Ardashir's son Shapur I (r. 240–272).[30] He is credited with engineering the death of the mystic heretic Mani, founder of Manichaeism, who had been a court favourite under Shapur I, the most tolerant of the Sasanian kings.

Kartir would be granted unprecedented authority by Shapur's sons, who viewed him as a pillar of their dynasty. With their backing or acquiescence he initiated pogroms against the various Christian sects, the Jews and other groups who did not worship Ahura Mazda and the eternal flame of Zoroaster.

In the West, Christianity was not yet the dominant religion at the beginning of the Sasanian era. Pagan mysteries and a pantheon of gods still had credence among the people. By this time Alexander had assumed almost god-like status. During the reign of Elagabalus (r. 218-222), a scion of the Severan family, Dio Cassius reports that a spirit, claiming to be the famous Alexander of Macedon, and resembling him in looks and general appearance, set out from the regions along the Ister, after first appearing there in some manner or other, and proceeded through Moesia and Thrace, revelling in company with four hundred male attendants, who were equipped with *thyrsi* and fawn skins and did no harm.[31]

The progression of this reincarnated 'spirit' of Alexander through the eastern empire demonstrates the power that the Macedonian king still held over the popular imagination. Dio does not make it clear what happened to him.

As for Ardashir, he was a very active character. By 226, he had occupied Ctesiphon and proclaimed himself the new Persian King of Kings (*Shahanshah*). Then he turned his attention to Rome. As a revivalist of the ancient Persian Empire, he believed that the rightful domain of the Persian world should extend to the Hellespont and should include all of today's Asian Turkey, Syria, Palestine and even Egypt. He wrote to the Roman emperor suggesting that he evacuate his forces from the eastern Mediterranean so that Persia might take up her ancient and rightful possessions once again. In Herodian's words:

He [Ardashir] claimed that it was now his task to renew this empire for the Persians just as they had possessed it in the past.[32]

Just as the Romans strove to humiliate Persia in imitation of Alexander, Ardashir sought to restore Persia to the greatness and territory of the Achaemenids at the expense of Rome.

Ardashir invaded Roman Mesopotamia in 230. So violent was his attack that the entire province was rolled up into the capital city of Nisibis (Turkish Nusaybin) which alone held out. The city had been under Greek and then Roman control since Alexander's victory at Gaugamela. Ardashir left an army to besiege the city and moved west to threaten Syria.

The emperor of the Romans at the time had come to the throne as a 14-year-old boy. His name was Severus Alexander (r. 222–235). He was the grandnephew of Septimius, nephew of Caracalla and cousin to Elagabalus.

The *Historia Augusta* said that he 'was given the name Alexander because he was born in a temple dedicated to Alexander the Great'.[33] Herodian had a different explanation. The boy's name was originally Alexianus until he became active in the government of his imperial cousin.

It was then that the name of Alexianus was changed to Alexander; the name of his grandfather became Alexander the Great, since the Macedonian was very famous and was held in high esteem.[34]

He was the first Roman to fight the new Sasanian dynasty. He intentionally took the throne name of the Macedonian hero and 'heard with pleasure...when they [poets] related the praises of Alexander the Great'.[35]

Another writer of the Severan era was Claudius Aelianus (Aelian) who mentioned Alexander of Macedon often in his work *De Natura Animalium* (*On the Nature of Animals*) because of the strange animals Alexander had encountered in Persia and India.[36]

In honour of his hero, the Severan Alexander took the step of restoring Macedonia's ancient privileges. He also presided over the games of Hercules that were held in honour of Alexander.[37] Upon his death it was charged contemptuously that he had 'wished to be a second Alexander the Great'.[38] He had some modesty, however. When he first became emperor, the Senate offered him the title of *Magnus* ('The Great') and he refused, saying that he had not yet done anything great.[39]

Later in his reign, though, he would adopt some of the symbols of Alexander. When he built public baths in Rome he named one of the bath-tubs 'the Ocean', and 'he had himself depicted on many of his coins in the costume of Alexander the Great'. When he was with his military friends he would offer a toast to the Macedonian.[40]

> In short, he made every effort to appear worthy of his name and even to surpass the Macedonian king and he used to say that there should be a great difference between a Roman and a Macedonian Alexander. Finally, he provided himself with soldiers armed with silver shields and with golden, and also a phalanx of thirty thousand men.[41]

Alexander the Great had soldiers outfitted with silver and golden shields in India and his infantry was formed in a phalanx. The Roman Alexander was perhaps the most blatant imitator of his namesake of all the Romans.

A modern historian has noted that a nude statue of the young monarch, now in the National Archaeological Museum of Naples, depicts him wearing the Alexander-inspired diadem. Though he is shown in an athletic pose, he is wearing the diadem rather than the laurel wreath which in ancient Greece symbolized athletic, not military, victory.[42] After Caesar's time it had become symbolic of military success without the disagreeable imperialistic implications. As the empire began to face eastward the diadem was becoming once again acceptable.

The young emperor assembled an army for a reckoning with the insolent new rulers of Persia. He would use the trappings and symbols of the great Alexander on his campaigns as he vowed to avenge the Persian outrage to Roman Mesopotamia. In the year 231, following the ancient tradition of the city of Rome, Severus

Alexander made public sacrifices before his departure to war. He then marched with his army out of the city. The people followed their popular young ruler across the Tiber, singing hymns and weeping with him at the sad necessity of his departure.[43]

The war with Persia, of course, was highly symbolic of the Macedonian Alexander's conquest and was seen that way. Over a hundred years later the historian Festus would remark, '[Severus] Alexander, as if reborn by some sort of fate for the destruction of the Persian race'.[44]

Unlike the Macedonian Alexander, his official entourage included his domineering mother Julia Mamaea. She was always influential in his decisions. Detractors accused her of being the real ruler of the empire through her influence over her impressionable son.

Along the way to Syria, the young Alexander gathered more legions as he passed through the provinces south of the Danube. Another legion was summoned from Egypt, and all were put to rigorous military training when they arrived in Antioch. Once again the Eastern troops proved unwieldy. Both a Syrian and the Egyptian legion mutinied. The emperor was forced to put down the uprisings and even disband an entire legion for its insubordination. Left without pay and honour, the disgraced men soon rallied around their eagle standard and begged their master to take them back. The emperor graciously relented.[45]

With his army in hand, Severus Alexander could not decide what to do next. A Roman army could invade the Persian homeland by three well-known routes. The first of these was through the mountainous safety of Armenia, where the Arsacid king urgently sought Roman protection. The second route was through the flat but dangerous plains of Mesopotamia. This was the path that the Macedonian hero had taken. The Romans now had interests there that needed protecting. Finally, there was the route southward along the Tigris and Euphrates valley to the heart of Iraq.

Unable to make up his mind, Alexander decided to take all three routes.[46] Committing one of the most basic of military blunders, he divided his forces in the presence of the enemy. The three Roman columns would not be able to support each other and did not coordinate their movements.

The northern arm of the Roman force moved through the hills of Armenia, gathering up Armenian allies along the way in order to invade Media. Persian opposition melted away before the slow but steady Roman advance into Sasanian territory. The Persian horse archers could not deploy effectively against the Roman infantry in the rugged hill country.

The Romans then invaded Media and plundered everything of worth they could get their hands on. As they rampaged about the land, the pleasant summer months waned into autumn. When an early winter came suddenly on them, the legions retreated to the safety of Syria. They were harassed in the mountain passes of Media and eastern Armenia by a relatively small band of Persians and Medians. Many of the invaders froze to death and fell where Mark Anthony's men had fallen before them.

Ardashir did not divide his forces as Alexander did. He abandoned the siege of Nisibis, while leaving a small blocking force in Media to harass the Romans there. He then focussed the bulk of his army upon the southern Roman force, which was headed down the Euphrates River toward Ctesiphon.

The Roman column advancing to the south found easy going at first. There was almost no opposition. Discipline became lax and the Roman lines wandered away from the protection of the Euphrates River on their right flank. From out of nowhere, Ardashir surprised them:

> The king attacked unexpectedly with his entire force and trapped the Romans like fish in a net; firing their arrows from all sides at the encircled soldiers, the Persians massacred the whole army.[47]

Meanwhile, the emperor, who had command of the central column, planned to follow in Alexander's footsteps through Mesopotamia. Inexplicably, he did not move from Syria. In that crucial summer of fighting against the resurgent Persians he did not leave Antioch, though some reinforcements were sent to relieve Nisibis.

Some accounts say he and much of his army were ill, while others claim that his domineering mother did not want him to risk his own life on campaign. He also may have been seduced by the pleasant groves of Daphne as Verus had been. As a result, his northern and southern forces were unsupported while he chose not to walk in the steps of his hero.[48]

The northern force straggled back into Syria much reduced by the ravages of winter, just as Antony's army had been three centuries before. They were compensated for their sufferings with the booty looted from Media. The pitiful remnants of the southern column limped back to Antioch with nothing to show for their efforts.

However, Ardashir's victory had been costly. The Romans fought fiercely and inflicted severe casualties on the Persian host. Ardashir was forced to lift his siege of Nisibis and abandon Mesopotamia to defend against the Roman attacks. The Roman garrisons there were reinforced and resupplied. More importantly, Syria was at least temporarily safe.

The expulsion of the Persians from Mesopotamia was the original goal of the expedition. The Persian departure from the siege of Nisibis and the wealth he brought back from Media allowed Alexander to declare victory and return to Rome in 233 for a triumph, his head covered with laurels.

The hyperactive Roman propaganda machine kicked into overdrive. Messages were received in Rome to the effect that the emperor had met and defeated a Persian host of over 120,000 heavy cavalry, 1,800 scythed chariots and 700 elephants, each bearing several deadly archers. Some later Roman historians would repeat the fantasy.[49] Upon his triumphant return to Rome, Alexander made a speech to the Senate in which he listed the vast number of forces arrayed against him and said that Ardashir was 'routed and driven from the field...in full flight'. His audience would have known that this was a reference to Persian King Darius III who fled from Alexander the Great at the Battle of Issus and at Gaugamela.[50]

The Senate dutifully voted their emperor the honour of a triumph, and the wealth stripped from Media made an impressive show. The conscript fathers of the Senate also voted to give the emperor the titles of *Parthicus* (they did not appreciate that the Parthian era was over) and *Persicus* for his victories.

Although Severus Alexander did restore Mesopotamia as a Roman province, it was merely a temporary setback for Ardashir. A peace treaty between Rome and Persia was negotiated and signed. At this time the Rhine frontier was threatened and the army was needed desperately in the West. The western imperative no doubt hastened the negotiations with Persia. Herodian noted the Persian's difficulty once peace was made:

> if once the Persian disbanded his army, it was difficult to reassemble, because it was not an organized standing force. Being really a horde of men rather than an army, with as much food supplies as each person on arrival brought for his own needs, they were difficult and reluctant to be torn away and leave their wives and families or their own land.[51]

The emperor, having made it clear to all that he was the new Alexander, rode off to protect another of Rome's river borders but was assassinated along with his mother in 235.

Two years after the death of Severus Alexander, Ardashir felt free of his treaty obligations to the deceased emperor and returned to the offensive in Mesopotamia. This time he was able to temporarily take both Nisibis and Carrhae, and he had the satisfaction of watching his son, Shapur, take Hatra in 240. Hatra, which in modern times has been occupied by ISIS, had continued to recognize the authority of the Parthians and obviously this could not be tolerated.

Not only did Hatra oppose the Sasanians, the city took the unusual step of requesting help from Rome. As early as 235 a detachment of Romanized Moors from North Africa helped to defend the city and left behind Latin graffiti to verify their presence.[52] Al-Tabarī noted that Shapur employed the services of several war elephants during the siege of Hatra.[53]

Al-Tabarī also tells the tale of a woman named Nadira, daughter of the Hatrian king, who betrayed her father and her city for love of Shapur. With her help he took the city. As part of the deal, he married her. However, he soon tired of her and put her aside because of her continuous complaints about the lack of creature comforts. When she whimpered about an uncomfortable mattress though it was made of silk, she anticipated (and perhaps inspired) Hans Christian Anderson's story of 'The Princess and the Pea'.[54]

The conquest of Hatra also found its way into Arabic folk poetry:

> Shapur of the Hosts attacked (Hatra) with war elephants, richly capari-soned, and with his heroic warriors. And he destroyed the stone blocks of the fortress's columns, whose foundation stones were like iron blocks.[55]

Before unleashing his son against Hatra, Ardashir laid siege to the fortress river town of Dura Europos and threatened Palmyra but the threat receded when he was compelled to move off to the east to meet other enemies.

When time permitted, Ardashir was free to pursue his natural enemy, the Parthian Arsacid who sat on the Armenian throne. From 226 to 238 he fought to overthrow the Armenian monarchy. At first, the Armenians acquitted themselves quite well. They gathered a strong army, strengthened by allied nations, and marched into Persia where their efforts met with some success. They pillaged Persian towns and farms and dragged great quantities of loot back to Armenia.

Frustrated with his long war with the Armenians, Ardashir resorted to that age-old weapon of war, treachery. He was able to find a disaffected Parthian nobleman of the Suren clan named Anak, who was willing to assassinate the newly ascended king, Khosrov II (d. 252), for a price. The traitor moved with his family from Persia to Armenia as though they were refugees escaping the wrath of the Sasanians. He soon gained the king's confidence and, in an unguarded moment, stabbed him to death. Horses were waiting for the assassin and he rode off for the safety of Persia. He did not make it. The king's guard caught up with him and executed him on the spot. His body was dumped into a local river. Back at the Armenian palace, the dying king commanded that every member of the assassin's family, men, women and children be put to death. His wish was granted.[56] The family of Anak the assassin were all killed save for an infant son. The boy's nurse spirited the child away to Cappadocia where he was brought up in a Christian household. As a man he would embrace that faith with missionary zeal, return to Armenia and become known as Gregory the Illuminator, the patron saint of Armenia.[57]

Meanwhile, with the Arsacid king dead, the Armenians fell into anarchy and the Persians poured through the undefended passes to conquer the entire country.

Yet, as so often happened in the painful history of Armenia, a young son of the assassinated king also escaped to Roman territory to continue the struggle in a new generation.[58]

Toward the end of his days, Ardashir decided to vest authority in his son Shapur and to take an honourable retirement from active life. Either he was becoming too sickly or (less likely) he wanted to enjoy life without the burden of authority. In any event, he laid down his sceptre for his son. It was a wise choice. It was around this time that Shapur captured Hatra.

Chapter 8

Shapur I, King of Kings

And we annihilated a Roman force of 60,000 at Barbalissus and we
burned and ravaged the province of Syria and all its dependencies.
                                    –Inscription at Naqsh-e Rustam[1]

By 241, the old enemies, Ardashir and Severus Alexander, were dead. Rome was once again in a dither about the successor to the last member of a ruling dynasty (the Severans). The different frontier field armies, provinces and even the Senate put forward their respective candidates and the legions shed their brethren's blood in a fratricidal orgy to find someone who could survive the assassin's knife. Few could. While the legions fought each other, the borders were left unguarded. Anarchy threatened all.

Succession, at least in this case, was much easier in Persia. The able Ardashir had an equally able son in Shapur I (r. 240–271), whom Ardashir had named as his co-ruler in 240, shortly before his death. Coins of the two men together announced the succession.

The name Shapur literally means 'the king's son'. According to Al-Tabarī, his mother was an Arsacid princess, which might explain his tolerance of different races and religions.[2] He would vex the Romans like none before him. In all, three Roman emperors would be humbled by his armies.

His coin shows us a man with a thick bull neck, sharp eyes and a nose possibly broken and healed improperly. His beard was close cropped and his lips pursed. The Byzantine historian Zonaras wrote that Shapur was a large man who towered over his subjects.[3]

While he was physically imposing, Shapur was one of the most learned of the Sasanian rulers. Jewish historians relate that he conversed freely with local rabbis.[4] He allowed considerable autonomy to Jewish cities and towns, permitting them to administer and adjudicate their own affairs and collect their own taxes. He showed them many signs of favour during his reign.

Once, he is said to have offered the Jewish community a fine white Nisaean horse (the kind reserved for royalty). If the Jews' promised Messiah were to come it was more fitting for him to ride a horse meant for a king rather than the donkey he was thought to ride.[5]

Shapur and other early Sasanian kings would include Greek, along with other languages, in their monumental inscriptions at Naqsh-e-Rustam. Art historian Matthew Canepa detects Dionysian themes in some of the early Sasanian art, a carryover from Hellenistic art popularized originally by Alexander.[6]

Greek continued to be the language of science and knowledge 'from India to the Mediterranean'. Persian authors would credit the study of Greek texts when composing their own writing. In Bactria, the site of a considerable Greek colony in Seleucid times, the Greek alphabet continued to be used until early Islamic times.[7] Sasanian kings, beginning with Ardashir, claimed to be descended from gods, a direct borrowing from Alexander and the Greek Seleucids.[8]

Shapur invited the philosopher and mystic Mani, who was born of Arsacid nobility (perhaps a relative of Shapur's mother), to his coronation and listened earnestly (we suppose) to his teachings. The mystic prophet, whose father may have been a Christian, was allowed to preach his blended message of Christian-like peace and Zoroastrian dualism throughout the empire.

Even though Mani preached against war, he sometimes joined Shapur on campaign at the king's invitation. It is the mirror image of Alexander and many Roman generals and emperors who favoured the company of philosophers and learned men while on campaign. We also must remember that the ancients liked bright colours, when we read that Mani's philosopher garb consisted of yellow and green striped trousers and a sky-blue overcoat.[9]

When Armenia and other client kingdoms learned of the death of the great Ardashir, there was rejoicing. Some of the subject peoples chose that time to rebel against Persian authority. This gave Shapur the opportunity to prove his mettle. Personally taking the field, he easily and ruthlessly crushed all dissent.

Then he put his mind to settling old scores with Rome. The records that have come down to us about Shapur and his wars against Rome are sketchy. Some of the Roman sources disagree with each other. The limited Persian references come to us from the monumental rock carvings in Iran and from a few mentions from later Islamic historians. These accounts are often at odds with Roman sources. As a general rule it can be said that the Romans tended to focus on Roman victories while the Persians focused on their own.

Shapur made at least three assaults on Roman territory during his reign. In the first campaign he unsettled the frontier area, sacking border towns and raiding as far as Antioch. The Sasanians, unlike the Parthians, were learning the art of siege warfare and used it effectively.

The breach of security along the eastern border shocked the Roman world. Yet the empire was weakened everywhere by the continual pressure of civil war and armed immigrant incursions across the Rhine and Danube frontiers. The intramural contests for the throne had left the distracted and mutually antagonistic legions in disarray.

Slowly the Romans were able to get their act together and send an army to contest the Persian violators of eastern Syria. The emperor of the moment was a young man named Gordian III (r. 238–244) who was but thirteen or fourteen when vested with the purple. His coins and statues show no signs of imitating Alexander. Perhaps to distance themselves from Severus Alexander and the Severan dynasty the emperors of this chaotic period chose not to copy the Macedonian or, just as likely, did not live long enough to do so.

In 242, with solemn Roman ceremony, sacrifices and public prayers, the emperor prepared for war. As part of the ritual, he opened the doors to the Temple of Janus for what would be the last recorded time.[10]

He set out from Rome for the East with an army augmented, for the first time, with large contingents of mercenary Goths and Germans in the ranks.[11] In addition to his troops, philosophers and scientists (probably his tutors) joined him on the march. Most notable among Gordian's companions was the 39-year-old Neo-Platonic teacher Plotinus, the most noted philosopher of his day.

A Greek born at Alexandria in Egypt, Plotinus was the student of the learned and mysterious Ammonius Saccas, one of the greatest teachers of antiquity, whose students also included the Christian mystic Origen and the sublime Longinus, who would later be executed as an enemy of Rome. Plotinus must have had some influence with Gordian. When he heard that the emperor planned a journey to the East, he invited himself along. He had in mind discussing philosophy with Indian mystics, as Alexander had done.[12] While Shapur had the mystic Mani with him on campaign, Gordian would have the Neo-Platonic Plotinus.

When Gordian arrived in Syria, Antioch was relieved from a loose Persian siege. By this time Shapur and the bulk of his army had already gone home, either because they had always planned to, or in anticipation of the Roman advance.

The remaining loot-and-hostage-laden Persians in Syria were disorganized, scattered and ill-disciplined. Their dissipated units were easily defeated piecemeal and the survivors retreated in haste beyond the Euphrates. The Romans, flush with easy victory, followed them across the river. There they defeated the Persians at Resaina (Ras el-'Ain) east of Carrhae (the site of modern fighting between ISIS and the Kurds), and retook both Carrhae and Nisibis.[13]

The Romans relieved a siege at Singara (Sinjar) to great rejoicing from the populace, before pushing southward between the rivers toward their intended target, Ctesiphon. Had he reached and conquered that city, he would most assuredly have been compared to Alexander. The architect of the Roman victories was a brilliant general named Timesitheus, the Praetorian Prefect and father-in-law of the emperor.[14]

In 244, Gordian fought a battle as far south as Falluja at a town called Misikhe (or Misiche). Both sides claim to have won that contest but the fog of war and history has obscured the truth. A Persian fire altar at Frayosh in Fars was dedicated to the victory, while Sasanian rock carvings at Bishâpur and elsewhere chronicle the event and suggest that Gordian was killed by Shapur. The inscription reads:

> On the edges of Assyria, at Misikē [on the Euphrates as it flows close
> to the Tigris], there was a great frontal battle. And Gordianus Caesar
> perished.[15]

The Bishâpur carving shows Gordian trampled under Shapur's horse. Roman records, of course, disagree. It is likely that it was Timesitheus who was killed at Misikhe. Following his death, supply problems plagued the army. Gordian was compelled to return to the safety of Syria, proud at having advanced so far into Iraq even though he was checked at Falluja.

In the spring, Gordian was planning to return to Rome to celebrate his victories. However, there seems to have been a good deal of discontent in the ranks. Contemporary historians say that his new prefect, a coarse and unlettered man known as Phillip the Arab, conspired against him. According to Zosimus, Phillip arranged for Gordian to be assassinated and then assumed the throne for himself.[16]

Zonaras tells a different story. He wrote that Gordian died when falling from his horse.[17] But no matter how he died, he was just as dead. A tomb and monument were erected at the site of his death at Zaitha, a fortress town between Circesium and Dura Europos in eastern Syria.[18] The new emperor, Phillip (r. 244–249), let out a story that Gordian had met with an accident and was inadvertently killed which apparently informed Zonaras' take on events.

Phillip quickly made a humiliating truce with the bewildered but delighted Shapur. Up to 500,000 denarii in gold was paid to the Persian to ensure the peace. The new emperor had no stomach for war in Iraq when his own empire needed to be won. In order to shore up his new imperial status he hastened to Rome to prevent rivals from contesting his right to the purple. The bulk of the army was gone from the East by 244. The shaky peace would hold for a decade.

Back in Rome in 248, Phillip would preside over the millennial anniversary of the founding of the city. The celebrations went on for days and included feasts, games, parades and a public holiday of thanksgiving. It would be the last time that state-sponsored secular games on this scale, including gladiatorial combats, would be held in Rome. The coming triumph of Christianity would put an end to the thousand-year-old tradition. As for Phillip, the Arabic emperor of Rome, he too would meet with an early death the following year at the hands of another claimant to the throne.

For the next several years both empires were distracted by troubles other than one another. Yet, when other disturbances subsided, the conflict between Rome and Persia would flare up anew.

Shapur's second series of campaigns against Rome began in 250 and lasted until 256. They formed a more widespread and coordinated attack. This time he was on the offensive. While he advanced with an army into the heart of Roman Mesopotamia, another Persian force based in eastern Armenia invaded Cappadocia.

Each side would blame the other for starting the war. The Sasanians wanted to end the Arsacid influence in Armenia, while the Romans demanded to approve the Sasanian choice of the Armenian king as they had done during Parthian times. That was unacceptable to Shapur. Roman interference in Armenia was all the excuse that the Persian king needed to ignite the next war.

In 252 (or 253), Shapur met a Roman field army on the banks of the Euphrates, east of Aleppo. At the Battle of Barbalissus, Shapur routed the enemy and bragged about it on the rock carving at Naqsh-e Rustam:

> And we annihilated a Roman force of 60,000 at Barbalissus and we burned and ravaged the province of Syria and all its dependencies.[19]

With the Roman army in ruins, Shapur was easily able to retake the city of Nisibis, the capital of Roman Mesopotamia. Shapur showed no signs of leaving Mesopotamia for home.

Instead, he began looking around to see what else he could lay his hands on. According to the rock carving at Naqsh-e-Rustam, Shapur captured some thirty-six cities on this campaign. His conquests included almost all of Roman Mesopotamia, Armenia and parts of Syria as far west as the hill-top fortress of Apamea (Qalaat al-Madiq).[20]

Shapur and his army were unstoppable. After his victory at Barbalissus, he crossed the Euphrates River. He was soon in front of Antioch. So swift and unexpected was his attack that the citizens of Antioch did not see him arrive until showers of arrows fell upon them as they sat in the theatre watching a play.[21] Persian troops gave themselves over to an orgy of looting, burning and killing. Any doors closed against them were reduced by use of a battering ram brought for the purpose.[22]

The Persians could have occupied the whole of Syria at this time. However, it seems that they had piled up so great a quantity of prisoners, gold and other precious commodities that there was a deep desire on the part of the soldiers to go home with their new riches, as Zosimus relates:

> Then, having razed absolutely every building, private and public, in the city with no one whatsoever interfering, they returned home with an untold

amount of booty, and in truth all Asia would have been acquired easily by the Persians had they not, overjoyed at the immense quantity of their plunder, in their zeal been concerned only about getting it back home safely.[23]

The treasures and population of Antioch were hauled to the Euphrates River where they were placed on boats or rafts and floated downstream to Persian Babylon. Syria would know a few years of exhausted and impoverished peace. Shapur, like his father, was making good on the Sasanian desire to imitate the Achaemenids and reverse the conquests of Alexander.

By 256, Shapur was back. This time he captured, and inadvertently sealed in a time capsule, the Roman outpost of Dura Europos on the west bank of the Euphrates River. The defenders had piled up tons of dirt and stones against the walls to strengthen them. In doing so they covered up the homes, temples, shops and privies that nestled against the wall. The buried ruins of the fortress would await modern archeologists to uncover a treasure of knowledge about Shapur and his contemporaries.

From the excavations we have learned that Shapur employed the arts of siege craft to take the city. Persian sappers dug under the wall, catapults were brought up, loaded and fired, while earthen ramps were built up to the height of the wall. Dura was doomed and, once destroyed, was never rebuilt.[24]

During that victorious decade only one nut was too tough to crack. We are told by the sixth-century Byzantine historian John Malalas, a native of Antioch, that Shapur laid siege to the city of Emesa (Homs). The siege was lifted when an adroit slinger on the walls struck the king with a lucky shot. He went home to nurse his wounds. He would be back.[25]

In 258, the Sasanian king could see the weakness of the Roman world. There was internal revolt in the provinces while foreigners rampaged seemingly at will in Europe. Shapur felt the time was right for another excursion to reclaim Achaemenid greatness.

With distracted Roman armies busy elsewhere, the Persians quickly overran the Arsacid-ruled and Roman-protected Lesser Armenia and threatened Cappadocia once more. Syria too was threatened.

Antioch of Syria was no small town in the ancient world. It was the third largest city of the empire, after Rome and Alexandria. The Persians had already sacked it once and this could not be tolerated again. The city authorities screamed for imperial help.

The emperor of Rome at this time was a popular old soldier named Publius Licinius Valerianus, now better known as Valerian (r. 253–260). In Malalas' words he was:

short, slender, with straight grey hair, a slightly upturned nose, a bushy beard, black pupils and large eyes; he was timorous and mean.[26]

This ageing warhorse defeated other claimants and donned the purple for the sake of the realm. Of all the troubles besetting the empire, including the persistent assaults of the Goths, it was the Persian threat that demanded his personal attention in 260. He left the affairs of the West to his imperial colleague and son, Publius Licinius Egnatius Gallienus and, though in his sixties, marched off to the East and his destiny. He had some early success chasing the Persians from the vicinity of Antioch and back across the Euphrates River.

It was said by contemporary historians that he brought 60,000–70,000 men with him to do battle with Shapur.[27] So large was this force that Valerian was able to leave a reserve at the town of Samosata to protect the important Euphrates River crossing there. Then he marched into Mesopotamia in Alexander's footsteps.

The two armies met in the spring of the year near Edessa (Urfa) uncomfortably close to Carrhae, the site of Crassus' defeat. Shapur had been in the area for at least a year in a loose siege of that city. We do not know how Valerian fell into the Persian trap. He certainly should have known better. It is probable that the Persians outnumbered the Romans. The Roman army at this stage did not have the tenacity, organization and discipline of the soldiers of old.[28]

The frightened citizens of Edessa, nominally Roman allies, stayed within their protective walls and nervously awaited the results of the conflict unfolding before them. They would embrace the victor, who most hoped would be Rome.

The Romans found that they faced a Sasanian army that differed greatly from that of the Parthians. While the Parthians had relied primarily on their swift horse archers and secondarily on heavy cavalry (called *Savaran* by the Sasanians), the Sasanians incorporated these, but added an engineering corps and a large conscripted army of light infantry and an elite heavy infantry. As at Dura Europos they employed all the instruments of siege craft. They also employed new battle tactics that the Romans had not seen before.[29]

Against the Roman heavy-infantry line the Sasanians would send a wave of mounted lancers to the attack. This would be followed by a second wave of mounted archers and a third wave of lancers again. Each threat required a different defensive response and the Romans were likely 'faked' out of position and overrun.

The battered Roman infantry instinctively dug in, creating an impromptu earthen fortress. Temporarily safe behind their ramparts, they were soon desperate for water, food and reinforcements. The reserves at Samosata, when summoned, refused to come to the aid of their comrades.

Shapur was easily able to intercept Valerian's supplies and communications. Then he settled in for a long wait to starve him out. Roman wags at the time suggested that there was treachery in Valerian's ranks. Edward Gibbon points the finger at the praetorian prefect, Macrianus, who as an anti-Christian would be vilified by later Christian writers.[30] Lack of water and food soon forced the Romans to desperate measures. Attempts to break out failed. At last, Valerian accepted Shapur's offer to negotiate.

The emperor was brought before Shapur for talks. The negotiations were a sham. Shapur had already decided the outcome. Once he had Valerian in his power, he simply took him prisoner. Valerian on the other hand apparently did not resist. Without their leader the encircled Romans lost the will to fight. The entire Roman army surrendered. Shapur had bagged the lot of them.[31]

Valerian was the only Roman emperor ever taken prisoner by an enemy. It was the worst military defeat that Roman arms had yet suffered. The effect in both countries was electric. In Persia, there was great celebration. The rock carvings at Naqsh-e Rustam and Bīšāpūr in Iran commemorate the event and Iranian school-children still learn of it today.

According to tradition, Shapur forced the emperor of Rome to kneel and used his back as a footstool to mount his horse. Valerian was sent back to Persia in chains and displayed before curious crowds of gawkers and mockers. When he died his skin may have been flayed, stuffed with straw and put on display – the ultimate expression of the taxidermist's art. This excessive humiliation may have been the hyperbole and imagination of later Christian historians.[32] Zosimus' account expresses the blow to Roman pride:

> Reduced to the rank of prisoner of war he [Valerian] died among the Persians, bequeathing the Roman name a heritage most shameful to future generations.[33]

As would happen so often in the third century, the different armies proclaimed their own favourites to succeed Valerian. In the East, one of Valerian's officials was proclaimed Augustus by his soldiers. This was the above-mentioned Macrianus. The author of the *Historia Augusta* would say of his family that:

> an embossed head of Alexander the Great of Macedonia was always used by the men (of the family) on their rings and their silver plate, and by the women on their headdresses, their bracelets, their rings and ornaments of every kind, so that even today there are still in that family tunics and fillets and women's cloaks which show the likeness of Alexander in threads of diverse colours.[34]

In recording this information the *Historia Augusta* went on to note that 'it is said that those who wear the likeness of Alexander carved in either gold or silver are aided in all that they do'.[35] This belief would endure for at least another century when St John Chrysostom (349–407), the Patriarch of Constantinople, would complain that people were still wearing coins or disks of Alexander on their heads and feet to ward off evil.[36]

In any event, the talismans of Alexander did Macrianus and his family no good. They were soon defeated and killed to unify the Empire under Gallienus (r. 253– 268), the son of Valerian. Apparently, Gallienus made no effort to ransom or rescue his father.[37] Though he did not fight the Persians personally he adopted some of the characteristics of Alexander in his coinage.[38] In his statues he is depicted with the *anastole* or cowlick on the forehead like that of Alexander and Pompey. Unlike Alexander, his lips are shown as pursed and his head is erect.

The captured Roman soldiers of Valerian's army were herded southward and settled in several Iranian cities including Dezful, northeast of Bosra. There the Roman PoWs were put to work on engineering projects such as dams, roads and aqueducts. Portions of a Roman-built bridge in Dezful still exist.[39]

There is at least one dam in Iran that was built by Roman engineers on the River Karun at Tustar (Shūshtär) during this time, the ruins of which remain. It is popularly known as Band-I Qaysar (Caesar's Dam).[40] In other locations, remains of aqueducts and bridges can still be seen. Alexander had settled some of his veterans deep inside Persia (most famously in Bactria) but they had come as conquerors, not PoWs. An unintended consequence of this more recent large-scale forced migration was an infusion of Greek learning and the introduction of Christianity deep within Persian territory.

The citizens of Antioch had been confident of their emperor and the army he took east with him. There was panic when they learned of the outcome of the battle at Edessa. Once again, Shapur's hard-riding cavalry sacked long-suffering Antioch. Anything not taken during the first attack was taken now.

With Valerian and his army neutralized, there was no organized Roman force east of Greece and Egypt that could stop the all-conquering Persians or other enemies in Western Europe. Shapur soon breached the mountain pass known as the Cilician Gates and raided into Anatolia as far as Ancyra (Ankara, the capital of modern Turkey). It was the deepest incursion of Persian arms since the Achaemenid dynasty. Roman client cities in the East hastened to make their peace with the victor.

In the desert, midway between Damascus and the Euphrates, sits the oasis town of Palmyra (Tadmor), site of modern troubles in a disintegrating Syria. This city was strategically placed in the desert by virtue of an abundant fresh (though sulphurous) water spring. Life was supported by irrigated fields, pastures for goats and orchards of the date-bearing palm trees from which the city took its Greek name. More importantly, Palmyra was an advantageous shortcut for trade between East and West along the wealth-bearing Silk Road, as well as trade with India travelling north along the Euphrates River from the Persian Gulf.[41]

The ruler of Palmyra at this time was a man named Odenathus who had inherited the status of a Roman senator from his father, a client king of the Severan emperors. However, the winds of change were blowing. With Persian victory everywhere else, Odenathus endeavoured to make peace with Shapur by sending him 'a long train of camels laden with the most rare and valuable merchandises'. Edward Gibbon, drawing on Peter Patricius' account described Shapur's response thus:

> 'Who is this Odenathus' (said the haughty victor and commanded that the presents should be cast into the Euphrates) 'that he thus insolently presumes to write to his lord? If he entertains a hope of mitigating his punishment, let him fall prostrate before the foot of our throne, with his hands bound behind his back. Should he hesitate, swift destruction shall be poured on his head, on his whole race, and his country'.[42]

His peaceful overtures rebuffed, Odenathus could see that there was no way out for him but through a bold strategy. He gathered the remnants of the Roman army in Syria, his own Palmyran forces and hard-riding desert Arab tribesmen.[43] He then set out into northern Syria to intercept portions of Shapur's army as it was casually and carelessly returning home.

Odenathus and his rapid deployment force were able to cut off stragglers and raid scattered Persian camps to 'liberate' the stolen goods and prisoners. They also managed to massacre some of the offending Persians. Among the trophies that Odenathus was supposedly able to capture were some of the wives and concubines of Shapur. If true, he was the first Western enemy since Alexander the Great to capture a Persian king's harem. However, Zonaras claims that it was a Roman named Callistus who captured the king's harem. Persian sources are silent on this event.[44]

The next year Odenathus followed up his success by raiding into Persian territory.

He crossed the Euphrates and recaptured Carrhae and Nisibis for Rome.[45] He then rode as far as the walls of Ctesiphon.

> When he [Odenathus] had advanced as far as Ctesiphon, not once but twice, he confined the Persians within their own fortifications; they were happy just saving their children and their wives and themselves.[46]

Jewish sources tell of Odenathus sacking some Jewish settlements in southern Iraq with great loss of life. The most important of these was the town of Nehardea (Tell Nihar) which contained a prestigious religious academy or university.[47] These attacks could have been in revenge for Jewish participation in the army of Shapur, or perhaps they were just easy targets.

During his triumphant campaign, Odenathus was not only able to retake Carrhae and Nisibis, he also intimidated the Persians out of Lesser (western) Armenia. He regained Mesopotamia for the Empire and did much to restore the Roman position in the Middle East. As the *Historia Augusta* put it, he 'restored the Roman power almost to its pristine condition'.[48]

Gallienus was appreciative of the efforts of Odenathus to avenge the insult to his father Valerian. He arranged for the Senate to proclaim the Palmyran an Augustus or 'Emperor of the East'. The proclamation only acknowledged the facts. Odenathus was already the de facto ruler of the eastern empire. For the first time since Aurelius and Verus the government of the Roman world was divided in half.

Odenathus ruled over what is now Syria, Israel/Palestine, most of eastern Turkey and northern Iraq. He was the protector of Lesser Armenia and dissuaded the Goths from pillaging the southern coast of the Black Sea. In an era of agonizing instability, his rule could not last for long. In 267, he was assassinated by a rival who was probably a relative.

The assassin hoped to take up Odenathus' crown but he did not count on his victim's wife, Zenobia. One of the most remarkable women of any age, Zenobia met the challenge of the usurper head on. She rallied her husband's forces and crushed the rebellion. Then, without the blessing of the Roman Senate, she assumed all of the titles and honours that they had once bestowed on her husband. She styled herself 'Augusta' or Empress, to the great chagrin of the senators in Rome, whose job it was to bequeath such honours. She considered herself the colleague and equal of the emperor at Rome. Now instead of Persia as an enemy, Rome began to see this self-proclaimed 'Empress of the East' as a real threat. For Persia it was a time of peace as Rome became preoccupied with this provincial insurrection.

Had Zenobia only maintained her husband's possessions she would have earned her place in history but she did more. She claimed to be a descendant of the famed Cleopatra of Egypt and therefore a scion of Ptolemaic royalty and the inheritor of the mantle of Alexander. She was even said to have been able to speak Egyptian.[49] It was not surprising then when she took advantage of Roman troubles in her Ptolemaic homeland. As with Cassius Avidius before her, Rome was again threatened by an internal heir to Alexander's greatness.

At that time the intrepid Goths had built or hired themselves a navy in the Black Sea. They boldly sailed through the Hellespont to terrorize the people of the 'wine dark' Aegean Sea and beyond. They would eventually raid as far south as Cyprus.

To counter this threat, Gallienus ordered the garrison in Egypt under General Tenagino Probus to meet and destroy the Gothic menace.[50] When the Romans sailed away from Egypt to meet the Gothic menace, chaos ensued. Unrestrained by the heavy hand of the Romans, rioting broke out among the mutually antagonistic racial, religious and linguistic factions in Alexandria.

One of these groups called upon Zenobia for help. Happy to oblige, the audacious queen sent an army to occupy the country of her famous ancestor in order to restore order in the name of Rome.

It was too much. Egypt was the breadbasket of the Roman world and the grain sent from that country to Rome fed the dependent populace. Without it there would be rack and ruin. Even though Zenobia continued to send the grain ships to Rome and claimed that she only occupied Egypt in the name of her imperial colleague in Rome, it just wouldn't do. Zenobia now controlled two of the empire's three largest cities, Antioch and Alexandria. It would be as if she ruled over today's Midwestern farm belt, Los Angeles and Chicago.

As related above, this was a time when philosophers were appreciated by monarchs. In the time before Christianity and Islam suppressed the ancient ways, the so-called pagan teachers were welcome at court. Zenobia embraced this practice. In Ctesiphon, Shapur had welcomed the vegetarian mystic Mani to his court. In Rome, Gallienus favoured Plotinus, that same Neo-Platonic teacher who had gone on campaign with Gordian III. The emperor even promised the philosopher that he would establish a city in Italy dedicated to the principles set down by Plato in *The Republic*.[51] However, the imperial patron of philosophy died in Milan at the hands of an assassin before he could bring this plan to fruition. His successors had neither the time nor the will for the project.

In the remote desert of Syria, Queen Zenobia was not to be outdone in the philosopher department. Her court was graced by a life-long friend of Plotinus named Gaius Cassius Longinus. Longinus had been a fellow student of Plotinus in Alexandria in his youth. Later he was the master of the prestigious Platonic school in Athens. He has long been credited with a discourse that survived from antiquity, entitled *On the Sublime* (though modern scholarship casts doubt on this).[52] The fourth-century writer Eunapius said of him, 'Longinus was in all branches of study by far the most distinguished of the men of his time'. He also said that he was 'a living library and a walking museum'.[53] In Palmyra, Longinus served as tutor to Zenobia's children and advisor to her court. Alexander had been tutored by a student of Plato (Aristotle). A new breed of Hellenistic princes would be taught by a scholar of Neo-Platonism.

Future generations would be inspired by Zenobia's courage and accomplishments. Geoffrey Chaucer would one day write of her in his *Canterbury Tales*:

> Zenobia, one time Palmyra's queen,
> As of her nobleness the Persians write

In arms was both so worthy and so keen
That none had greater fearlessness in fight
Or boasted of a lineage more bright.[54]

While he lived, Gallienus had strengthened the army to include a greatly expanded elite corps of heavy cavalry. The lessons learned in the wars with Persia had taught the Romans that a strong contingent of armoured horsemen was a powerful offensive weapon. He apparently intended them to be a loyal imperial force along the lines of Alexander's Companions or Persia's Immortals.

Perhaps he dreamed of using his new cavalry arm as shock troops to reinvade Persia but he never got the chance. He was continuously at war with enemies from without and usurpers from within the Empire until his assassination in 268.

Replacing Gallienus was an army general named Claudius II Gothicus. In the short two years left to him before disease took his life he decisively defeated both Germanic and Gothic invaders. To celebrate his victories, coins were struck in at least one city in Anatolia that have been identified as 'Alexander-coins' which were probably meant to promote the comparison between Claudius and Alexander.[55] The victorious emperor did not live long enough to receive more comparison, but his successor did.

By 270 Rome was at last blessed with a capable, if ruthless, emperor who lived long enough to make a difference. Lucius Domitius Aurelian (r. 270–275) was a military man through and through. He might have previously been a captain of cavalry in Gordian's expedition to Persia. He was comfortable with the Eastern people. Like Alexander the Great, he would adopt some Persian formalities and fineries at his court. Like Alexander, Aurelian had a temper. Eutropius, echoing complaints about Alexander, tells us that Aurelian 'was a man of ability in war, but of an ungovernable temper, and too much inclined to cruelty'.[56]

Sextus Aurelius Victor compared him favourably to both Alexander and Caesar and called Aurelian 'scarcely different from Alexander'.

That man was not unlike Alexander the Great or Caesar the Dictator; for in the space of three years he retook the Roman world from invaders.[57]

Aurelian was born to poor parents in the province of Lower Moesia (Bulgaria). Rising through the ranks of the army, he would become one of Rome's greatest soldier emperors. From the moment his army proclaimed him emperor he was constantly at war. His coin shows us a man with a thin, taut face, close-cropped hair and beard, and steely eyes. It is not unlike the coins of the other no–nonsense soldier emperors.

Before he could turn his attention to Zenobia, he first had to deal with rebellions at home and two successive barbarian invasions of Italy itself. In several fiercely fought battles, he turned the Germanic invaders around. Yet for a time even Rome was threatened. Like Alexander, he knew that he had to secure his homeland before beginning Eastern conquest.

With the emperor's blessing, the citizens of Rome began to build a protective wall around their city for the first time in 500 years. It was a massive undertaking that would eventually have a circumference of 12 miles (19km), be 12 feet (3.6m) thick and stand 20 feet (6m) high. It had to be built by civilians as the army had its hands full elsewhere. Still largely intact in many places, it is still known today as the Aurelian Wall.[58]

Next, the new emperor dealt with the Goths south of the Danube River who had plagued his predecessors. He forced the invaders to retreat northward beyond the river into Dacia (Romania), which had been a Roman province. Aurelian now formally abandoned Dacia to the Goths permanently.

Within the bankrupt empire he tried to reform the debased Roman coinage. Coins were only worth the value of the precious metal that they contained. So bankrupt was the Roman treasury by that time that silver coins were made of baser metal and given a silver splash coating, much like American coins today. This led to a debilitating inflation at home. Aurelian's solution was to increase the silver content of the coins to restore faith in Roman currency. He did not have enough precious metal to mint pure silver and gold coins. The half measure would have to do.[59]

To bring more revenue to the imperial treasury he would have to restore the eastern Mediterranean to his authority. As soon as he could, he headed for the East to deal with Zenobia, who was busy expanding her realm to include most of Anatolia.

As Aurelian travelled across Asia Minor and Zenobia's forces retreated before him, city after city hastily reaffirmed its allegiance to Rome. Aurelian would meet Zenobia in battle on the plains just east of Antioch in Syria. Her army was anchored by her own heavy cavalry. It is very possible that many of them were Persian mercenaries.

When Aurelian observed that the Palmyrans placed their cataphracts (heavily armoured cavalry) in the front lines, in the Sasanian manner, he ordered his vulnerable infantry to the safety of the opposite bank of the adjacent Orontes River.

His own light cavalry of Moorish and Dalmatian horsemen did battle with the heavily armored cataphracts. The swifter Moors, at Aurelian's command, retreated before the charging lancers, taunting them and exhausting the heavily laden horses in the heat of a sweltering Syrian summer day. When the Palmyrans and their horses, both in heavy armour, became exhausted by the heat and had emptied their quivers and lost their lances, the light cavalry of Aurelian, at a signal, turned on their exhausted and scattered enemy and soundly defeated them.[60] Another battle may have been fought in the same manner near the crossroads city of Emesa (Homs), with similar results.

Her army now in tatters, Zenobia was forced to retreat to her desert strong-hold of Palmyra. There she desperately sought the assistance of the old enemy, King Shapur I of Persia. Unfortunately, that fabled warrior was either dead or on his death bed. Internal concern for the succession to his throne outweighed any concern for the struggle in Syria. Better to let Persia's enemies fight it out among themselves.

Zenobia tried to escape to Persia but she was captured. She was then sent to Rome where she formed the centrepiece in Aurelian's well-deserved triumph. In the parade she was fettered with gems and chains of solid gold so heavy that a muscular slave had to help her carry them.[61]

Also displayed in the parade were magnificent gifts to Aurelian sent by Shapur's eldest son and second successor King Varahran I (r. 273–276). These included a magnificent purple robe, richer and more vibrant by far than anything associated with the Roman imperial colour. There was also a splendid war chariot captured in Palmyra. It was covered in precious stones. Aurelian rode behind Zenobia in his own ceremonial war chariot pulled, it was said, by four hearty stags.[62]

At the end of her ordeal, Zenobia was given an honourable retirement in compensation for the humiliation of being led and ridiculed through the streets of Rome. Zenobia's court philosopher Longinus was not so lucky. He was made the scapegoat for her evil ways and the vengeful Aurelian had the man executed.[63]

Aurelian's own glory was fleeting. Having vanquished all external and internal foes, he too was fatally bitten by the Alexander bug. He had already taken up many of the practices of an Eastern court with its manners, lavish court dress, fawning eunuchs and effeminate customs. He was becoming Easternized, as Alexander had been before him. In the words of Aurelius Victor:

> That man [Aurelian] first introduced among the Romans a diadem for the head, and he used gems and gold on every item of clothing to a degree almost unknown to Roman custom.[64]

The soldier emperors had become enamoured with a god known as Sol Invictus (Unconquered Sun), a solar deity popular in the ranks. Aurelian was the first to establish this god in the pantheon of other Roman gods. His modern biographer, Alaric Watson, noted that the 'association between solar imagery and political power in the ancient world was entrenched by Alexander the Great'.[65] Aurelian was taking advantage of the association. The imperial coinage would associate emper-ors with this deity until the conversion of Constantine to Christianity.

In the early summer of 275, a few months after his triumph, Aurelian set out to settle the score with the Persians who had humiliated his predecessor, Valerian. He progressed as far as Thrace, where, in October of 275, he was struck down by one of his own officers. Once again an assassin forced a regime change in Rome, saving Persia from impending invasion.[66]

Chapter 9

Diocletian: Roman Revival

> The victorious army, on returning from Persia, as they had lost their
> emperor Carus by lightning, and the Caesar Numerianus by a plot,
> conferred the imperial dignity on Diocletian.
>
> –Eutropius[1]

ight years would pass after the death of Aurelian before another aggressive soldier, with the grand-sounding name of Marcus Aurelius Numerius Carus (r. 282–283), assumed the purple. The Roman world still sought revenge for the insult done to their popular emperor Valerian.

The army had already mutinied against Carus' predecessor, Emperor Probus (r. 276–282), who had sought to take them to Persia.[2] Probus, like Aurelian, Julius Caesar and Caracalla, was assassinated while making preparations to invade Persia. When Probus died, the army declared for Carus as their emperor.

We see no imitation of Alexander in the coins or statues of Carus and we must be wary when the twelfth-century Christian writer Zonaras tells us that when 'Carus came to power, he crowned his sons Carinus and Numerianus with the imperial diadem'.[3] While it is tempting to think that he is referring to the diadem as Alexander and the Romans of the republic thought of it, we must remember that the word had an altogether different meaning in the gilded age of the Byzantine Empire of Zonaras' time.

Carus adopted the foreign policy of his predecessors. Whether the soldiers liked it or not, the invasion of Persia was on. He led the reluctant soldiers once more to the East to redeem Mesopotamia. Carus ignored the lessons of the past by neglecting to secure Armenia, which still retained its Sasanian master. This time it did not matter.

It was a bad time for the Persian King Varahran II (r. 276–293). A grandson of Shapur I, he did not inherit his grandfather's tolerance or military prowess. One of his brothers usurped the eastern provinces and kept the kingdom in civil turmoil for years. In a bid for the favour of the powerful and self-righteous priest Kartir and the Magi, Varahran II had the philosopher Mani killed, if he had not already been put to death by his father Varahran I.[4]

Kartir now reached the pinnacle of his power and influence. He was an important underpinning of the Sasanian throne even while usurping much of its power.

The grateful king, desperate for allies, gave him the title 'Saviour of Varahran's Soul'. The price was high. Kartir became the power behind the throne. From this time on the religious establishment in league with a few noble families would often dictate the successor to the Sasanian throne.[5]

Varahran and his army were occupied with civil war in faraway Afghanistan trying to hold on to the fragmenting Persian realm. Carus easily overran Mesopotamia without opposition. Then he sped south along the Euphrates River to Seleucia and Ctesiphon. When the few Persians in the area at last stood to fight, they were crushed on the field. Carus occupied both cities and sent patrols into the interior to scout out his next moves.[6]

As in the past, when the Romans were able to conquer the capital city of Persia, they weren't quite sure what to do next. The Romans hesitated after their victory. (In 2003 the Americans found themselves in a similar situation in Iraq.)

Then fate took a hand, as it almost always did in the contests between Rome and Persia. This time it would be in spectacular fashion. In late July a violent storm roared over the Roman camp sending repeated claps of thunder and lightning all about. When it was over the emperor was found dead in his tent.[7]

The soldiers, brave but exceedingly superstitious, were sure that Carus had been struck and killed by lighting, a very bad omen. Death by lightning was considered the wrath of the gods upon the offending victim. They wanted no more of this evil magic.

The legionaries loudly demanded to return to Roman territory. All too happy to comply, the less-superstitious generals declared victory and quickly marched back to the safety of Syria. Persia was again saved by the sudden death of a Roman emperor.

The *Historia Augusta* suggests that Carus was the victim of an ancient curse.

> many declare that there is a certain decree of Fate that no Roman emperor may advance beyond Ctesiphon, and that Carus was struck by the lightning because he desired to pass beyond the bounds which Fate has set up.[8]

There was some truth to this superstition because every emperor who crossed, or tried to cross, the Tigris River (Ctesiphon was on the east bank) up until that time had met an ignoble end. It seemed impossible for a Roman to match the fortune of Alexander.

So many emperors had died (and would die) while fighting the Persians that their deaths fueled the musings of Omar Khayyám over 700 years later:

> I sometimes think that never blows so red
> the rose as where some buried Caesar bled.[9]

With another emperor's death, the army once again began the process of choosing a new ruler. When the dust settled both of Carus' sons were dead.[10] The winner of the imperial contest was Diocles or, as we know him, Diocletian (r. 284–305). He would be the last of the great pagan emperors. His reign lasted for twenty years. It would be the first time in a century that an emperor remained alive, let alone ruled, for so long a time. Malalas reports that he was:

> tall, slender with a shrivelled face and both his hair and beard completely grey; he had a fair-skinned body, grey eyes, a thick nose, and a slightly hunched back; he was very magnanimous and an avid builder.[11]

Relieved of the responsibility of subduing Persia and carrying on Carus' scheme of further conquest, Diocletian set about the task of renewing the *Pax Romana* and restoring the grandeur of old. He was another administrator and builder in the mould of Augustus and Hadrian. His first act was to negotiate peace with Varahran II so that each monarch could be free to pursue interests elsewhere in their kingdoms.

Before the outbreak of peace there were other battles to fight. Much of Diocletian's time was spent in the field discouraging the growing number of immigrant peoples that wanted to get inside the Roman borders. When not fighting outsiders he had to deal with disgruntled rebels within the weakened realm.

No matter what other pressures were imposed on the Roman world, there always seemed time to meddle in the affairs of Armenia. It had been over forty-six years since the Sasanians had successfully invaded that country, killing its Arsacid ruler and sending his infant son Tiridates (Trdat III) fleeing to the protection of the Roman court. Educated in the Roman manner, Tiridates grew up an exceptionally vigorous youth. He excelled on the battlefield and as an athlete in the Olympic Games.[12]

In 287, Diocletian was in a position to promote Tiridates' hopes to assume the crown of Armenia. That country was ripe for revolution. The Sasanian overlords had taxed the population heavily for the construction of palaces, fire temples and forts. The formidable Persian Magi had broken the statues and shrines of the traditional Armenian gods and replaced them with the eternal flame of Zoroaster.[13] The restless Parthian nobility of the country had no love for their Sasanian rulers. Many longed for an Arsacid restoration.

Now Tiridates, the son of an assassinated Arsacid king, rode into Armenia at the head of a Roman army of liberation. His countrymen rose up against the tyranny of their Persian masters. Armenia was quickly cleansed of enemy outposts and influence. Recently built Zoroastrian shrines and fire temples were desecrated and thrown down, their eternal flames extinguished. The house of Arsacid was restored to power amid popular rejoicing.

The timing of the Roman invasion could not have been better. Within Persia the periodic bloodletting of a dynastic struggle was underway. The contending candidates were Nerseh, an elderly son of the revered Shapur I, and the third Varahran, son of Varahran II.[14] They were too preoccupied with fighting each other to support their kinfolk in Armenia.

By 293, the deadly contest for the Sasanian succession was decided. Nerseh (r. 293–302) prevailed over his nephew and consolidated his authority over the country. His coin shows us a wide-eyed, full-faced man. He had a prominent nose and wore an earring dangling a large pearl. His beard was short, but his hair flowed out from under his crown and reached to his shoulders.

In a mirror image of the Roman dynastic struggles, Nerseh found that once he had a firm grip on the country he could renew the ancient conflict with the Romans. Once again the *casus belli* was Armenia.

Tiridates III (r. 287–330) established himself in Armenia during the Persian civil war and began raiding into Persian territory (which Armenia claimed). By 296, Nerseh felt it was time to deal with Armenia. Persian light and heavy cavalry flooded across the border into Armenia and forced Tiridates to flee for the second time in his life to the protection of his Roman allies.

Diocletian was in no mood for Persian aggression. With the new threat he ordered Galerius Maximianus, his trusted son-in-law, to proceed from his station on the Danube to assume command of the Syrian legions. Galerius' assignment was to wrest Armenia back from Persia. As we already know from ages past, the ill-disciplined Syrian legions were not the right instrument to carry out the imperial will against Persia. Nevertheless, they would have to do.

Meanwhile, following their successful invasion of Armenia, the Persians were becoming active in Roman Mesopotamia. That is where Galerius went to challenge them. Forgetting the lessons of the past, Galerius was thinking more of Alexander's success on this same route than of Crassus' defeat. He marched into the vast openness of the Mesopotamian highlands without securing his northern flank in Armenia. Nor did he have a plan to counter the active Persian cavalry. Galerius, with the aggrieved Tiridates in tow, stumbled into battle with the Sasanian heavy cavalry, the *Saravan,* near the historic battlefield of Carrhae.

Aurelian had been able to get his vulnerable infantry out of the way of the hard riding Palmyran *Saravan,* Galerius could not. The Persians had time to bring up reinforcements and Galerius found himself outnumbered and out manoeuvred.[15] Like Crassus before him, he learned the hard way that unsupported infantry could not stand up to disciplined and coordinated Persian light and heavy cavalry.

The Roman army of Syrian garrison troops was enveloped by the fast-moving horse archers and lancers who were supported by swarms of pesky light infantry. The latter killed the wounded and robbed the dead. The Syrian legionaries, none too brave to start with, broke and ran. Tiridates barely escaped capture by swimming across the muddy Euphrates River in full armour, using his wooden shield as a float.[16]

One can imagine the fear and trepidation Galerius felt when he presented himself humbly before an enraged Diocletian. The poor, disgraced son-in-law was made to run alongside of the emperor's carriage for over a mile (1.6 km).[17] Galerius pleaded for the opportunity to set things right. After his master's fury had subsided, the two men planned for the next campaign.

At about the same time that the Persian campaign began, the Egyptians, angry with Diocletian's new tax laws, revolted against the Romans. The emperor was forced to divide his forces in order to prosecute both the invasion of Persia and the suppression of revolt in the empire's most important agricultural province.[18]

The emperor now sent for hardened troops stationed along the Danube. These men were veterans of tough fighting, privations and hard marches. Many of them had been with Carus and Diocletian in the heart of Iraq. They knew how to fight Persians. Among their number was a large contingent of Gothic auxiliaries.

This time, 25,000 seasoned veterans marched with Galerius. Meanwhile, Diocletian would take the humbled Syrian legions with him to Egypt. When the heat of the summer of 298 waned, the emperor marched southward toward the Nile, while Galerius crossed the Euphrates.

Rather than repeat his mistake in Mesopotamia, Galerius marched through the foothills of Armenia, safe from cavalry raids and among a population that genuinely wished him and Tiridates well. Galerius had learned from the now-long Roman experience: secure Armenia first.

It was well known by this time that the Sasanians, like the Parthians before them, did not like to fight at night. At sundown the Persian armies would break off the contest and retire to their camps to resume operations in the morning. The story is told that one night, as the two armies rested within sight of each other, Galerius with just two mounted companions scouted the Persian camp personally.[19] He noted that the numerous Persian horses were tied and hobbled and the posted guard was small. Returning to his own camp he quietly had his men awakened. He ordered them not to wear any armour or gear that might make unnecessary noise. The men prepared for a night engagement. The Romans softly approached the sleeping camp of the enemy and positioned themselves in the dark. Just before dawn, trumpets sounded and the Romans attacked in a headlong rush of yells and war paeans.

The sleepy camp of horse archers, heavy cavalry and light infantry was at an extreme disadvantage. It took time to unhobble and mount frightened horses. The archers had to laboriously string their bows and secure their quivers. All these actions took time and the running, shouting, sword-wielding Romans allowed them no breathing space. The feeble resistance was crushed as the confused enemy fled into the first rays of the sun. The attackers gave themselves over to an orgy of slaughter and looting.

Nerseh was wounded in the fight, but escaped. As was to be expected, the king's tent complex was rich in adornments and treasure. Galerius captured a great amount of loot, including the king's wife Arsane, his sisters and his children along with several Persian noblemen. Eutropius explains:

> After putting Nerseh to flight, he (Galerius) captured his wives, sisters, and children, with a vast number of the Persian nobility besides, and a great quantity of treasure.[20]

According to the *Historia Augusta*, Galerius, like Alexander before him, treated the family of the Persian king with every respect and honour. The spoils of this war made a splendid backdrop to the triumph that Galerius would enjoy. A stone relief of this victory is commemorated in the Arch of Galerius at Thessaloniki in Greece, where he had taken up residence.[21]

Like Alexander, Galerius had defeated the Persian king, captured women of his family and harem, enriched himself with Persian treasure and absorbed Persian territory. He was even given credit by some of his contemporaries for going beyond Persia as Alexander had done. According to the *Historia Augusta*, 'our most venerated Caesar Maximian [Galerius] has shown, to conquer the Persians and advance beyond them'.[22]

The *Panegyrici Latini*, a collection of speeches and poems, some of which extol the virtues of various emperors, offers an example of the excessive flattery aimed at Galerius:

> Yet you see, Emperor, that I cannot find anything with which to compare you in all antiquity unless it be the example of the race of Hercules. For even Alexander the Great now seems insignificant to me for restoring his realm to the Indian king when so many kings, O Emperor are your clients.[23]

The Romans chased Nerseh and his surviving bodyguard as far as Adiabene on the east bank of the Tigris River. Our sources are not as clear as we would like but it seems that Galerius may have even captured the Sasanian capital, Ctesiphon.[24] Diocletian's modern biographer, Stephen Williams, speculated on Galerius' frame of mind:

> Galerius may well have envisaged total conquest of Persia, fulfilling for himself the dream that had captivated and eluded so many Roman generals of repeating the feat of Alexander.[25]

Upon hearing the news of the great victory, Diocletian ordered Galerius to halt his progress. He knew of the legends that predicted bad luck if the Romans should cross the Tigris. He also knew that he could not let his underling get all the glory, even if he was his son-in-law. He travelled as far as Nisibis (now back in Roman hands) to greet Galerius on his return from battle. With victory came forgiveness and a future crown. Perhaps two future crowns. One of Galerius' officers on this particular Persian campaign was the future emperor Constantine.[26]

It was not long before a Persian ambassador named Apharban humbly entered the Roman camp to negotiate a peace and secure the release of the king's family, now housed and cared for in the pleasant suburb of Daphne, in the foothills above Antioch.[27]

Apharban, trained in diplomacy and flattery, tried to put a favourable spin on the situation. He praised the valour and success of the Roman victor and appealed to his vanity and mercy. Rome and Persia, he suggested, were like a man's two eyes, 'which ought mutually to adorn and illustrate each other'. Galerius angrily reminded him of the treatment received by Valerian at the hands of Nerseh's father, Shapur I, when the Persians were victorious.[28]

In hard bargaining Diocletian demanded and received the return of Mesopotamia. In 300, a treaty would be signed that redrew the common border eastward to the banks of the Tigris River. Five small territories beyond the river were ceded to Armenia while Tiridates was restored to the Armenian throne.

The increasingly important country of Iberia was to have a pro-Roman king who would secure the passes through the Caucasus Mountains against the ever-more hostile peoples in the north. In all it was an extremely lenient treaty. Its terms would last for the next forty years.

With the addition of these new provinces, Rome reached the farthest eastward she had enjoyed since the time of Septimius Severus. Diocletian and Galerius enjoyed a magnificent triumph in Rome.[29] The declining fortunes of the Empire were momentarily reversed.

Galerius' military success against Persia gave rise to his own strange but familiar imitation of Alexander: 'He insolently dared to affirm that, in the fashion of Olympias, the mother of Alexander the Great, his mother had conceived him after she had been embraced by a serpent'.[30] On the very eve of the triumph of Christianity, virgin births were still attributed to divine serpents.

As for Diocletian, he enjoyed the addition to his treasury that the Persian booty supplied and he began to use some of the loot personally. His silken footwear was embellished with gold, pearls and precious stones. The rest of his wardrobe was likewise enriched with a cloak of purple and gold. On the other hand, when Alexander the Great introduced such finery at his court in imitation of the Persians, it almost spawned a revolt.[31]

Diocletain also put the money to work constructing a fortress-like palace at Split on the Adriatic coast. Significantly it was divided between public and private spaces. The soldier emperors who had spent their time in the field were at the mercy of assassins. Diocletian would withdraw into his own reclusive space and live.

There is a postscript to Diocletian's victory over the tax resisters in Egypt. A triumphal column was raised in his honour in Alexandria. Future generations would mistakenly call it, 'Pompey's Pillar'. In fact it was a monument to Diocletian. The Greek inscription can still be read:

> To the right and good emperor, the protector god of Alexandria, Diocletian, who has never been beaten.[32]

In these few words the emperor or, more likely, his admirers, claimed that he is greater than Alexander as 'protector god' who, like Alexander, 'has never been beaten'.

Chapter 10

Shapur II: The Great One

[Shapur II] led an expedition into the land of the Romans, took a
great number of prisoners there, and planted them in the city of Irān-
Khurrah-Shapur, which the Arabs call al-Sūs.

—Al-Tabarī[1]

A fter twenty years of rule, in an act worthy of the Roman farmer
Cincinnatus (519–430 BC) or the American President George
Washington, Diocletian voluntarily laid down his crown in AD 305 and
retired to private life. Unfortunately peace did not follow Diocletian's retirement. Wars and revolts throughout the Roman world plagued the new emperors (for now there were two Augustii and two subordinate Caesars, as created
by Diocletian).

After his victory over Nerseh, Galerius actively sought Diocletian's retirement
so that he could be the ruler of the eastern Empire. When his dreams came true
they turned into a nightmare. Galerius (r. 293–311) as emperor was in way over
his head. He would eventually beg Diocletian to come out of retirement to help
him. No amount of pleading could entice the retired emperor from his vegetable
garden. He now much preferred cabbages to kings.

Civil peace was not restored until another powerful leader, Constantine (sole
ruler from 324–337), pulled together the reins of the empire. The new emperor
was 'tall, ruddy, magnanimous, peaceable and dear to God'.[2] As we have seen, he
was no stranger to conflicts with Persia.

Although the use of Greek was waning in Sasanian Persia it was still used
to communicate between the two empires. According to Eusebius, Constantine
wrote a letter to Shapur that was translated from Latin to Greek 'so that it would
be more accessible to the (Persian) readers'.[3] This vestige of Alexander's conquests died hard.

The comparisons between Constantine and Alexander would not be long in
coming. His great admirer Eusebius would write:

our emperor began where the Macedonian ended and doubled in time
the length of his life, and trebled the size of empire he acquired.[4]

The reference to 'trebled the size of empire' disingenuously refers to Constantine being crowned emperor when he only controlled Britain, Gaul and Spain. He had to fight to reunite the empire.

In our own time, Professor Michael Tierney noted that 'there is a striking similarity between the careers and achievments of the Emperor Constantine and Alexander the Great'.[5] Tierney opens his study of the emperor and his city with a lengthy comparison of the two men:

a. Both were great conquerors never once defeated.
b. The speed and certainty of their movements seemed to defy the rules of war.
c. Each claimed to have received a divine revelation.
d. Both were men of overmastering passions which caused terrible deeds.
e. Each was the founder of a new type of state, the beginner of a new historic epic.

Outside the imperial court there is some numismatic evidence of popular respect for Alexander during this time. We have already seen that, at least since the time of the imperial pretender Macrianus (approximately AD 260), people wore amulets featuring Alexander's likeness to ward off evil.

The Boston Museum owns a collection of contorniates (bronze medallions) which were used as tickets to public events. These disks contain the likeness of iconic heroes such as Augustus and Trajan. One of the museum's contorniates dating to the age of Constantine features the likeness of Alexander on the obverse. He is depicted wearing the skin of the Nemean lion, an enduring association that still resonated at the beginning of the official Christian era.[6]

A gold medallion minted in the early fourth century, now housed at the Bibliothèque Nationale de France in Paris, depicts Constantine and Alexander side by side, each the equal of the other.

The imperial coinage helped to burnish the emperor's image as a strong leader. His modern biographer David Potter would write:

Constantine's [coin] portraits are beardless, youthful… his style echoes that of Augustus and way before him, Alexander the Great whose military skill he emulated.[7]

The dawning of the new era brought a strange amalgamation between the old pagan traditions and the new Christian sensibilities. In the Cabinet des Médailles (Cabinet of Medals) of the Bibliothèque Nationale in Paris are several medallions depicting Alexander as Hercules on the obverse, with images and the name of Jesus Christ on the reverse.

Most of Constantine's surviving statuary depicts him as the solid Roman soldier that he was. However, at least one surviving bust now in the collection of the Capitoline Museum in Rome shows us Constantine with his head slightly inclined to the left and his lips slightly parted, signs of an imitation of Alexander.

In later years, during the reign of Valentinian I (r. 364–375), a medallion would be struck featuring Alexander wearing the Herculean lion skin headdress but with the facial features of Constantine.[8] The growing clout of the Christian Bishops however would soon put a stop to this odd synergy. It would not do to have Alexander's god-induced birth and his claims to be the 'son of God', and even a god himself, overshadow their claims for Jesus of Nazareth.

Some of the Christians then coming to positions of influence were already trying to put an end to the reverence for Alexander. The Christian historian Orosius, born late in the fourth century, was a contemporary and friend of St Augustine. He was scathing in his condemnation of Alexander, calling him 'blood-thirsty' and 'wicked'.[9] St Augustine himself ridiculed Alexander. He relates the story of a time when Alexander captured a notorious pirate.

> For when [Alexander] had asked the man what he meant by keeping hostile possession of the sea, he answered with bold pride, 'What do you mean by seizing the whole earth? Because I do it with a petty ship, I am called a robber, while you who does it with a great fleet are styled emperor'.[10]

Their vitriol echoes that of Seneca and Lucan in the first century.

In the eastern half of the dissolving empire it was different. They were closer to the Persian threat. Some of their writers drew upon Alexander for inspiration. One of these was the Syriac Christian named Aphrahat (c. 280–345), who lived near Mosul in today's Iraq. His surviving writings, called the *Demonstrations*, included several references to Alexander the Great. This can be seen as a reflection of the continuing interest in Alexander during the time of Constantine.[11]

Another writer of the era was Flavius Polemius, a powerful enough man to be named a consul in 338. He was beholden to the Constantine dynasty and loyal to them. He translated a version of the *Alexander Romance* into Latin and, 'was moved to produce a book that compared Constantine's son Constantius to both Alexander…and Trajan'.[12]

In any event the western church fathers could not totally erase the memory of Alexander. Even into the Middle Ages, the *Romance* continued to be read and one of its prominent features, the ascension of Alexander into heaven, became 'a popular motif on misericords, pavements, and roof-bosses in cathedrals throughout Europe'.[13]

In Persia, it was a time to focus on domestic affairs. King Hormizd II, (r. 301–309) the son of Nerseh, attended to the country's legal system and internal concerns. His most important foreign policy move was to marry off his daughter to an Armenian prince in order to spawn some loyalty to Persia.[14]

Upon the death of Hormizd, his oldest two boys were put to death by the Magi as being unfit to rule. A third son was imprisoned.[15] The Magi and ruling nobles put the living sons aside and chose the as-yet-unborn son of the late Hormizd to succeed to the throne. Their plan was to raise the boy up in their own image, pious and patriotic. According to legend, while the child's mother, one of Hormizd's concubines, was still pregnant, the Magi symbolically placed a crown on her swelling belly, hoping that the child would be a boy. To their relief, he was. Shapur II (r. 309–379) became king on the day he was born.

He would live to the age of seventy years and every day of his long life he would be the King of Kings of Sasanian Persia.[16] During his reign the Sasanians achieved the 'height of centralization in Iran'.[17] The man who was born to be king had wide eyes set in a slender face. His prominent ears were framed by long bushy hair and close-cropped beard. His childhood was still a time of peace between the two quarrelling empires. The outward tranquillity seems to have been the product of Constantine's strong hand, but when Shapur came of age things would change.

While an uneasy peace was maintained with the Romans, Persia's other neighbours sought to take advantage of the boy king. The Arabs especially were active in raiding, looting, and even settling in Fars province from across the Persian Gulf. They also migrated easily out of the Arabian Desert and into Roman Mesopotamia. The restless Arabs may have raided all the way to Ctesiphon.[18] It was an omen of things to come.

As Shapur reached manhood there were momentous undertakings in Armenia. King Tiridates III (Trdat), who had been raised in Constantinople and assumed his crown with Rome's blessing and protection, brought something new to his homeland: Christianity. It is likely that he picked up his new faith while being educated by his Roman tutors. He must have studied the teachings of Christ secretly because he was at court during the last persecution of the growing sect under Galerius. Armenian sources, on the other hand, tell of a conversion while he was king.[19] The conversion is attributed to Gregory the Illuminator. If true, it would be the ultimate irony since Gregory's father had murdered the father of Tiridates. In 301, Tiridates proclaimed that Christianity would be the official religion of Armenia. In doing so he anticipated Constantine's conversion by a generation.

Meanwhile, Shapur II thoroughly grasped the reins of power at the tender age of sixteen. He would vex the Romans for the rest of his life. In the beginning of his personal rule, he pulled together the distant parts of his empire to consolidate his power. As part of this process we hear of him commanding a naval expedition in the Persian Gulf to admonish the Arabs for their intrusions upon his territory.[20]

On land, meanwhile, his handpicked force of 1,000 cavalrymen ravaged the eastern Arabian Peninsula, exacting a brutal vengeance on the Arab tribes that had raided Persia. From then until the Muslim conquests, the Sasanians controlled both sides of the Persian Gulf.[21] It was a sign that he intended to expand his realm like the Persians of old.

While Christianity was gaining adherents on both sides of the border, Shapur sided firmly with the Magi and began a pogrom of heavy taxation and persecution of the minority sect.[22] As might be expected, Constantine championed the cause of the Christians wherever they might live, even Persia. Religious fervour fanned the flames of war.

In 336, Shapur turned his attention to the Roman world.[23] His timing was perfect. The aging Constantine was near the end of his long and eventful life and would die within a year. The combination of Constantine's power and Shapur's youth had kept the peace on the common border for a generation. We say this with some uncertainty, because some sources hint that he fought a Persian campaign. These include chronicler John Malalas who wrote:

> He [Constantine] began a campaign against the Persians, was victorious and made a peace treaty with Shapur, the emperor of the Persians. It was the Persians who asked to have peace with the Romans.[24]

In any event, the uneasy 'peace' of forty years was coming to an end. The bone of contention between the two titans was, once again, Armenia. Tiridates III, having bequeathed Christianity to his kingdom, died in 330. As the new religion spread in Armenia, it ran afoul of the Magi who had also made inroads in the country (especially the eastern half) for the fire and sun loving Zoroaster. Like their modern counterparts, the Ayatollahs, the Magi were intolerant of others.

Another dispute between Persia and Rome was the status of Mesopotamia, which Galerius had retaken from Shapur's grandfather Nerseh. The fact that the Romans controlled territory that Persia considered its own was insufferable. It wasn't long before Persian or allied Arab raids were reported to the Roman authorities.

In his new capital city of Constantinople, the aging Constantine was moved to action. In 366, he mobilized his army from distant frontier posts and informed his foreign allies, particularly Armenia, to be prepared for the invasion of Persia. The Persians took note. Shapur sent envoys to negotiate for peace or stall for time.[25] It was too late. Constantine had already been aroused and peace was no longer an option. Like Alexander, he would not listen to Persian offers of peace. That winter he prepared for war.

On 27 February 337, Constantine celebrated his sixty-fourth birthday with every expectation of settling accounts with Shapur. His campaign was to be a grand tour, including a pious baptism on the banks of the sacred River Jordan in Palestine.[26] Preparations continued but by Easter Sunday Constantine complained to intimates that he did not feel well. Still he planned to set out on a journey of conquest. He would have with him a number of Christian clergy. Just as former rulers had travelled with philosophers, Christian kings would travel with priests and Christian Bishops and scholars. A special 'prayer tent' was made to accommodate the aging warrior's pious meditations.[27]

Constantine finally left his capital but not to conquer. He hoped to heal at a hot springs and continue his march to Persia. But in May of 337 he died in a villa at Nicomedia (İzmit in Turkey). The powerful hand of Constantine was forever stilled. His nephew and future emperor, Julian, remarked that his uncle had succumbed 'in the midst of his preparations for war'.[28] He left his heirs with a huge burden by leaving his son Constantius an unfinished war with Persia that would end tragically with the death of Julian in 363.

His death was the signal for Shapur II to unleash his own forces upon Armenia and Mesopotamia. Armenia caved in quickly. Her leaders after Tiridates were weak and willing to trade land for peace. All of the lands that had augmented the Armenian realm a generation earlier at the expense of Media were lost. In Mesopotamia, Shapur roamed the countryside at will, defeating timid Roman field armies. The battle we know most about was near the desert town of Singara (Sinjar), the site of modern-day conflict.

Singara was the southern anchor of the Roman province of Mesopotamia just as it is a southern anchor of the Kurdish region in modern times. It had been in Roman hands off and on since 197, when Septimius Severus had conquered and fortified it.[29] The town was built astride a seasonal stream that flowed with winter rains trickling down from the surrounding peaks of the Jebel Sinjar to the north. The city walls allowed the runoff to flow through the fortress town and the welcome water was siphoned off into cisterns and reservoirs for use during the scorching summer months. The walls also enclosed empty land for farming or grazing, and an adjoining hill, which housed a strong citadel.

Garrison duty there could not have been pleasant. The mid-twentieth century traveller Freya Stark visited the town and wrote:

> From the rise of the Roman camp where a pale streamlet trickles one can look out and see no horizon—only perpetual wind and dust.[30]

The Romans fortified the oval town as best they could. Shapur II had earlier tried to take Singara in 334 but failed because of troubles on the eastern borders of Persia, which had demanded his attention. He would return.

The new Roman emperor in the East was Constantius II (r. 337–361), a son of Constantine the Great. He was just nineteen when his father died, but he had already served in Antioch as the eyes and ears of his monarch. After his father's funeral, which was said to have been unsurpassed in its pageantry and the out-pouring of grief and love from the people, Constantius divided the administrative responsibilities of the Empire with his two brothers.

The anonymous writer of the *Itinerarium Alexandri* dedicated the work to Constantius and compared him to both Alexander and Trajan as a conqueror of Persia. He hopefully boasted that Constantius, 'In truth, you will…equal the famous Alexander.'[31]

Robin Lane Fox points out that the author of the *Itinerarium* 'compliments Constantius on his "successful beginning" and military readiness for a Persian expedition'. The successful beginning meant the placing of a Roman candidate on the throne of Armenia in 339, securing that country in preparation for an attack on Persia. The author goes on to note that Alexander and Constantius were both the same age (twenty-two) when they invaded Persia.[32]

Nine wars (seasonal campaigns) would be fought between Rome and Persia during Constantius' reign. He would personally lead the army in two of them.[33] There were both defeats and costly victories:

> The fortune of Constantius was different [from Constantine's]; for he suffered many grievous calamities at the hands of the Persians, his towns being often taken, his walled cities besieged, and his troops cut off.[34]

While the Romans were busy with problems on the Danube, the Persians struck Mesopotamia. In 337, Shapur drew his forces up outside the important city of Nisibis for two months, trying to starve the citizens into submission. His siege engines and earthen ramps could not breach the walls but his engineers had another idea.

The Mygdonius River, now called the Jaghjagh, flows through the city. The Persians found a point upstream where they could dam the river, which was swollen with the early spring mountain runoff. Meanwhile, they strengthened the banks of the river to direct the flow of water so that when they burst the brimming dam the force of the water would rush upon the earthen walls of Nisibis. As expected, the mud brick walls dissolved in the rush of water. Shapur then had to wait for the flooded field to dry before he could attack. By the time the mud dried out, the desperate defenders of Nisibis had rebuilt the damaged section of the wall and a frustrated Shapur was forced to retire empty-handed.

The next year Constantius brought his army into Mesopotamia to confront the Persians. There was no one to fight. Shapur had gone home and disbanded his host of peasant conscripts. The border regions were ripe for conquest and the Romans crossed the Tigris on a bridge of boats and despoiled the countryside. Once again Rome (at least briefly) occupied the province of Adiabene or Assyria. There was no Persian resistance.[35]

By 346, Shapur was once more on the move. He again laid siege to the long-suffering city of Nisibis. This time he remained before the city for three months without result. In 348, Shapur returned to Mesopotamia. He had conscripted a vast army of peasants and paid mercenaries, which was unusual for the Persians at that time. They bridged the Tigris in three places and marched across day and night unopposed. The Greek writer Libanius said of them:

> there was no type of military equipment which did not complement their army, archers, mounted archers, slingers, heavy infantry, cavalry and armed men from every part.[36]

Shapur's force was augmented by war elephants. Once across the river he established a strong camp in the desert scrub about 19 miles (30k) from Singara.

The Romans drew in their advanced guards and awaited the Persian approach. The emperor was said to be residing within the walls of Singara at the time. Shapur brought up his army and occupied the surrounding hills to the north with archers and spearmen. On the plains to the south he pushed forward his heavy infantry. In the battle that was fought there the Romans advanced their own heavy infantry in the blazing summer sun.

The Persians could not stand up to the disciplined Roman advance. They broke and ran for the safety of their own camp with the Romans in hot pursuit. After the heated chase, the sweat-soaked Romans broke through the line of Persian light infantry, archers, elephants and cataphracts that protected the Sasanian camp. The Persians fled in disarray. With that initial success, the Roman discipline dissolved as they gave themselves over to looting and the desperate search for water with every expectation that the battle was won.

Then the Persians did something completely unexpected. During the night the bulk of the army reassembled itself in the surrounding hills and came alive. In the first known Persian night battle, they struck back.[37] While the westerners were totally distracted with their nocturnal looting and revelling, Shapur sent his dismounted archers quietly forward. The Persians surrounded their captured camp and unleashed volleys of arrows out of the darkness toward the light of the torches and campfires.[38] Drunken and frightened Romans fell like flies under a withering and terrifying barrage they could not see. At length, disciplined Roman heavy infantry marched into the night to dislodge the archers.

In the morning, the surviving Persians began their long, mournful retreat across the Tigris, destroying their bridges when they had crossed. It is possible that some of Constantius' army crossed the Tigris in pursuit before being recalled.[39] The town of Singara was saved. Even though the Persian crown prince and the treasury of the camp were captured, the Romans considered this battle a defeat because of the losses they suffered during the night battle.[40]

In 350, Shapur moved in a different direction. He captured and imprisoned Tigran VII, the king of Armenia (r. 339–350). He had the poor man blinded so he was ineligible to resume his kingdom.[41] When the people rose up and evicted the Persians from their country, Tigran's son, Arsaces II or Arshak (r. 350–367), took up the duties of his disgraced and mutilated father.

In the spring of that year, Constantius quit the East with the flower of his army to deal with troubles in Europe. Shapur saw his opening. He mobilized his army and returned to Mesopotamia. He went back to Nisibis for his third attempt to take the stubborn city. Nisibis was one of the most fought-over cities in this long conflict. It had changed hands many times during the prior four hundred years. For the past forty years, it had been in Roman hands. Shapur wanted it back.

Once again, Persian engineers went to work manipulating the river. This time they seem to have built dams upstream and down so that a portion of the city was inundated by an improvised lake. They built rafts and attacked the weakened walls across the new moat, but this impromptu navy was repelled by diligent archers and stone-throwing *ballistae*. Shapur abandoned the rafts; but soon a 150-foot section of the earthen walls of dried mud brick dissolved and collapsed into the temporary moat.

Shapur did not wait for the defenders to rebuild their defences. He ordered an immediate attack. The attackers on foot, on horseback and on elephants soon were mired in deep, boot-sucking mud. Their advance slowed to a crawl and they became easy targets for archers amid the rubble. As the determined attackers got closer, archers, slingers, spearmen and *ballistae* took their toll. As the elephants became bogged down and stung by arrows and stones they panicked and trampled the infantrymen near them.

The siege lasted a hundred days and again resulted in failure. Shapur might have continued the siege, but news of invasions of Persia from the northeast compelled him to draw up his army and march away. He would be away fighting in Khorasan for the next five years (353-358).[42]

In that autumn of 353, Shapur faced the new enemy on his eastern border. The Persians called this new foe the Chionites.[43] In another century, tribes related to these mounted warriors would be in the West and become known to the Romans as Huns.

The wars with other enemies presented both sides with renewed opportunity. When either the Roman or the Persian armies defeated an enemy, they would absorb contingents of the defeated army into their own fighting forces as auxiliaries. While the Romans brought Goths and Franks with them to fight Shapur, he employed defeated Eastern enemies to fight the Romans. The practice of using foreign mercenary soldiers in these wars was not new but it was a growing practice.

Chapter 11

Julian: The Soul of Alexander

He was deluded into the belief that his exploits would not only equal,
but exceed those of Alexander of Macedon; so that he spurned with
contempt the entreaties of the Persian monarch. He even supposed
in accordance with the teachings of Pythagoras and Plato on 'the
transmigration of souls', that he was possessed of Alexander's soul,
or rather that he himself was Alexander in another body.
                                                    –Socrates Scholasticus[1]

O f all the Roman invasions of Iraq, the expedition of Julian holds the most
detailed information for the historian. This chapter summarizes the
account of Ammianus Marcellinus and others.

Like Claudius before him, Julian was a bookish and introverted minor member
of the royal family (he was the son of Constantine's half-brother) and was never
expected to rule. When Constantine died in 337, he bequeathed the empire to his
three sons. Julian was left out of the inheritance. Instead he went to Athens where
he studied quietly with his Neo-Platonic tutors.[2]

There he cultivated a love for Graeco-Roman culture and tradition. His classical teachers nurtured in him a contempt for Christianity, the new religion that his
uncle had bequeathed to the Empire. Julian had been brought up as a Christian in
the court of Constantine. It was a time in his life that he was miserable. When he
turned his back on the Nazarene faith, he was saddled forever with the label 'The
Apostate' by his Christian detractors.

By 355, Julian's cousin, the Emperor Constantius II (r. 337-361), was the sole
surviving son of Constantine. He was completely preoccupied with the threat of
the Persians in the East. He needed someone he could trust to lead the armies in
the West, where the Alamanni had settled on the west bank of the Rhine, raiding
deep into Gaul and threatening the Roman heartland. He appointed Julian to be
the Caesar in overall command in the West.

An intense youth with an active mind, Julian surprised everyone by personally
taking the field in 357 and, in a pitched battle at Argentoratum near Strasbourg,
soundly defeating the Alamanni. Germanic settlers were evicted from lands west
of the Rhine.[3]

Further, he took his army across the river to destroy barbarian villages, boats and bridge-making materials. By his offensive actions, he made Gaul momentarily safe from Germanic raids.[4]

He soon became a popular favourite with his troops and the people of Gaul. His popularity grew when he lowered taxes and streamlined the imperial government in the West. His growing popularity soon came to the attention of cousin Constantius in Constantinople, but not in a good way. The royal court was rife with jealous eunuchs, sycophants and yes-men whose gossip soon poisoned the emperor against his successful cousin and potential rival. Yet a popular relative was the least of Constantius' problems.

The real problem for the emperor was that the Persians still harboured designs to retake Roman Mesopotamia as well as ancient Achaemenid lands. The Persian king echoed the founder of the Sasanian dynasty. Shapur made it very clear in a letter he sent to Constantius.

> I have often repeated what I am now about to say. Even your own ancient records bear witness that my ancestors possessed all the country up to the Strymon River [the Struma in western Bulgaria] and the frontier of Macedonia. And these lands it is fitting that I who ...am superior to those ancient kings in magnificence, and in all eminent virtues, should now reclaim.[5]

In 355, the Romans hoped to make a more permanent peace with Persia and invited Shapur to send representatives to Antioch to discuss a truce. Shapur took this as a sign of weakness and instructed his delegates to make exorbitant territorial demands. As might be expected, these were unacceptable to the Romans and the talks collapsed by 358.

In 359, Shapur returned to Mesopotamia and brought with him a numerous and fierce new ally, the Chionite Huns with whom he had recently been at war. The historian Ammianus Marcellinus, to whom we are indebted for much of the story of Constantius and Julian, wrote of standing on a hillside overlooking the Tigris River and seeing a terrifying sight:

> we saw the whole expanse of country before us, stretching to what we Greeks call the horizon, covered with columns of troops, headed by the king in gleaming robes.[6]

The Romans took long-rehearsed precautions. The land of northern Iraq was scorched and wells were poisoned or filled in with sand. No crop or green field would be left to sustain the thousands of horses that the Persians always brought with them. The Romans herded livestock away and the terrified peasants were gathered up into fortified cities.[7]

Yet abundant spring wild grass remained, and local guides knew where to dig shallow holes in the sand to reveal hidden aquifers. Shapur II confidently crossed the Tigris with his great army. On either side of him rode the king of the Albani and the king of the Chionites. He bypassed his nemesis city of Nisibis and headed straight for the Euphrates and the riches of Syria. The Persians sent flying columns of cavalry ahead of their main army to break up any Roman concentrations and intercept their communications. They tried to prevent the scorched earth policy being carried out by their enemy, but with mixed success.

Now fate took a hand on the Roman side. The spring thaw had swelled the Euphrates to flood stage and Shapur could not cross the swollen river. The battered Roman field army, which had been bested by Shapur several times, was glad of it. Syria was for the moment safe from pillage.

Frustrated at the river's edge, Shapur turned his disappointed host to the north, where the land had not been scorched. They received the surrender of a few Roman outposts before coming upon the strong city of Amida (Diyarbakir in Turkey) whose imposing black basalt walls sat astride the west bank of the upper Tigris River. So strong were the walls that they are still today among the best-preserved city walls in the world.[8]

Shapur is said to have brought with him over 100,000 fighting men. Embedded with the city's 20,000 soldiers and civilians was our war correspondent, Ammianus Marcellinus. He relates the despair that the citizens felt at first seeing the Persian host:

> Seeing such countless peoples, who had gathered over a long period to set the Roman world ablaze, concentrated on our destruction, we abandoned all hope. From that moment the one thing we all longed for was to find a way of ending our lives with glory.[9]

The Persian king approached the city with his grand army, supported by a contingent of elephant-mounted warriors brought forward for the occasion. He replaced his crown with a war helmet resembling a golden ram's head so he could be distinguished anywhere on the field.

Amida turned out to be a tough nut to crack. Shapur may have lost 30,000 men in a seventy-three-day effort to take the heavily fortified city. Grumbates, the king of the Chionites, lost a son in the battle.[10]

The Persians brought forward battering rams and catapults. Mobile towers were constructed that topped the city walls. Earthen mounds were built up against the ramparts. The defenders were worn down by constant attacks. When the city fell, Shapur allowed both Chionite and Persian to have their way with the town. He could hardly have stopped them. When their blood lust was spent, most of the surviving defenders were deported deep within Persia (Ḵuzestān) to spend their lives in labour.[11] Ammianus (if we are to believe him) was lucky to have escaped at the last minute through an unwatched water gate. After destroying Amida, Shapur crossed the Tigris River into his own country for the winter, to rest the army after their Pyrrhic victory.

In the spring of 360, he crossed into Mesopotamia and captured Singara after a siege, though it was garrisoned by at least one legion (I Parthica). Magnanimous in victory, he spared the citizens and surviving defenders.[12]

He next approached the riverside city of Bethzabde (Cizre in southeastern Turkey). This city, sitting astride a pleasant and fertile valley of the Tigris, was fortified with double walls and three legions as defenders; II Armeniaca, II Flavia Virtutis and II Parthica. Once based in the comfort of Rome, II Parthica had opposed Constantine at the Milvian Bridge and was punished by their current duty.

A long siege ended in defeat for the town. An exasperated Shapur, furious at the refusal of the garrison to yield, gave the city over to looting and murder. The two towns (Singara and Bethzabde) had taken so long to overcome that the season was late and winter setting on. Shapur decamped for his own country.

Constantius' response to the summer of loss was slow and inexplicable. He certainly had one eye on events in Europe where mutiny and invasion were brewing. Still, he made a slow progress against Shapur and did not arrive at Bethzabde until after Shapur had refortified it and manned it with stout defenders. Constantius laid siege to it until the rainy season prevented further action.

As might be expected, there was a great deal of fear in Antioch and throughout the entire Roman East about the numberless new threat of Persians and Chionites. The Syrians fully expected Shapur to return the next year when the Euphrates might not be in flood. However, that year saw a strange stalemate. Shapur sent only a small number of cavalry to make continued threats to cross the river.

Meanwhile, the problem with cousin Julian had been brewing since Constantius wrote to him in Gaul. The emperor ordered his cousin to send four auxiliary legions to the East at once, along with hundreds of other picked men, the cream of the Western army.

The emperor's sycophants sought to kill two birds with one stone. First, the seasoned and victorious veterans along the Rhine would stiffen the resolve of the Eastern army against the Persian host. Secondly, the move would strip Julian of his power as a rival to the throne. To refuse the order would be treason, punishable by death.

When the soldiers on the Rhine heard the orders, they were furious. They loved their commander Julian, but even more they loved their homes and families in Gaul. Like soldiers in our own time and for the same reasons, they did not want to go to war in far off Iraq.

Most of Julian's legions were made up of the sons and grandsons of immigrants. These men were recruited from Germanic tribes who had crossed the Rhine in earlier generations and settled in to life under the Roman banner. Recruited, armed and trained in the Roman manner they spoke their own dialect of camp Latin and fought under Roman generals like Julian. Ethnically they had no connection to the sons of Italy. In many cases they had enlisted only to defend their own homes against the new waves of armed immigrants that threatened their farms and towns. They had a tacit understanding with the army that they were not to be sent across the Alps to fight elsewhere. That is just what was now demanded of them.

They would not have it. The legions of Gaul, rather than obey the order of the distant emperor in Constantinople, spontaneously proclaimed Julian to be their emperor. This put him in a very tight spot. To refuse the army's proclamation was certain death, for they would abandon him in an orgy of anarchy. To accept their acclamation meant civil war with his cousin Constantius. Mindful of his fate he decided that the die had been cast. He must assume the purple or else. In a very great irony, the army that revolted because it did not want to go to Iraq now had to follow its new emperor to that very place.

Julian wrote to the major cities of the empire to explain why he was rebelling against the emperor. The only surviving letter was written to the citizens of Athens and addressed to Themistius, his teacher there. In the letter he proclaimed that he was adopted by the god Helios. Julian had become the son of a god. It must have had a familiar ring to it for Alexander and the later Roman emperors had claimed to be born of the gods. By this time in history it also had a decidedly anti-Christian tone.

He reminded the Athenians that he was the champion of philosophy by which he meant Athenian philosophy. Elsewhere in the letter he wrote, 'For a long while I used to think that I was to rival Alexander the Great and the Emperor Marcus (Aurelius)'.[13]

Constantius learned of the perfidy of the Western legions while he himself was on campaign in Mesopotamia, trying to recapture the towns taken by Shapur. It was a half-hearted attempt as he had to keep his forces ready to contend with Julian's rebellion. That is just what he resolved to do thanks to a key piece of intelligence.

Late in 361, he learned that the Persians, who had threatened to cross the Euphrates River, had gone home. Constantius was suddenly free to contest the throne with his cousin. Constantius had been sole emperor for twenty-four years. Authority lay heavily upon him as he led his army to an uncertain fate.

Fortunately for all concerned, he died on the journey in November of 361, in Cilicia, at age 40.[14] On his deathbed he made the reluctant but wise decision that would keep the empire intact and at peace with itself. He named Julian his successor and heir. Civil war was avoided and Julian was proclaimed emperor by the entire Roman world.

Constantius, though he spent much of his time fighting the Persians, is not included in the list of emperors who were compared to Alexander. His wars, like those of Marcus Aurelius, were defensive in nature. They were not the crowd-pleasing invasions and occupations of other lands and the confiscation of their riches. Instead the emperors were now fighting wars to protect the lands, distant from Rome, which earlier emperors had gained at great cost. Eutropius said of Constantius, 'His fortune is more to be praised in civil than in foreign wars'.[15]

It would await the next emperor for a new invasion of Persia with all the glory, wealth and fame that might be gained. That would be Julian, the last emperor to openly avow his admiration for Alexander over Christ. As his friend Libanius would write: 'Alexander the Great was very dear to Julian'.[16]

Next to Alexander Severus, Julian was the quickest of the emperors to compare himself to Alexander. Perhaps because so much of his writing and that of his admirers and detractors survive, we have a clearer picture of how he viewed himself.[17] Even so, he was not unaware of his hero's faults. In his *Panegyric in honour of Constantius* he noted:

> They say that Alexander, when he had broken the power of Persia, not only adopted a more ostentatious mode of life and an insolence of manner obnoxious to all, but went so far as to despise the father that begat him, and indeed the whole human race. For he claimed to be regarded as the son of Ammon instead of the son of Philip, and when some of those who had taken part in his campaigns could not learn to flatter him or to be servile, he punished them harshly.[18]

The Last Offensive

In December 361, having command of the combined army, Julian triumphantly entered a sceptical Constantinople with the zeal of a reformer. He soon set the city on edge with his proclamations, tax reforms and urgent orders.

He purged the palace of eunuchs and other hangers-on that bled the public purse, and tried to simplify the tax collection to provide some relief for the peasants. As with modern day tax reformers, Julian began to be resented by strongly entrenched special interests.

His second reform alienated him from his subjects. He publicly renounced the Christian faith and reversed the imperial policy of his cousin Constantius and uncle Constantine. Julian was out of step with the new age.

Like the brilliant (and foolish) generals and emperors of the past, he ignored criticism and pushed forward his own agenda. That agenda had everything to do with defeating the Persians and regaining the lands of Mesopotamia. He knew instinctively that victory would make all other considerations moot. At the height of his fame,

> He was often heard to repeat an anecdote of Alexander the Great, who on being asked where he kept his treasure, generously answered: 'In the hands of my friends'.[19]

While in Constantinople, Julian appointed a man named Claudius Mamertinus to be one of two Consuls for the year 362. In gratitude, Mamertinus made a speech to the Senate in which he made allusion to the empire's grasp of land even beyond Persia. We are reminded of the poets who flattered Augustus when he suggested that the Roman world was universal.

> The Rhine, the Danube, and the Nile, and the Tigris with its twin the Euphrates and the two oceans which receive and return the sun and whatever is between the confines of these lands, its rivers and shores.[20]

All these lands, he claimed, belonged to Rome, or at least they would just as soon as Julian conquered them.

Meanwhile the imperial intelligence service informed Julian that the Chionites who had so powerfully augmented Shapur's army had gone home. Either their commitment to Persia had been paid, or they tired of their great losses and small gains.

The new emperor shifted his headquarters to Antioch in July of 362. On his journey to that city he and the army are said to have deliberately camped on the field of Issus where Alexander had defeated Darius III.[21]

Diplomacy was not Julian's forte. He was a blunt and straightforward man, used to philosophical certainty and unquestionable command. His army of simple western peasants understood and obeyed. The East was different. Complex loyalties of tribes and clans, unwritten alliances, circus factions, language, ancient feuds and modern hatreds had to be attended to and, like modern American leaders, Julian did not understand it at all. Nor did he care to. He was gruff with his Armenian and Arab allies. We are reminded of Crassus. He expected their support and told them so. In a letter to the Armenian king, he warned what would happen if Armenia did not support his invasion plans:

Be assured that you will be an easy victim of the power of Persia when your hearth and home, your whole race and the kingdom of Armenia all blaze together.[22]

When Shapur got reports of the intense preparations for war being carried out by Julian, he sent a letter offering to make peace. This time the Romans viewed overtures for peace as weakness. Julian turned him down flat. He dismissed warnings against the Persian campaign just as Alexander ignored Chaldean Magi who warned him against entering Babylon.[23] Julian ignored all pleas for peace, as Alexander, Trajan, Constantine and, of course, Crassus had done.

After his death Julian would be scorned by Christian writers. Among them was Socrates Scolasticus who would write:

[Julian] was deluded into the belief that his exploits would not only equal, but exceed those of Alexander of Macedon; so that he spurned with contempt the entreaties of the Persian monarch. He even supposed in accordance with the teachings of Pythagoras and Plato on the transmigration of souls, that he was possessed of Alexander's soul, or rather that he himself was Alexander in another body.[24]

As late as 761, one Christian cleric would insult another by calling him 'a Julian'.[25]

In March of 363, Julian and the army left Antioch and crossed the Euphrates River over a pontoon bridge. The people of Antioch prayed for his success but were glad to see him go. His first stop was at the town of Carrhae, a town already etched deep into the Roman psyche.

Aside from the tragedy of poor Crassus, the little town of Carrhae had other unfortunate memories for the Romans. The popular emperor Caracalla was murdered near there by an aide while he was making a pilgrimage to the Temple of the Moon, and Galerius had lost his first battle near the town.

The same Temple of the Moon that Caracalla sought, Julian found in disrepair owing to the Christian contempt for all things pagan. He ordered it to be restored. After praying to the ancient gods, the emperor proceeded with his campaign and made the first of many tactical and strategic mistakes.

He detached as many as 30,000 men from his main force to join up with the Armenians to harass the Persians in Media.[26] Importantly, after their feint into Iran they (including the Armenians) were to move south along the eastern bank of the Tigris River just as Alexander had done. To lead the Median column he entrusted his maternal cousin, Procopius. He would never see him again.

Once they were away, Julian moved southward along the Euphrates River where he was joined by a fleet of over a thousand riverboats that he had enlisted, confiscated or built. Some were made of wood and others of animal skins. Fifty of these were warships.[27] Others were for use as pontoons when bridging rivers but most were supply ships carrying everything from food, tents, firewood, weapons, animal fodder and siege engines.

When Gordian III made his trip down the Euphrates, he had with him the famed philosopher Plotinus. Julian could do no less. The brave soldier was still a scholar at heart, and he was most comfortable in the company of learned men. The philosopher Priscus, a Neo-Platonist like Plotinus, had been one of Julian's teachers at Athens and an advisor at his court. Julian wanted the philosopher's company on the long journey. When time allowed, Julian would enjoy the intellectual conversation and friendship he could only have with the pagan philosopher.

Heedless of all warnings, Julian moved south. We know more about Julian's invasion of southern Iraq than that of any other Roman or, for that matter, Alexander himself. Our sources for previous invasions do not tell us in detail of the difficulty in overcoming Persian defences.

Julian confronted fortress after fortress on his line of march along the Euphrates. They had to be subdued or bypassed. We do not hear about these stout defences from Trajan, Verus, Severus or Carus. Thanks to Ammianus Marcellinus we have a detailed account of Julian's invasion of Iraq.

Why didn't the other Roman invaders have the same problems that Julian had? Why were they only confronted by Persian field armies if at all? The answer may be obvious. As we have seen the Sasanians valued Roman military ways more than the Parthians. They purposely built stout defences. Mud brick walls and buildings in Iraq were mortared with pitch, an abundant material in a country with so much oil. This made them incredibly strong. By Julian's time the Sasanians had prepared themselves for Roman incursions.[28]

After several pitched battles to reduce Iraqi fortress cities, Julian came to the Sasanian capital of Ctesiphon. He 'fixed his camp for some time at Ctesiphon'.[29] The city lay before Julian, defiant. The Sasanians were proving to be good students of Roman architecture and Ctesiphon was now well protected. It would require a long siege during the brutally hot Iraqi summer to take the city.

Julian considered his options. The diversionary force he had sent to the north was expected to join him here at Ctesiphon with the Armenian allies. He did not know that the Armenians refused to join the coalition to invade Iraq, and had deserted the Roman banner as they had done long ago to Crassus and Antony. The remaining Roman force was stranded in Media. They could not break through the Persian forces led by Shapur II to rejoin Julian in the south.

Julian was in a quandary. He did not have sufficient forces to take Ctesiphon, and he did not know the whereabouts of Shapur and his army. All the country over which he had travelled had been laid waste, and could not sustain his army should they retreat that way. It was now mid-June. If he stayed before Ctesiphon, he might be trapped there by the combined Persian army in the heat of summer while his provisions dwindled.

Fully one third of his available men were tied up in the manning of the supply boats and warships that he brought with him. If they could be freed up, he might have the reinforcements he needed to breach the walls of Ctesiphon. In a rash move, perhaps encouraged by Persian deserters, someone ordered the ships to be burned.[30] Almost immediately, the legionaries understood the disastrous implications. Their siege engines had gone up in smoke, as had their all-important bridge building equipment and their precious provisions. All that was saved they would have to carry on their backs.

Julian was at all times aggressive and made the best of a bad situation. He ordered his army, now augmented with the out of work sailors and stevedores, to march north along the east bank of the Tigris. The fields could still allow them to live off the land as they sought new conquests closer to home. Libanius thought that Julian's goal was the plain at Gaugamela where Alexander defeated Darius III.[31]

Meanwhile, Shapur, after compelling the northern Roman force to retreat, had rushed his army southward to join up with the Surena and destroy Julian. Their numbers were augmented when the Arab horsemen who had been Julian's strongest cavalry contingent saw that the tide was turning. They bolted and joined the enemy.

The Romans continued their hot and dusty march along the eastern banks of the Tigris. Their long column, including wagon train and prisoners, extended for four miles (6.4 km). Without their precious boats, they were unable to cross the Tigris River. Their food ran low as they passed the scorched and smoldering fields they had hoped would sustain them. The Persians harassed them and forced them into exhausting skirmishes that sapped their strength and slowed their progress.

As the Romans, now fully conscious of their peril, reached the area of modern Samarra, the enemy hit them sequentially in the rear, centre and front. When Julian learned of the first attack on the column's rear, he rushed to be in the thick of the fighting without taking the time to don his body armour. No sooner had he neared the scene of fighting at the rear of his long column than he learned of an attack on the front of the extended line of march. He wheeled his horse about to meet the new threat. His loyal bodyguards struggled to keep up. Then the enemy attacked the centre of the Roman column as well.

In the confusion of battle, the emperor's guards became separated and Julian found himself in the thick of the fighting. A spear of unknown origin pierced his side and mangled his liver before it could be pulled out. He fell from his horse and was quickly carried away to shelter. Hearing of his wound, his troops lost all discipline and chased after the fleeing enemy, cutting down all within their reach. In the night, Julian died of his wound and along with him any offensive spirit the army might still have.[32] He died at nearly the same age as Alexander and the spirit of Alexander died with him.

The commanding generals met in conclave to choose a new emperor from their own ranks. The compromise choice for the purple was Jovian (r. 365–366).[33] He was a staff officer from the Danubian frontier, son of a popular general and a nominal Christian.

When Shapur learned of Julian's death, he wrote to the Romans:

> God has brought you into our power and has made us to prevail over you, in return for your violence toward us and your trampling over our land. We hope that you will perish there from hunger without our having to wield a sword against you in battle or to point a spear at you; but dispatch to us a leader (to treat with us), if you have appointed a leader over you.[34]

The new emperor was not of a martial spirit like his predecessor. After marching the army to the north as far as Dura (Ad-Dawr between Samara and Tikrit), he reluctantly met with Shapur and made considerable concessions, in order that his army might cross the river unhindered and return back into its own territory.

By the humiliating peace that Jovian signed, Rome was forced to cede some of Armenia and most of Mesopotamia that it had ruled for two hundred years. The common border was moved back to the Euphrates River. Shockingly, the new emperor gave away the brave and now Christian city of Nisibis which had defied and defeated Shapur on three occasions. It was now to be abandoned by its brave citizens to the victorious Persian. Singara, already in Persian hands, was officially surrendered. Julian's grand expedition to Iraq had come to nothing. Worse, Syria was open to attack and the Eastern Empire began its age-long decline.

Jovian's desperate giveaway of Mesopotamia to save his army could in no way inspire comparison to Alexander. Rome had fallen on hard times and it would only get worse.

Chapter 12

The Sasanian wars with Byzantium: The waning of Alexander

Persia, a land formerly darkened with the gloom of idolatry, barbarous
to the last degree and wholly given over to unlawful practices.
–St. John Damascene[1]

After a reign of only nine months, Jovian was found dead in his bed under mysterious circumstances. The periodic struggle for dynastic control of the empire continued. The winner, once again chosen in military conclave, was another Christian general, Valentinian (r. 364–375). He at once divided the empire in half, taking for himself the West while appointing his brother Valens (r. 364–378) to be emperor of the East.

With a shrinking military pool of young men available or willing to join the army, the emperors in Constantinople began to hire mercenary troops. Soon Goths, Slavs and Huns would guard the eastern frontier along the banks of the Euphrates River. The sons of the fierce warriors who had breached Roman defences along the Rhine and Danube in recent memory would become the sentinels of Rome along the Euphrates.

In Constantinople, Valens mirrored popular sentiment and repudiated Jovian's disgraceful treaty. Valens had served in the household guard of both Julian and Jovian.[2] Defeat at the hands of Shapur was insufferable.

In 378 Valens was prepared to fight Persia for control of Mesopotamia. However, before he could make his move Persia was saved from Roman invasion by fate. This time salvation would come in the form of a host of Visigoths who had clamoured across the Danube River into Thrace early in 376. Herded by the even-more-aggressive Huns to the east, hundreds of thousands of Visigoth immigrants forced their way across the Danube for protection and refused to leave. Valens, distracted by this unexpected threat, quickly signed an agreement with Shapur's representatives, giving up the Roman claim to Armenia. He then hastened to meet the Visigoths (and his own death) at the disastrous Battle of Adrianople (August 378).[3]

Shapur II died the next year at the age of seventy. He had inherited a shaky throne at his birth. In the seven decades of his reign the Sasanians had wrested from Rome the lands of Mesopotamia, Assyria, Armenia and Iberia. He had successfully turned back a major Roman invasion, killed an emperor, humiliated another (Jovian), and expanded his realm in all directions. After his death, Persia moved into a period of internal preoccupation. While contending warlords weakened the Persian homeland, Armenia and Iberia would again slip their leash. Peoples in eastern Persia felt their own need for liberation. The empire that Shapur II had so painstakingly built began to erode, while challengers for the vacant throne contended with one another.

Meanwhile the Romans of Constantinople, after the disaster at Adrianople, did their best to strengthen their position along the common border. There was a tenuous peace, more of a cold war, between the two superpowers for many years.

With the death of Valens, an emperor came to the throne in Constantinople worthy of the name. He was Theodosius I (r. 379–395), called 'the Great', the last ruler of a united Empire, such as it was. During his reign he would often be compared to Alexander and the victorious Roman generals of the past. In the work known as the *Panegyrici Latini*, a contemporary writer named Pacatus Drepanius compared Theodosius favourably to Scipio Africanus, Hannibal and Alexander.[4] However, the comparison to Alexander was empty flattery.

Another court flatterer was a man known to us as Menander Rhetor. He is credited with a treatise on how to give 'epideictic' or show speeches to an important man. He describes the proper etiquette one should use when addressing an emperor. Included in his suggestions is the importance of comparing 'the reign of Alexander with the present (emperor)'.[5]

Yet another flatterer was a court poet named Claudian who suggested that Theodosius' son Honorius (r. 384–423) may one day 'hold sway over farthest India, be obeyed by Mede (Persian), unwarlike Arab or Chinese'. Addressing the young Honorius in person he predicted that 'You shall be as great' as Alexander.[6] Of course the boy did no such thing.

The flattery is reminiscent of Ovid's predictions of future Eastern victories for Gaius Caesar, four hundred years earlier. It also demonstrates a continuing line of Roman desire for the elusive conquest of Asia that had been a part of the Roman mindset since Republican times.

Theodosius himself flattered his son Honorius. He advised him not to be too hasty to take up the sword and reminded him of Alexander and his father Philip:

> It is said that Alexander, conqueror of Persia, wept at the constant news of Philip's fortune, telling his companions who rejoiced in his sire's valour that his father left him nothing to conquer. In you I see a like spirit.[7]

Admiration for Alexander did not prevent Theodosius from outlawing paganism which led to the destruction of pre-Christian temples, especially in Alexandria,

Egypt, the most famous of the cities founded by his hero, the Macedonian conqueror.[8]

Imitation of Alexander took another twist at court as the Byzantines of Constantinople adopted oriental ways of 'emperor worship'. The emperors themselves took on the airs of Persian despots and it was expected that all who came before them would pay homage in what the Greeks called *proskynesis*, a deep bow often to the point of prostration.

Just as Alexander had attempted to adopt some Persian customs, the Byzantines accomplished this to a very high degree. Alexander's Macedonians and the Italians of the Republic would not have tolerated it but the Latin speaking emperors in the Greek east end of the disintegrating empire had no problem with this form of imperial showmanship.[9]

The Byzantines romanized Alexander as did earlier Romans. In an early version of the *Alexander Romance*, a 15-year old Alexander wins a chariot race at Olympia. In a later version, the venue is changed to Rome and he competes in the colours of one of the Roman racing factions.

One modern historian, H J Gleixner, in his 1961 dissertation *Das Alexanderbild der Byzantier*, noted that 'Alexander is represented in a manner reminiscent of the Byzantine Emperor'.[10] In Richard Stoneman's translation of a Greek-language Alexander Romance called *He Phyllada tou Megalalexantrou* (*The Book of Alexander the Great*, he quotes K Mitsakis as writing: 'Alexander was born an antique pagan, but died a Byzantine Christian'.[11] As we have seen, some Moslem writers of the Middle Ages would claim Alexander as an Islamic hero. The Byzantines could do no less.

The Persians, now without the guidance of a powerful king like Shapur II, determined to ingratiate themselves with the new emperor. When Theodosius was crowned, the Persians sent rich gifts of gems and silks as an offering of friendship and peace.[12] No doubt these gifts served to fuel his Alexandrian ambitions in mind if not in deed. Yet, behind the glad-handing, there remained the issue of Armenia. Negotiations, begun by Ardashir II (r. 379-383), the brother of Shapur II, continued during the reign of his son Shapur III (r. 383–388).[13] The resulting treaty allowed Persia to swallow up fully four fifths of Armenia, leaving just one fifth (Lessor Armenia) for Constantinople.[14]

Though disadvantageous to Rome, the resulting treaty of peace with Persia freed Theodosius to act in the West. As with Alexander and the best of the Roman generals and emperors, Theodosius secured Armenia, or at least a portion of it, before going to war elsewhere.

By 399 in Persia, a son of Shapur III, Yasdagird I (r. 399–420), came to power. He showed a ready willingness to promote peace. Trade and commerce with the West expanded. For a time Christianity flourished even at his court. In 410 the first synod of the Nestorian church was allowed to convene in Ctesiphon.[15] Since the Nestorian sect was persecuted in Roman territory it was allowed, though monitored, in Persia.

The treaty also allowed for prisoner exchanges and the bones of Christian martyrs were returned to Roman territory. They received burial in the old Armenian capital of Tigranocerta, which was renamed in their honour as Martyropolis (today's Silvan in southeast Turkey).[16]

Relations had improved to the point that by 408 Theodosius' son and heir, the emperor Arcadius (r. 395–408), requested that King Yasdagird serve as a guardian for his infant son Theodosius II (r. 408–450). The worried father wanted to insure that internal plots in the capital did no harm to the boy. Yasdagird accepted the charge and sent one of his representatives, Antiochus, to Constantinople to be the boy's tutor, constant companion and insurance against foul play.[17]

The good will could not last. Relations deteriorated between Rome and Persia over the Christian issue. Peace ended with Yazdagird's premature death. According to legend, he was preparing for a hunt when he was unexpectedly kicked by a mysterious white horse, a story which is usually considered to be an allegory.[18] His battered body lingered briefly before dying. While highly thought of in the West for his pacific nature, Zoroastrian interests at home gave him the posthumous title of 'The Sinner'.[19]

With the passing of Yazdagird, war between Constantinople and Ctesiphon flared up anew. Ominously the new conflict had religious origins. Christianity had been growing in numbers and influence within the Persian realm despite the intolerance of the Magi. However, some Christians were even less tolerant than the Magian priests. Late in the reign of Yazdagird, a few zealot Christians took it upon themselves to destroy some Zoroastrian fire temples in the name of Christ. For the offenders, martyrdom quickly ensued.[20] Yazdagird abandoned the Christians and sided with the Magi. The wrath of the priests was aroused and a state-sanctioned pogrom of Christians began throughout the Persian realm. These events continued after the reign of Yazdagird and grew in intensity. Christian refugees soon streamed across the border into Syria, where they were granted asylum in the now-fervently-Christianized Roman Empire. The Persians demanded that the Romans hand over these heretics for punishment. The Romans refused.

The simmering hatreds exploded into war. On the throne in Constantinople sat a boy of seventeen whose guardian had been Yazdagird. Theodosius II (r. 408–450) was the grandson of Theodosius I and the only son of Arcadius.

The Persian leader who followed Yazdagird was his son, a man named Bahrám V (Gōr) (r. 421-439). His mother was the daughter of the Jewish Exilarch, the leader of the Jews in 'exile' in Persia.[21] While Bahrám V is credited with Jewish maternity, he was raised away from court among the Lakhmid Arabs of al-Hira in

Mesopotamia.[22] He was not the first choice of the Persian nobility. They wanted to bypass the discredited old king's offspring in favour of one of their Sasanian relatives. When Bahrám's older brother tried to claim the crown, he was assassinated. Bahrám refused to accept this insult to his family. He rallied an army from among his Lakhmid friends to help him take the throne. He was victorious. Significantly, it was the first time that the Arabs imposed a ruler on another country.

Meanwhile, the Romans actively encouraged and aided the Christians within the Persian realm. Very probably they were using them to spy and undermine the Sasanian regime. When Bahrám began an active persecution of the Christians. Byzantine Rome would not stand for it.

Theodosius II would preside over both of the Roman-Persian wars in the fifth century. In 421 the Romans struck first. The Roman general Ardaburius attacked Armenia and the Persian province of Arzanene (southwest of the saline Lake Van) where he routed a Persian garrison and enslaved his prisoners.

From there the fighting shifted to Mesopotamia, where the Romans laid siege to the long-suffering city of Nisibis. The siege failed when Bahrám Gōr advanced his army to protect the city. There was no effort on the part of the Romans to march further into Persia.

Meanwhile in Europe, the rapacious Huns threatened Constantinople itself. The Romans, fearing a war on two fronts, made peace with Persia.[23] This mini-war had lasted only one campaign season. For Theodosius II it was never about imitating Alexander but a defence of the Christians in Persia.

This war with no name turns out to have been a signal event in the history of the Middle East. The hardening of attitudes of piety on both sides led to the first religious wars. The ongoing wars between the Greco/Roman Empire and Persia were now seen as holy crusades long before the 'crusades' of the Middle Ages. Neither pagan Rome nor the Macedonia of Alexander's time made 'holy war' on Persia in the name of Zeus or Jupiter. Wars of religion were something new and are with us yet.

The 'powers that be' in Persia, even before the embrace of Shiite Islam, were narrowly focused on their own national faith. The Magi, like the Ayatollahs, were the defenders of the faith.

The Romans were frustrated by the Persian army which by this time had matured significantly:

> all the companies were clad in iron, and all parts of their bodies were covered with thick plates, so fitted that the stiff-joints conformed with those of their limbs; and the forms of human faces were so skillfully fitted to their heads, that since their entire body was covered with metal, arrows that fell upon them could lodge only where they could see a little through

tiny openings opposite the pupil of the eye, or where through the tip of their nose they were able to get a little breath. Of these, some who were armed with pikes, stood so motionless that you would have thought them held fast by clamps of bronze.[24]

Growing Sasanian power coincided with a weakening of military resources and resolve in the West. While Rome, east and west, confronted the onslaughts of Vandals and Huns, the emboldened Sasanians attacked the remaining Roman interests in Mesopotamia.

In 440, the second Roman–Persian war of the fifth century broke out. Compared to the war of 421–422, there were no major battles and the Romans quickly came to terms. A donative of gold and the return of some doomed Persian deserters to Ctesiphon ransomed the peace. A new treaty called for the cessation of construction of new forts on the common border.[25]

Theodosius II had good reason to want peace with Persia. Things were not going well in the West. In 439, the Vandals occupied Carthage and raided the southern coasts of Europe. In 441, Attila and his Huns decisively defeated a Roman army along the Danube and threatened both Rome and Constantinople. By 446, Britain would be abandoned.

While the Persians were occupied with the outnumbered Christians and invasions of Hephthalite Huns (sometimes called 'White Huns'[26]), the Romans had their hands full with the Huns of Attila. The twin assaults on the two empires had the result of keeping the peace between them for over fifty years. Once other challenges had receded, the tensions along the Euphrates River heated up once again. Hostilities resumed in 502, over the same unresolved issues: Armenia, trade, religion and the border.

All the while, Arab tribes were growing in numbers and power and although they were still surrogates of the two empires, their independent raids into Syria were repulsed only with difficulty.

The Eastern Roman emperor was now Anastasius I (r. 491–518). He was favoured by the widow of his predecessor Zeno (r. 474–91). To stay on the throne he ruthlessly crushed rebellions from the brother of the late emperor. He then staved off incursions from the aggressive Bulgar people in the Balkans and the Isaurians in Asia Minor (for which he was awarded a triumph) before taking on the Persians.

Anastasius had three panegyrists to sing his praises and compare him to the heroes of the past. They were Christodorus of Coptos, Priscian of Caesarea and the Christian writer Procopius of Gaza (not the same man as the historian of Justinian). Christodorus and Priscian compared the emperor's victories favourably to the early Roman general Pompey, who had also been active in Asia Minor. The Gazan Procopius saw him as being better than Alexander. Procopius would have us believe that the emperor was greater than Philip of Macedon who devastated the towns he overran. He even gushed that Anastasius was a better ruler than Alexander the Great.

King Kavad I, or Kawād, (r. 488–531) was Anastasius' Persian counterpart. During the reign of his father, Peroz (r. 459–484), the Romans helped to pay for his wars with enemies north of the Caucasus Mountains to prevent them from reaching Roman territory.[27] However, in the climactic Battle of Herat in 484, Peroz had been killed by the victorious Huns. Kavad secured his throne with the support of an army of allied Huns whose hostage he had been. The Huns had to be paid for their services and they soon formed a large part of Kavad's army as well as his household guard. Kavad applied for financing from Constantinople but Anastasius refused, hoping that the two enemies would war on one another.[28]

By this time the minority Christian community in Persia had grown large enough to splinter into factions. The two largest were the Nestorians and the Monophysites, who disagreed on the spiritual and physical nature of Jesus. In coming years the doctrinal differences between the Christians would take on racial, linguistic and nationalistic tones that would make reconciliation impossible.

It was relatively easy for the Nestorians to plant doubt in the mind of King Kavad about the loyalty of their rivals. The Magi noticed this and smiled. The Nestorians were proclaimed the only allowable Christian sect in Persia and pogroms of the Monophysite faithful soon followed.

In Constantinople, the emperor was offended by the persecution of the Persian Christians. The pious Anastasius, a devote champion of the Monophysites, was the self-proclaimed protector of his sect everywhere, even within Persia. A re-run of the war of 420-21 was imminent.

In the peace treaty of 442, Rome had pledged to help pay to maintain a Persian garrison in the pass known as the Caspian Gates to guard against the northern barbarians. However, sentiment in Constantinople ran against subsidizing the Persian army and Rome's contributions soon lapsed. Kavad, desperate for funds, demanded that the Romans renew their donative for the Persian garrison in the important pass, or face war. Anastasius answered that the Persians must surrender Nisibis in exchange. Kavad refused and negotiations stalled.[29] Kavad's desperation for money led him to take the offensive against the wealthier Roman world.

In August of 502 he led his allied army into Armenia, quickly captured the border fortress of Theodosiopolis (Turkish Erzurum) and annexed the Roman portion of Armenia.[30] At the same time, an allied Bedouin Arab force attacked Palestine and Jerusalem, where they ravaged the countryside and looted any town not protected by walls and a vigilant garrison. The always-pesky Arabs were demonstrating an increasing ability to wage war.

By October, the main Persian force was in front of Amida, where they began a three-month siege of that city.[31] Once captured, everything of value was stripped from Amida. Statues and marble flooring, tapestries, the wealth of the church, all fell prey to the victors. The plunder was piled on to rafts and floated down the adjacent Tigris River to Iraq. Kavad wintered in his new city.

With Amida in Persian hands, the war seemed to run out of steam. The Persians had suffered great losses. They exhausted the available forage for their animals and local food for their remaining soldiers. The Arabs and Huns who formed much of the Persian fighting force were ready to go home to spend their loot, mourn their dead and treat their wounds. In the spring, Kavad and the army departed leaving behind some 3,000 troops to garrison his prize and keep an eye on the 10,000 surviving citizens.

Thus began the more-or-less-continuous wars of the sixth century. These wars would be of limited scope. Objectives, on both sides, would include the sacking of a town or two and the pillage of the countryside round about. There would be no Alexander-style bold thrusts into either Persian or Roman territory beyond Antioch or central Anatolia. For Constantinople these would be defensive wars or offensive battles meant to sting the enemy rather than destroy him.

The Roman counter to Kavad's offensive would begin in April of 503. Four separate armies of up to 50,000 men in total moved against the Persians. It was the largest field army the Romans had deployed in the East since Julian's time.[32] The armies gathered at Edessa and Samosata where they crossed the Euphrates independently and moved against their assigned targets. One Roman force would besiege Amida while another attacked Nisibis. Neither siege was successful. In any event it would be August before Kavad could reassemble his allied army and respond.

The new division of forces was a weakness that would plague the Byzantines for the rest of their days. An emperor was no longer willing to vest total power in one ambitious commander. So the army was divided among several generals so that no one man could threaten the increasingly isolated throne. The division of the Roman command into four groups had the effect of nullifying their size and strength. Each commander was jealous of his authority. The troops were mutinous and despised the hardships of campaigning. In one instance a Roman commander fled at the approach of the enemy, leaving his camp to be plundered. The indomitable spirit of the early Roman Empire and, for that matter, of Alexander, had abandoned the Roman cause.

In the presence of the Persian enemy another of the Roman armies, under a commander named Aerobindus, made a tactical blunder. Rather than harass the enemy in conjunction with other Roman forces, he ordered a retreat westward across the Euphrates to Syria and so could not interfere with the Persian advance.

This allowed Kavad to defeat two other Roman columns piecemeal.[33] Victorious in the field, Kavad came to the city of Edessa and demanded gold to spare the inhabitants. The garrison was defiant and refused to pay. While they haggled, the Arab horsemen allied to Persia looted the countryside. With victory over the Roman field armies and a new winter coming on, Kavad withdrew without further success.

Upon his return home he had other troubles. Bands of predatory Huns not allied with him, or perhaps renouncing their alliance, drew his attention elsewhere in the Persian empire. While the king was thus occupied in the East, his generals conducted the war against Rome.

The Romans again took the offensive. In 504 they raided Persian lands in Armenia and Mesopotamia and wrested from them some of their Arab and Armenian allies who, out of convenience, defected to the Byzantines. Roman sieges of Nisibis and Amida were nearly successful as the defenders were reduced to severe privations. At Amida the surviving populace nearly starved to death, as the small Persian garrison continued to hold out against a tight Roman blockade.[34] After a prolonged war of three to four years, an exhausted Kavad sued for peace. Anastasius was able to purchase the final victory 'by certain modest favours' to Kavad.[35] In effect, Amida and other captured cities were ransomed and the Persians returned to their side of the border. Constantinople was so rich that using money to make a problem go away soon became a standard procedure in the foreign policy of the city and its empire.

Anastasius had been able to restore the borders *ante bellum* but at great cost. Courtiers may have continued to flatter their monarchs that they were every bit as powerful, clever and brilliant as the Macedonian conqueror but increasingly their silky words rang untrue.

After the lost cities were reclaimed, the Romans began a programme of repopulating the war-ravaged eastern frontier by bringing in and settling a mixture of Goths, Bulgars, Vandals, retired soldiers and others. While Kavad would be preoccupied on his northeastern frontier for the next ten years, the Romans would refortify the long border between them.

Fourteen miles (22.5 km) west of the Persian controlled town of Nisibis sat a small strategically located village called Dara(s). Today its ruins sit in Turkey on the sensitive Syrian border. Anastasius was determined to fortify the town as a new border post to guard against Persian attacks from Nisibis. So intertwined had the state and church become that the emperor entrusted the construction of a fortress at Dara to the newly appointed Christian Bishop Thomas of Amida. The cleric moved to Dara and supervised the layout and construction of a church. He did more. He ordered huge quarries to be dug into the surrounding hills and great stones soon emerged for building walls and fortifications.[36] A ring of two walls encompassed a commanding hill and surrounding flatlands. Higher hills funnelled a seasonal stream through the city and cisterns were dug to capture a portion of it. Baths and storehouses were built along with the church, porticoes, housing and granaries.

This double-walled city was built and fortified much to the displeasure of the Persian enemy. The city sat astride the main road that the Persians traversed to invade Syria, and so was strategically important. Kavad protested but was distracted by other troubles. Anastasius soothed his rage with gold. Dara would stand against the Persians for the next 60 years.

In the fullness of years, Anastasius passed from this world in 518. His rival Kavad would live on until 531 to vex the next Roman emperor, the ambitious but illiterate Justin I (r. 518–527). As Kavad aged he gave much thought to his successor. To secure the succession for his favorite son Khusro, Kavad proposed to Justin in 524 that the emperor adopt Khusro and become his guardian. Negotiations were begun, but they soon broke down as other issues poisoned the talks. Some at the Roman court feared that adopting the Persian into the royal family would make him an heir to the Byzantine throne. That was unthinkable. The final Roman offer of an adoption of Khusro as a 'barbarian charge', rather than as a son of the emperor, was unacceptable to the Persians and humiliating to Khusro. He swore revenge against the insulting Romans and he would have it.

Before Kavad's death, Khusro assumed much of his father's authority. The Sasanian empire reached its zenith under Khusro I (r. 531–579). Khusro was known favourably in Persia as 'Anushirvan' (The Immortal Soul). He had been born to Kavad during one of his periods of exile and soon became his father's favourite. The new king was a hot-tempered young man. He was prone to fly into a rage when displeased. He built cities, crushed a communistic rebellion (the Mazdakites), strengthened his authority over the nobles and Magi and expanded the war against Rome.[37]

The Romans in their turn had men who were equal to his challenge. In 527, Emperor Justin (r. 518-527) died and his nephew and co-ruler Justinian (r. 527-565) took his place. Even in the sixth century of the Christian era, when the Western empire had long since collapsed and been divided among invading peoples, the Latin-speaking Justinian still viewed himself as the emperor of the whole Roman world.

He is famous for his wars to reclaim the West. During his long reign he laboriously and at great expense attached North Africa, southern Spain and much of Italy to his authority. Before trying to reunite the empire he had to secure his eastern border against threats from Persia.

One of the flash points was the twin kingdoms of Iberia and Lazica (present day Georgia on the eastern coast of the Black Sea). Traditionally Persian client states, they had taken to Christianity early. Though Constantinople swore to protect them and established Byzantine garrisons in Lazica, these proved heavy handed and unpopular. This resulted in a call for help to the Persians, who invaded both countries and evicted the Romans.

Justinian's response was to send a brilliant young officer to right the situation. His name was Belisarius. In the introduction to his 2009 biography of Belisarius, historian Ian Hughes laments that 'his story is now relatively little known, especially when compared to the giants of the ancient world, such as Julius Caesar, Alexander the Great or Hannibal'.[38] Another of the few to tell his story was the imminent classicist Robert Graves (author of *I, Claudius*) who wrote a flattering novel, *Count Belisarius*, about his hero. Belisarius was compared favourably to Alexander by the greatest [modern] Roman historian of them all, Edward Gibbon.[39]

The main contemporary material available to all historians about Belisarius comes from Procopius (500–565) who served for a time as Belisarius' secretary. Curiously Procopius, who was in a better position to compare Belisarius to Alexander, never did. Instead in one short phrase he compared his emperor Justinian to the Macedonian:

> they [the Persians] were bringing as charges against Justinian the very things which would naturally be tributes for a worthy monarch, namely that he was exerting himself to make his realm larger and much more splendid. For these accusations one might make also against … Alexander the Macedonian.[40]

While Justinian had other capable generals, it was Belisarius who stood out. Having received his orders from the emperor, Belisarius, rather than sail through the Black Sea to Lazica and Iberia to contest those countries, instead occupied the recently completed fortress at Dara. From there he threatened the nearby Persian city of Nisibis. In 530 his outnumbered forces won a stunning victory against the aging Kavad at the Battle of Dara.[41] On the eve of battle, Belisarius addressed his army with disparaging words about the prowess of their Persian foe:

> their whole infantry is nothing more than a crowd of pitiable peasants who come into battle for no other purpose then to dig through walls and to despoil the slain.[42]

In the same year, another Roman general, named Sittas, won a major victory over Persia in Armenia.

In the next year a Persian army invaded Syria but Belisarius had placed his army between the Persians and the rich Syrian cities. He then herded the intimidated Persians back toward the border from a distance. But his troops were spoiling for a fight. Contrary to his own instincts, Belisarius gave into his troops' desire to fight the enemy. The result was the Battle of Callinicum on Easter Sunday of 531, in which the Romans were badly mauled.[43] Still the Persians continued their retreat to their own country nursing their wounds.

Meanwhile, Justinian sought allies among other nations. He wrote to the Christian king of Ethiopia and proposed that the African kingdom join in the war against Persia. It was a logical request. Ethiopia had recently occupied Yemen with 3,000–4,000 troops utilizing Roman shipping. They would occupy the country from 523 to 574 and threaten Persian control of trade with India.[44]

Ethiopia had no navy of its own and could not transport its troops without Roman ships.[45] On more than one occasion the Ethiopian king promised, at Justinian's repeated urging, to attack Persia and once even set his army in Yemen into motion but nothing ever came of his promised alliance with Constantinople other than the temporary conquest of Yemen and an unsuccessful assault or raid on Mecca later in the century in 570, within a year of Muhammed's birth.[46]

Although some of the conflicts were on a small scale, the fighting between the two enemies, Rome and Persia, now stretched from the Black Sea to the Indian Ocean. It was war on a broad front. But all of it was of secondary importance to Justinian.

In Mesopotamia, a peace treaty with the new Persian king Khusro I (r. 501–579) was duly signed and Belisarius was recalled to Constantinople. There he was given command of a Roman force against the Vandals of North Africa, centred in what is now Tunisia. In two pitched battles he destroyed the Vandal kingdom and by 534 North Africa became the first province that had been lost to Rome to be restored to Justinian's neo-Roman Empire. Belisarius moved on to occupy Sicily.

By 536 the garrison left in Africa rebelled against Constantinople. To calm the situation Justinian dispatched one of his commanders, Germanus, who was also his cousin. Upon his arrival, according to historian J A S Evans, Germanus delivered a speech to the mutineers 'with words which are a faint echo of those Alexander the Great once used when the Macedonians rebelled against his policies'.[47] If an Alexander connection occurs to Professor Evans, it would also have occurred to Germanus and the rebellious legionaries.

While the speech may have been a good one, he needed to be conciliatory, hand over back pay and empathize with the soldiers. It worked to a point. In 536 Belisarius had to return to Carthage to further soothe the passions of the mutineers. He stabilized the situation and loyalty to the emperor was restored.[48] The Romans then turned their attention to Italy. Belisarius defeated the Ostrogoths to capture Rome in 536 and Ravenna by 540.

In 540, accepting an invitation to act in concert with the Ostrogoths against Constantinople, Khusro I invaded Syria and sacked Antioch.[49] The destruction of Antioch was such a blow to the government of Justinian that a contemporary observer noted that, 'There was not a farmer or taxpayer left to the treasury'.[50]

Justinian made a hasty peace with Persia and sweetened it with gold but when Khusro continued his interference in the Roman protectorate of Lazica, Belisarius was sent in angry response. He arrived in Syria in 541 while Khusro was in the north consolidating his position in Lazica.

Instead of pursuing Khusro, Belisarius laid siege to Nisibis. He was unable to subdue the heavily fortified city but his incursions into Persian-controlled Assyria east of the Tigris River compelled Khusro to abandon his plans and return to defend his kingdom. If Belisarius had made a dash for Ctesiphon in southern Iraq, Khusro would have been badly out of position to defend it. The fear of an Alexander-inspired invasion was enough to compel the king to return home.

In 542 Belisarius' presence in Syria was enough to turn a Persian invasion force around without having to do battle.[51] When Belisarius arrived on the scene he ordered all the garrisons of Syria to report to him. Yet against the numerous enemy he could muster fewer than 15,000 troops. Of these only his 7,000 household cavalry were reliable.

When the King of Kings learned that his old adversary Belisarius barred his path, he hesitated. Khusro sent an ambassador to the Roman camp to ascertain their strength. Belisarius moved out from his pitiful camp to a forward position. He selected his best warriors, displayed them in active and aggressive postures and athletic contests keeping them in motion, and well-armed so that the ambassador would see what fearsome opponents they were.

> he [Belisarius] dismissed the envoy, who went to Khusro and said that he had seen the general Belisarius, a man who was exceptionally intelligent and brave, and soldiers such as he had never beheld before…He advised Khusro not to get involved in a fight with them in case he was defeated and lost the entire Persian empire.[52]

Unable to determine the number or quality of the Roman troops, the Persian king lost his nerve. By a brilliant stroke of reputation, diplomacy and guile, Belisarius was able to intimidate the Persian back into his own land. The Romans won a desperately needed bloodless victory.

Rawlinson had a different take on the Persian retreat. He suggested that bubonic plague had broken out in Egypt and spread panic before it. When Khusro learned of it, he decided not to tempt fate and kept himself and his army safe from harm.[53]

While Belisarius kept the Persians in check, affairs in Italy disintegrated and Justinian was forced to recall his general to stabilize his emperor's efforts there.

With Mesopotamia and Syria exhausted and impoverished. The war in the East shifted its focus to Lazica and Iberia. From 541 to 562 the two superpowers fought for control of the Black Sea and the two kingdoms at the sea's eastern shores. Finally King Khusro accepted that the kingdoms were Roman protectorates in exchange for gold.[54] The truce was to last for fifty years, but as usual it excluded Armenia which, almost predictably, became the cause of troubles that broke the peace after only ten years.[55]

During the reign of Justinian, a seemingly insignificant event would eventually change the relationship between Europe and Persia. In 552, some silkworm eggs were smuggled into Constantinople from China in hollow bamboo tubes. Within a few decades the Western world had its own independent silk industry.[56] The reliance on imported silk from China and the odious Persian middleman would decline and with it the fortunes of the Sasanians.

As for Belisarius, he served his emperor well but in all ages successful generals frequently make their masters jealous and distrustful. Justinian frequently starved Belisarius of men and supplies. The fact that he could still win victories with little imperial support burnished his image as a brilliant general. Justinian would have been further ahead to favour his best general.

Justinian died in 565 and was replaced by Justin II (r. 565-574) who was the husband of Justinian's niece, Sophia. A devout Christian, he took offence when Zoroastrian officials set up fire altars in Armenia. Justin appointed his cousin Marcian, also a nephew of Justinian, to be the commanding general in a new Persian invasion. In 573, following some victories over local Persian forces, Marcian laid siege to Nisibis and was confident of victory. Back in Constantinople, it seemed to take too long for the city to fall and gossipy courtiers poisoned the impressionable emperor's mind against Marcian.

It was alleged that the general had eyes on the throne. Justin bought into the folly and had Marcian relieved of command on the eve of what might have been a successful siege of the long-suffering town. Disgusted, Marcian packed up and left with his household guard during the night. In the morning, the troops, noting that he was gone and with no new commander placed over them, panicked. They fled to Dara. Khusro's army came up and seized all of their abandoned equipment.[57] He then mounted his own siege of Dara which was successful. In Constantinople, Justin's impotent rage at the twin defeats fed a growing madness and for a short while the Roman world was ruled by insanity.

The mad emperor Justin was persuaded by his wife in a moment of lucidity to share the throne with his trusted friend Flavius Tiberius Constantius as Caesar in 574.[58] Taking the reins of empire firmly in his own hands as Justin sank into dementia, Tiberius II (r. 574–582) consolidated his authority by spending the money that Justin had assiduously squirreled away in the treasury.

In the East at least he had some measure of success. He bought mercenary allies where he could. The Alani, from north of the Caucasus, had largely sided with Persia. They were paid twice as much by Tiberius II to side with Constantinople. He impressed their representatives by meeting with them personally.

With his expanded army, Tiberius was able to buy a year's truce with Persia along the eastern border with gold. Only Armenia was exempt from the purchase price.[59] Once the ink was dry and the gold delivered (45,000 solidi) the Persians moved on Armenia.

By 575 Khusro had ruled for over forty years. He was old and tired. His hair was white when he led his army in person for the last time. His aim was to suppress the rebellion in Armenia. In the ensuing conflict the Persians met with initial success, advancing into the Roman portion of Armenia and threatening neighbouring Cappadocia. Then they were forced from the country by a Roman general named Justinian (a great-nephew of the former Emperor Justinian).

In the crucial battle the Romans scattered their foe and fought their way into the Persian camp. They seized the king's tent, treasury and extinguished the sacred eternal flame that always attended him. Even the war elephants were captured and sent to Tiberius along with the other spoils.[60] The king hastily escaped with his life, but more of his army was lost trying to cross the Euphrates River which, in the hills of Armenia, flows dangerously swift. General Justinian won a complete victory.

Defeated, the Persian survivors returned home for the winter season. Justinian took advantage of the retreat of the Persian field army to march all the way to the Caspian Sea, took ship and raided into Persian territory during a mild winter before returning to western Armenia.[61] It was the first time that the Romans had attacked Media from the sea.

In 576 or 577, a new Persian army led by a general named Tamkhosrau managed to defeat Justinian's army. Justinian was relieved of command by the emperor and ordered home. There was no sorrow at the Byzantine court over Justinian's defeat. This daring member of the royal family had already been implicated in a plot against the emperor. It is likely that the rest of his life was spent under house arrest.

Tiberius then appointed Maurice, his friend and Captain of his bodyguard, to command the eastern armies (*magister militum per Orientem*).[62] Maurice ravaged Mesopotamia. Singara was captured to the delight of the Romans. Raiding parties were then sent across the Tigris burning, looting and killing.[63] He won sufficient victories that he was rewarded with the hand of the emperor's daughter Constantina in 581. In August of that year Tiberius II died without a male heir and Maurice was proclaimed emperor by the court and army alike.[64]

There was much to do. The Lombards were active in Italy, the Avars had imposed themselves south of the Danube and the Slavs ravaged the Balkans. Then too there was Persia. Khusro I died in the spring of 579. Maurice now had to contend with his son and successor Hormizd IV (r. 579-590).

All the while Romans and Persians continued to fight one another over limited objectives. A city might be sacked by one side or the other, allied Arab tribes fought one another or raided the territory of either side with increasing aggression. The mutual carnage would continue until the death of Hormizd at the hands of a palace coup in 590.

He was succeeded by his son Khusro II (r. 590-628). He came immediately under attack by a Persian general named Varahran Chobin, who had won significant victories against the Byzantines to the west and Göktürks to the east. Feeling wronged by Hormizd, Chobin, the scion of a Parthian clan, took advantage of the weakness of Khusro to usurp the throne for himself in the summer of 590.

Khusro escaped Ctesiphon and fled to Roman territory where Maurice took him under his wing.[65] The ousted Sasanian king was provided with money and a Roman army to back his right to rule. He marched back to Ctesiphon, gathering allies as he went. The rebel army deserted their new Parthian king and Khusro II was returned to his throne.

Now it was Chobin's turn to flee. He sought asylum among the Turks but was murdered by his host.[66] Khusro in gratitude to Maurice gave over the fortress of Dara and much of Armenia to the Byzantines. In addition, the odious annual payment of gold from Constantinople to Ctesiphon for the defence of the Caucasus frontier was suspended. Byzantine authority in the East almost equalled that of Septimius Severus. The timing was perfect, for Maurice was able to move his army to confront his western enemies with his eastern border secure.

There must have been some criticism of the emperor for placing a 'client' king on the throne of Persia when he could have just as easily fulfilled the age-old Roman desire of annexing the vast kingdom as Alexander had done. Theophylact Simocatta, the court historian of Maurice, rebutted this point of view by arguing that removing the Persian king would create a power vacuum that would be filled by new enemies of Rome. As an example he offered up the experience of the 'insane' Alexander of Macedon whose death resulted in contending 'tyrants' and empires which tore the Macedonian empire asunder.

> Alexander became an immature sport of fortune and, when she smiled on him a little in mockery, he swaggered in his mastery of Europe, undertook to master the sea, desired to hold the sceptre of Babylon, yearned for Indian power, threatened to subjugate Libya, and constrained his kingdom to expand as far as the sky is spread and the sun's eye shines with

sparkling rays. He attempted to subjugate the temporal universe to a single unitary power. But, sooner than this, ambition was quenched along with power, and affairs proceeded once more divided up into leadership of multiple tyranny.[67]

Simocatta repeats the long-held belief of one portion of the Roman literati that Alexander was an evil presence. From Seneca and Lucan to St. Augustine, there was always a disapproving voice to Alexander's conquests and personal flaws. Simocatta directly dismissed those among the Romans who admired Alexander and believed his feats should be duplicated. He took his place among the Macedonian's detractors.

Chapter 13

Heraclius and Khusro II: Greek Tragedy

When Heraclius perceived the perilous state the land of the Byzantines
was in, with the Persian armies devastating it, their killing of the
Byzantine warriors, their carrying off into captivity of the Byzantines'
women and children, their plundering of the Byzantines' wealth, and
their violation of the inmost parts of their realm, he shed tears before
God and made humble petition to Him. Imploring Him to rescue him
and the people of his kingdom from the Persian armies.

—Al-Tabarī[1]

The conflict of Rome and Persia was prolonged from the death of
Crassus to the reign of Heraclius. An experience of seven hundred years
might convince the rival nations of the impossibility of maintaining
their conquests beyond the fatal limits of the Tigris and Euphrates.
Yet the emulation of Trajan and Julian was awakened by the trophies of
Alexander, and the sovereigns of Persia indulged the ambitious hope of
restoring the empire of Cyrus.

—Edward Gibbon[2]

At long last Rome succeeded in placing its candidate on a Persian throne.
There were a few years of friendship between the two empires. With
peace in the east, Maurice could shift his army to contend with his
western enemies. One of his more far reaching moves was to appoint one of his
eastern generals, Heraclius (the elder) to be the Governor-General of Africa
(Tunisia).

Maurice was successful in holding off the Lombards in Italy, the Avars on the
Danube and the Slavs in the Balkans. In doing so it was the army that paid the
price in hardship and death. When ordered to winter in a bleak fortress north of
the Danube in enemy territory, they recalled their grievances, real and imagined,
and rebelled. Proclaiming one of their generals named Phocas to be emperor, they
marched on Constantinople. Maurice was captured and killed along with all six of
his sons as Phocas took power in the capital.

As was customary, the new Emperor Phocas (r. 602–610) dispatched representatives to the courts of other lands to announce the regime change. In Persia Khusro

decided to take things personally. Maurice had been his friend and protector and had even called the Persian king his 'son'.

The envoys of Phocas were imprisoned and eventually killed. Khusro had found the perfect excuse for war to undo the odious concessions he had made to Maurice as the price of Roman support.[3] As it was, all of Persia resented the gains the Romans had made at their expense. They undoubtedly blamed Khusro for it. Now he could make amends. With all of Persia restored to his authority he was ready to take back what he had given away.

From 603 to 610, the Persians slowly and methodically captured every Roman city and fortress east of the Euphrates River, and all of Armenia. Meanwhile in North Africa the Governor General, Heraclius, the loyal appointee of Maurice, refused to recognize Phocas as emperor and stopped remitting taxes to the capital. In 610 he went one step further. He dispatched his son, Heraclius the younger, to contest the throne.

In 610, the younger Heraclius captured and killed the usurper Phocas and was proclaimed emperor himself. His would be a star-crossed reign. However, the civil war among the Romans depleted the troops available to fight the Persians (and other enemies). Khusro continued his conquests while in the west Spain and most of Italy were forever lost to the empire.

Heraclius (r. 610–641) tried to make Khusro understand that Maurice had been avenged but the Persian king had tasted victory and he liked it. He now did something that none of his Parthian or Sasanian predecessors had done. After sacking Antioch in 611, the Persian army did not return home as it always had before. Instead Persian troops stayed and occupied the city and countryside.[4] That same year other Persian armies accepted the surrender of Apamea and Emesa. Syria was now to become a part of the resurgent Persian Empire.

Khusro II believed that he had as valid a claim to the throne in Constantinople as anyone else as the 'son' of Maurice. Therefore he was the legitimate heir to the Roman throne and, according to Theophanes, he was ready to seize it.[5]

In 613, Persian forces invaded Palestine and occupied Jerusalem. The siege of the holy city lasted but twenty days.[6] The church's most holy relic, the 'True Cross' of Jesus, and the city's Christian Patriarch, Zacharias, were carried away into Persia as trophies of war.[7]

While one Persian army was conquering Palestine, another Persian force struck deep into Asia Minor. This army marched unopposed all the way to Chalcedon (modern Kadiköy) a city on the Bosporus opposite, and in sight of, Constantinople. A siege of the city was begun in conjunction with an army of Avars who arrived from the Balkans at the city's western gates in 617.

In June of 619, the Persians occupied Alexandria in Egypt and by 621 all of Egypt was in their hands. Khusro II had restored Persia to the glory of Cyrus II

(BC 549–530) by extending the empire almost to the boundaries of its Achaemenid magnificence. The entire Persian world rejoiced.

The Sasanian victories allowed Khusro to live in unparalleled splendour. An Islamic writer, Hamza Isfahani, would glowingly say of him:

> Khusro Parvez [the ever victorious] had 3,000 wives and 12,000 slave-girls who were musical performers. He had 6,000 men who served as guards. As many as 8,500 horses were earmarked for his riding. He had 960 elephants and 12,000 mules for carrying the baggage. He also had 1,000 camels.[8]

Khusro's achievements had not gone unnoticed in Arabia where Muhammad was quietly gathering followers. He saw the situation clearly and wrote, 'The Romans are vanquished in a near land and they, after being vanquished, shall overcome'.[9] In Constantinople, Heraclius began to reverse the situation and fulfill Muhammad's prophecy.

The propagandists in Constantinople began to link the emperor with Alexander. Heraclius' modern biographer Walter Kaegi tells us that 'He and his writers sought to associate his name with famous names from antiquity: Alexander, Scipio and Constantine I'.[10]

Dutch historians Gerrit J. Reinink and Bernard H. Stolte named an entire chapter in their study of the Syriac *Alexander Romance* and the writings of George of Pisidia, 'Heraclius: The New Alexander'.[11]

George of Pisidia was a contemporary and on friendly terms with Heraclius while the Syriac *Romance* was written around the same time. Both are thought by Reinink and Stolte to be a hopeful prophesy that Heraclius would duplicate Alexander's victories over the Persians. The two Dutchmen see other ways that Heraclius copied Alexander. They point out that in the Syriac *Alexander Romance* the Macedonians took up the battle cry, 'God help us!' According to them, this was the same battle paean used by the army of Heraclius. It has its origin in a manual on war called the *Strategicon of Maurice* which was attributed to the Emperor Maurice. As we cannot vouch for the accuracy of the Syriac *Romance* we do not know if Heraclius copied Alexander or if he was made to look as if he had.[12]

Byzantine historian J B Bury, in his study of the later Roman Empire, also saw the connection between Heraclius and Alexander. Taking the other point of view, the Iranian historian Irfan Shahid, while addressing a gathering at Dumbarton Oaks in 1972, dismissed Bury's comparison as being superficial.[13]

Most of the emperor's first ten years in power were spent in defensive fighting including breaking a siege of Constantinople by the Avars. By 622, Heraclius was ready for offensive action. He landed his army in Bithynia to train his men, until then cooped up by city walls, to fight in the field. From there he marched into Cappadocia where he defeated a major Persian force at an unknown location and relieved Persian pressure on Constantinople.

The victory in Cappadocia is not well documented. It has been referred to as the 'Battle of Issus', though it did not take place there.[14] The reference to Issus could very well have been made by the emperor's propagandists to associate him with Alexander in the hearts of the people.

The climactic war between Rome and Persia carried on for several more years as Heraclius, taking command in person, defeated one Persian army after another. The last major battle between the two arch rivals was the Battle of Nineveh in 627, which was fought near the site of Alexander's final battle with Darius III at Gaugamela in 331 BC.[15] Heraclius was victorious. Walter Kaegi suggests that Heraclius was 'probably unaware' of the proximity of the two battles.[16] This is highly unlikely. Many Roman generals and emperors had crossed the Tigris in the area of Gaugamela even if it were just as raiding parties. They include Trajan, Caracalla, Galerius, Constantius, Belisarius, and Maurice. In the case of Trajan and Caracalla at least it seems that they were daring the Parthians to fight them on the ancient battlefield. The historian Libanius thought that Julian was on his way to Gaugamela during his doomed retreat from Ctesiphon. Heraclius knew exactly where he was and would have welcomed the comparison to Alexander.

The battle was not well documented by Byzantine historians. Instead they described it in terms of a personal triumph by the emperor, who was described fighting gloriously in hand-to-hand combat while mounted on his favourite horse, Dorkon. He is even credited with killing three Persian soldiers and severing the head of the Persian commander Rhazates. Despite the similarities to Alexander personally fighting at Gaugamela mounted on his horse Bucephalus and charging at the Persian king, the contemporary Byzantines attributed his success instead to his unwavering faith in Christ.[17]

Following his victory, Heraclius marched southward toward Ctesiphon along the east bank of the Tigris River. He did not invest the Sasanian capital because bridges he needed to cross over intervening canals had been destroyed.

As it was he did not need to go any further. Khusro was overthrown and killed in a palace rebellion and his son placed on the throne. It was the end of the Sasanian dream to restore the borders of the Achaemenid Empire. Having reached the very pinnacle of fame and fortune, Khusro was toppled and brutally killed by his own people. He was the last effective king of Sasanian Persia.

After 700 years of war a Roman almost duplicated the victories of Alexander. Heraclius had toppled a Persian monarch and gained (or recovered) great swathes of territory and wealth that the Persians had stripped from Roman cities.

One horde of treasure discovered and confiscated by the Romans was at Takht-e Soleyman in northwestern Iran. Here Heraclius found an ornate throne room including celestial and astrological images which served to illuminate the power of King Khurso. Like Alexander before him, Heraclius destroyed the Persian throne.[18]

Alas, the unprecedented Roman triumph was ephemeral. Even though the border between eastern Rome and Persia reverted to conditions in effect in 591 it would not remain so for long.

During the long conflict between Heraclius and Khusro II, and unknown to either of them, there lived amongst the Arabs a man who would end up being greater in the light of history than either monarch. He of course was Muhammad, who overshadowed them both to such an extent that we barely know of either the Roman emperor or the Persian king today. In military terms Muhammad's greatest contribution to his people was the unification of the Arabic tribes to one devout purpose.

For a few years Heraclius was allowed to taste the fruits of his brilliant success. In great ceremony he restored the 'True Cross' to Jerusalem and received universal praise from his subjects. Then the impoverished Arab tribesmen exploded out of the desert, aflame with the new faith of Islam. Muhammad was by that time dead, but his successors (called *caliphs*) were able to lead an energized and vigorous people against both exhausted empires and overcame them.

In the year that Heraclius died, the Moslems took Alexandria in Egypt with all its riches and grain. All that Heraclius had worked so hard to reconquer was lost to him and the empire. At the same time, all of Sasanian Persia would collapse and be replaced by Islamic rulers. In time Islam would supplant Zoroastrianism as the Persian state religion, though many pre-Islamic rituals would survive into our own time.

The Arabs ended the long rivalry between Rome and Persia in their own favour and opened a new chapter in East/West relations in which Alexander would play a diminished role. However events today give rise to reflections of the past and the Roman experience may yet be visited upon new generations.

> The armies of Rome will mass to meet the armies of Islam in northern Syria…It will initiate the countdown to the apocalypse.
>
> –ISIS[19]

Conclusion

The imitation of Alexander may more rightly be called the 'comparison to Alexander'. Not until the third century did an emperor (Caracalla) even claim to be like Alexander (his reincarnation). Before that time republican generals and the early emperors were more modest. Caligula may have claimed to be a god, like Alexander, but he was thought 'mad' for doing so. It is not the emperors themselves but our extant literary sources that compare the great men of Rome with the Macedonian.

Livy is one ancient writer who, in his 'Digression', compares a Roman to Alexander. He opines that Lucius Papirius Cursor, a general active in the service of Rome during the lifetime of Alexander, could have defeated him had he invaded Italy. Papirius then was the first Roman to be compared to Alexander.

Alexander for all his greatness was a man of serious flaws. He was a tyrant. He drank too much and was prone to lethal fits of anger that imperilled the lives of his friends. Early in the third century, Aelian would write, 'Alexander himself is said to have drunk more than any man'.[1] Cicero, who compared Caesar favourably to Alexander, nevertheless feared that he might become a tyrant as well.

To the republican-minded senators of Rome, Alexander took on too many of the trappings of monarchy. If generals and emperors of the republican era and the early Principate sought to imitate Alexander they avoided any association that could be seen as mimicking a king. Not until the third century AD, when soldier emperors were continually absent from Rome and senators no longer played a significant role in government, would the rulers of the empire wear the diadem, the very symbol of Alexandrian kingship.

Still, Roman generals and emperors sought ways to identify themselves with the Macedonian conqueror. This is seen in the campaigns they fought, in the statues, monuments and coins they commissioned, the dress they affected and their devotion to the gods favoured by Alexander.

Roman citizens relished the victories of their growing empire and thought of themselves as the natural successors to Alexander and his empire. This is reflected in Alexander-themed art work stolen from Greece or art copied from Greek originals such as that found in the homes of the people of Pompeii, Herculaneum and elsewhere.

This also explains the popularity of plays and mock sea battles called *naumachia* that extolled Greek victories over Achaemenid Persia. By reflection they told of Rome's own victories, real or imagined, over Parthia and later the Sasanians.

If Alexander was considered 'great' it was for his military accomplishments. This is always associated with his conquest of Persia and reaching the outer Ocean at India, a distance incomprehensible to the Romans of the Mediterranean. The imitation of Alexander had almost by definition to include war against the Parthian and Sasanian successors of the Achaemenid Persians.

As the republican armies moved eastward to conquer the Hellenistic successor kingdoms to Alexander they frequently faced much larger forces and often overcame them. They even believed that by overthrowing Macedonian-ruled kingdoms they might actually be defeating Alexander. This fuelled a confidence in Roman abilities to overwhelm the larger but less well equipped and disciplined armies fielded by eastern peoples.

When at last Pompey's army came into contact with the Parthians they seemed docile. Pompey's legates, Afranius and Gabinius, easily trespassed on Parthian territory without consequence. However, when Crassus, following in the footsteps of Alexander, sought to slash his way to the outer Ocean he was soundly defeated and killed by a Parthian force one quarter the size of his own army.

Mark Antony, seeking revenge and his own Persian conquests, was also defeated by Parthian arms. Antony, having failed at aggressive war, sought to imitate the forms of Alexander through association with the gods and his personal appearance, ultimately without success.

From then on every Roman leader of consequence had to deal with Persia in one way or another. Augustus, trying to appear the republican at home, adopted Alexander's forms of control over the empire but not his kingship. The surviving work we have of the poets of his age predicts a future in which Augustus or his heir would expand the empire to India and the Ocean. These dreams would endure and be repeated into Byzantine times.

The Julio-Claudians inspired by Augustus turned largely to diplomacy. It was not until Trajan that a Roman would again attempt to imitate Alexander's conquests. Like Alexander, Trajan established a foothold east of the Tigris River and then followed the southerly flow of the Euphrates River, protecting his right flank at river's edge. He was supported by warships and supply vessels until he reached the wealthy cities of Babylonia which Alexander had conquered and where he died.

Lucius Verus, Septimius Severus, Carus and Julian would also adopt this strategy, giving Rome some claim to Alexander's greatness in achieving military success against a Persian kingdom. Yet none of these Roman conquerors could retain a Roman presence in Persia for very long. Eventually guerilla warfare, hunger and disease would expel the invader.

Just as the Romans dreamed of Alexandrian conquest at the expense of Persia, so the Persians dreamed of Achaemenid-like conquest at the expense of Rome. For the most part they did not have the resources to back their claim. After the fall of the Parthians the successor dynasty, the Sasanians, would inherit this dream of Persian control of Achaemenid lands in the eastern Mediterranean.

For most of the duration of Sasanian control of Persia, they fought Rome to a standstill in a mind-numbing series of battles, one after another for nearly four centuries, succeeding only in destroying the cities and farms that lay between them. Not until Khusro II, early in the seventh century, would the Sasanians, oh so briefly, restore the lands of the Achaemenids to Persian control.

At the same time that the Sasanians presented a serious threat to Rome, the cult of Alexander was revived and reverence for the old hero spread amid the imperial court of Heraclius and the public forum alike. Then it spread to the battlefield where Heraclius nearly duplicated the feats of Alexander. His Persian counterpart Khusro II, like Darius III, was killed by his own people. His son and successor acquiesced to all of Heraclius' demands. It was not necessary for the Romans to occupy Persia.[2]

Long after the end of the rivalry between Rome and Persia, Alexander would still be remembered in different cultures. Islamic scholars believe that he is mentioned in Surah 18 of the Quran as the *Dhul-Qurnayn* or 'two headed one'. The Hebrew bible is thought to make an allusion to him in Daniel 8:1-21 and he is mentioned by name in 1 Maccabees 1-9. In Greece he became legend through a book associated with the *Alexander Romance* called the *Phyllada*.[3] In more modern times he is remembered through the paintings of Charles Le Brun (commissioned by French King Louis XIV), the best-selling novels of Mary Renault and the 2004 film by Oliver Stone.

An echo of the ancient Sasanian dream of restoring the Achaemenid Empire can be seen in Iran today in the form of support for factions in Iraq, Syria, Lebanon, Yemen and Gaza. At the same time, continued western involvement in Iraq, Syria and Afghanistan and belligerence to Iran are an echo of Alexander's incomparable conquest. The wars and insurgencies being fought today thus find their very deep roots in antiquity and the rapacious life of Alexander and his Roman imitators.

Endnotes

Preface

1. Khayyám, Omar, *The Rubáiyát*, translated by Robert Graves & Ali Shah (Garden City, NY: Doubleday, 1968), XIX.

Introduction

1. Agathias, *Greek Anthology*, TE Page et al (eds), translated by WR Paton (Cambridge MA: Harvard University Press, 1916), II.25.8.
2. Andrew Stewart, *Faces of Power: Alexander's Image and Hellenistic Politics* (Berkeley, University of California Press, 1993), p 10. Stewart here is distilling the lost work of Callisthenes, through later writers of antiquity who quoted him. See also Plutarch, *The Life of Alexander*, 27. 9, in Plutarch, *Lives*, translated by Bernadotte Perrin (Cambridge MA: Harvard University Press, 1963).
3. Richard Stoneman, *Legends of Alexander the Great* (London: Everyman, 1994), pp ix-xiii
4. Michael Tierney, 'Constantine the Great and His City', in *Studies: An Irish Quarterly Review*, Vol 23, No 89 (March, 1934), pp 59-70.
5. H H Scullard, *Scipio Africanus: Soldier and Politician* (Ithaca: Cornell University Press), p 237.
6. Diana Spencer, *The Roman Alexander: Reading a Cultural Myth* (Exeter: University of Exeter Press, 2003).
7. Angela Kühnen, *Die imitatio Alexandri in der Rrömischen Politik* (Münster: Rhema Verlag, 2008).
8. G J D Aalders, *Germanicus und Alexander Der Grosse*, <Historia: Zeitschrift für Alte Geschichte, Vol 10, No 3 (July 1961), p 383.
9. Erich S Gruen, 'Rome and the Myth of Alexander', in T W Hillard et al (eds), *Ancient History in a Modern University* (Grand Rapids: William B Eerdman's Publishing, 1988), pp 178-91.
10. Anthony Kaldellis (ed and trans), *The Byzantine Family of Michael Psellos* (Notre Dame: University of Notre Dame, 2006), p 171.
11. Stewart, *Faces of Power*, p 365.
12. Peter Holliday, 'Roman Triumphal Painting: Its Function, Development and Reception' in *The Art Bulletin*, Vol 79, No 1 (Mar 1997), p 135. Holliday, an art historian, suggests the mosaic was removed from the eastern Mediterranean and transplanted to Pompeii. Andrew Stewart in *Faces of Power*, p. 331, says that the mosaic was taken to Italy in 146 BC. There is also a surviving bronze and silver

statue of Alexander the Great on horseback found at Herculaneum now owned by the *Beni Archeologici di Napoli*.

13. See Stewart, *Faces of Power*, for a discussion of Alexander's statues; also Niels Hannestad, '*Imitatio Alexandri* in Roman Art', in Jesper Carlson (ed), *Alexander the Great. Reality and Myth*, (Rome: L'Erma di Bretschneider, 1993).

14. Plutarch, *The Life of* Caesar, 61, in Plutarch, *Lives*, translated by Bernadotte Perrin (Cambridge MA: Harvard University Press, 1963).

15. Ferdowsi, *The Epic of the Kings: Shahnameh, the National Epic of Persia*, translated by Reuben Levy (Chicago: University of Chicago Press, 1967).

Chapter 1: Rome and Parthia

1. Julian, *To the Alexandrians*, 433C, translated by Wilmer Cave Wright (Cambridge, MA: Harvard University Press, 1949-61).

2. C E V Nixon and Barbara Saylor Rodgers, *In Praise of Later Roman Emperors: The Panegyrici Latini* (Berkeley: University of California Press, 1994), 12.5.3.

3. Marta Sordi, '*Alexandro Magno e l'eredita disiracusa*' in *Aevum*, 57 (1983), pp 19-23. However Lionel J Sanders believes her case is weak: 'The Dionysian Narrative of Diodorus', in *Hermes* 15, Vol 116, No 1 (1988), p 54.

4. Quintus Curtius Rufus, IV.4.18 and X.I.15, translated by John C Rolfe (Cambridge MA: Loeb Classical Library, Harvard University Press, 1962). Alexander proposed to travel in the west as far as Spain.

5. Sextus Julius Frontinus, *Stratagems*, I.II.3, translated by Charles E Bennett et al (Boston: Harvard University Press, 1961); Justin, *Epitome of the Philippic History of Pompeius Trogus*, translated by John Yardley (Oxford: Oxford University Press, 1997), XXI.VI.1; Paulus Orosius, *Seven Books of History against the Pagans*, 138, trans. Irving Raymond (New York: Columnia University Press, 1936).

6. Theophylact Simocatta, *The History of Theophylact Simocatta*, translated by Michael & Mary Whitby (Oxford: Clarendon Press; New York: Oxford University Press, 1986), iv. 1. 1-iv. 16. 28. 13. 1-8.

7. Arrian, *Anabasis*, 1. 15. 4, trans E Iliff Robson (Cambridge MA: Loeb Classical Library, Harvard University Press, 1961).

8. Orosius, III.18.3; also Livy, 8.24, translated by T J Luce (New York: Oxford University Press, 1998).

9. Justin, XVIII.1.

10. Plutarch, *Life of Pyrrhus*, 8.1, in Plutarch, *Lives*, translated by Bernadotte Perrin (Cambridge MA: Harvard University Press, 1963).

11. Plutarch, *Pyrrhus*, 19.1.

12. Julian, *The Caesars*, 324C.

13. Ammianus Marcellinus, translated by Walter Hamilton as *The Later Roman Empire* (London: Penguin, 1986), 24.1.3.

14. Edward Gibbon, *The Decline and Fall of the Roman Empire* (New York: Alfred A Knopf, 1994) IV.41.

15. Plutarch, *Pyrrhus*, 21.

16. Titus Maccius Plautus, *Mostellaria*, edited by Frank R Merrill (London: Macmillan, 1972), pp 775-7. Peter Green notes that this play also marks the earliest time in the surviving literature that Alexander is called 'The Great': *Classical Bearings: Interpreting Ancient History and Culture* (Berkeley: University of California Press, 1998), p 201. This point is also made by Diana Spencer in *The Roman Alexander*. For a discussion of Plautus' plays see Edith Hamilton's book, *The Roman Way* (New York: WW Norton & Co, 1932), chapters 1-3.

17. Livy, 9.17.2; See also Morello, 'Livy's Alexander Digression (9.17-19)', *JRS*, Vol 92, (2002), pp 62-85.

18. Livy, 9.16.9.

19. Livy, 9.19.17; R Morello, 'Livy's Alexander Digression', p 63; W B Anderson, 'Contributions to the Study of the Ninth Book of Livy', *TPAPA*, Vol 39 (1908), pp 89-103, argues that the digression was a youthful exercise, not an integral part of Livy's '*History*'.

20. Spencer, *The Roman Alexander*, pp 47, 50.

21. Chamoux, François, *Hellenistic Civilization*, translated by Michael Roussel (Oxford: Blackwell Publishing, 2003), p 27.

22. Livy, 9. 17; A E Wardman, 'Plutarch and Alexander', *The Classical Quarterly*, Vol 5, No ½ (Jan-Apr 1955), p 101. During the early imperial period Stoic writers would be especially critical of Alexander. See Seneca, *Epistulae Morales ad Lucilium*, 94, 62-63, cf 91.17, 119.7: and Lucan, X.26-28; see also Spencer, *The Roman Alexander*, p 117.

23. Seneca, *Naturales Quaestiones*, translated by Thomas Corcoran (Cambridge MA: Harvard University Press, 1972), II.i-xvi.1; Lucan, *The Civil War* (*Pharsalia*), translated by J D Duff (London: Heinemann, 1962), X.14-52. For a discussion of Seneca and Lucan's writing about Alexander see Stoneman, *Legends of Alexander*, intro. xxvii-xxx.

24. Lucian, *Dialogues of the Dead: Philip and Alexander*, translated by M D Macleod, Vol VII (Cambridge, MA: Loeb Classical Library, Harvard University Press, 1961) p 395.

25. John Warry, *Warfare in the Classical World* (New York: Barnes & Noble, 1998) p 162.

26. Lucius Annaeus Florus, *Epitome of Roman History*, translated by E S Forster (Cambridge, MA: Harvard University Press, 1929), I.23.2-3.

27. Gareth C Sampson, *The Defeat of Rome in the East: Crassus, the Parthians, and the Disastrous Battle of Carrhae, 53 BC*, (Philadelphia: Casemate, 2008), p 14. We must rely on ancient sources for these numbers.

28. Polybius, *The Histories*, translated by W R Paton (Cambridge MA: Harvard University Press, 1954), 5.49; Athenaeus, *The Deipnosophists*, translated by Charles Burton Gulick (London: W Heinemann Ltd, 1927), 12.540.b.

29. Nepos, *Hannibal*, translated by J C Rolfe (London: Harvard University Press, 1960), XXIII. VII. 5-VIII. 2; Justin, XXXI.3-6.
30. Grainger, John D, *The Roman War of Antiochos the Great* (Leiden: Die Deutsche Bibliothek, 2002), p 79; The Russian historian Michael Rostovtzeff refers to the Hellenistic age as the 'Macedonian Age' in *The Social and Economic History of the Roman Empire* (Oxford: The Clarendon Press, 1957), p 182.
31. Fronto, *Preamble to History*, 5, translated by H R Haines in *Correspondence*, (Cambridge MA: Harvard University Press, 1920).
32. Appian, *History of Rome*, translated by Horace White et al (New York: The Macmillan Co, 1912), 8.
33. For a study of Roman ties to Troy see Luis Pastor's article 'Troy, between Mithradates and Rome', http://www.pontos.dk/publications/books/bss-9-files/bss-9-13-ballesteros-pastor.
34. Strabo, *The Geography of Strabo*, Vol 1, translated by Horace Leonard Jones (Chicago: Loeb Classical Library, 1917), 13.1.27; see also Lionel Pearson, *The Lost Histories of Alexander the Great* (Chico: Scholars Press, 1983), pp 40-41.
35. Velleius Paterculus, *Compendium of Roman History*, translated by Frederick W Shipley (London: Loeb Classic Library, 1924), I.11.4; Erich S Gruen, *The Hellenistic World and the Coming of Rome*, p 259. One discriminating Roman, Q Metelius Macedonicus, took equestrian statues by Lysippus which had been commissioned by Alexander himself.
36. Cicero, *Pro Flacco*. For more on Roman attitudes toward the Greeks see Andrew Erskine, 'Greek Gifts and Roman Suspicion', *Classics Ireland*, Vol 4 (1997). See also Edith Hamilton who says that Cicero spoke this way in the courts, 'as he was bound to do', *The Roman Way*, p 75.
37. Virgil, *The Aeneid*, translated by W F Jackson Knight (Baltimore: Penguin Classics, 1971), II.48-9.
38. Juan Cole, *Napoleon's Egypt: Invading the Middle East* (New York: Palgrave Macmillan, 2007), p 17.
39. Quintus Curtius Rufus (Curtius), *History of Alexander*, translated by John C Rolfe (Cambridge, MA: Loeb Classical Library, Harvard University Press, 1962), V.X.5.
40. Curtius, VI. II. 14; Justin, XLI.1.
41. Curtius, VI. VI. 1-10. Trans. John C. Rolfe
42. Robin Lane Fox, *The Search for Alexander* (Boston: Little Brown & Co, 1980), p 423.
43. Ellis H Minns, '*Parchments of the Parthian Period from Avroman in Kurdistan*', *JHS*, Vol 35 (1915), p 22; Richard N Frye, *The Heritage of Persia* (Costa Mesa: Mazda Publishers, 1993), p 158.
44. Warwick Wroth, *A Catalogue of the Greek Coins of the British Museum: The Coins of Parthia* (Chicago: Argonaut Inc, 1967), p 275 (Table B). For a discussion of the diadem see Matthew Canepa, *The Two Eyes of the Earth: Art and Ritual of Kingship Between Rome and Sasanian Iran* (London: University of California Press, 2009) pp 196-200.

45. Charles Seltman, *Greek Coins* (London: Methuen & Co, 1965) pp 152 and 215: 'The coins alone tell us that Alexander started a new epoch'; Fry, *Heritage of Persia*, pp 158-9.
46. Colledge, Malcolm, *The Parthians* (New York: Frederick A Praeger, 1967), pp 74 and 170; Seltman, *Greek Coins*, p 236.
47. Philostratus, *The Life of Apollonius of Tyana*, translated by F C Conybeare (London: Harvard University Press, 1969), I. XXXI.
48. Plutarch, *Crassus*, 33.3; Note: Euripides wrote *The Bacchæ* while residing at the court of Macedonian King Archelaus I sometime before 399 BC; see also Richard Stoneman, *Alexander the Great* (London: Routledge, 1997), p 12.
49. Tacitus, *The Annals of Imperial Rome*, translated by Michael Grant (Middlesex: Penguin Books, 1987), XII.13. In particular Hercules.
50. Colledge, *The Parthians*, p 125. The Parthians often used Seleucid dating on their coins.
51. Sir Percy Sykes, *A History of Persia* (Oxford: Clarendon Press, 1922), p 27.
52. Tacitus, *Annals*, VI.31.
53. Simon Hornblower (ed), *Greek Historiography* (Oxford: Clarendon Press, 1994), p 241.
54. Neilson Debevoise, 'Parthian Problems', *The American Journal of Semitic Languages and Literatures*, Vol 47, No 2 (Jan 1931), pp 78-80.
55. Wolfram Grajetzki, *Greeks & Parthians in Mesopotamia and Beyond* (London: Bristol Classical Press, 2011), p 12.
56. Philostratus, II.XVII.
57. Philostratus, II.XLII; II.XXIV and II.XLIII. The ruins of Taxila are 20 miles (32 km) north-west of Islamabad in Pakistan.

Chapter 2: First Impressions

1. Juvenal, *The Satires of Juvenal*, intro A.F. Cole (New York: Putnam & Sons, 1906), 10.133-173. In this passage, Juvenal compares Alexander to Hannibal.
2. Michael Attaleates, *The History*, translated by Anthony Kaldellis, Dumbarton Oaks Medieval Library 16 (Cambridge, MA: Harvard University Press, 2012), 27.11.
3. Nepos, *Hannibal*, 13.2; Lucian, *Dialogues of the Dead*, 115.
4. Frontinus, *Strategems*, I.II.1.
5. Frontinus, *Stratagems*, IV.III.8-10.
6. Lucian, *Dialogues of the Dead*, XII; Juvenal, *Satires*, 10, 165-170.
7. See Gruen, *Rome and the Myth of Alexander*, p 182 for a discussion and sources for this story.
8. Aulus Gellius, *Attic Nights*, translated by John C Rolfe (London: William Heinemann Ltd, 1961), 7.8.1-6 & 6.1; Plutarch, *Alexander 2*; Spencer, *The Roman Alexander*, p 172.

9. Nixon and Rodgers, *Panegyrici Latini*, pp 458-9.

10. Scullard, *Scipio Africanus*, p 237; See also Robin Lane Fox, *Alexander the Great* (London: The Dial Press, 1974), p 217; Livy, 44.44.1-3.

11. Adrienne Mayor, *The Poison King: The Life and Legend of Mithradates* (Princeton: Princeton University Press, 2010), pp 26 and 37.

12. Mayor, *The Poison King*, p 67.

13. One such coin is housed at the Bibliothèque Nationale in Paris.

14. Arthur Keaveney, *Sulla: The Last Republican* (New York: Routledge, 1982), p 37; Mayor, *The Poison King*, p 134.

15. Luis Pastor, 'Marius' Words to Mithridates Eupator', *HZfAG*, Vol 48, No 4, 4th Quarter (1999), p 506; Memnon, 18.2, Codex 224, *Photius: Bibliotheca*, Rene Henry (ed), Roger Pearse. (© *Les Belles Lettres, Paris*).

16. Pseudo-Callisthenes, *The Greek Alexander Romance*, translated by R. Stoneman (London: Penguin Books, 1991), 1.29-30.

17. Thucydides, *History of the Peloponnesian War*, translated by Steven Lattimore (Indianapolis: Hackett Publishing Co, 1998), 5.89.

18. Mayor, *The Poison King*, p 30. Mayor suggests that Sulla acted on his own, p 136.

19. Note: Chaeronea was also the site of a Macedonian victory over an army of Athenians and Thebans in 338 BC. In that battle King Phillip II commanded the right wing and his son, the future Alexander the Great, fought on the left wing. The location of that battle could not have been lost on the Roman public.

20. Justin, XI.9.

21. Plutarch, *Sulla*, 5.4. Plutarch gives the name of the Parthian king as Arsaces. Just as future Roman emperors referred to themselves as Caesar or Augustus, Parthian kings also took the name of the founder of their dynasty, Arsaces. The name of the Parthian king at this time was Mithradates II; see also Justin, XLI.4-5.

22. Frye, *Heritage of Persia*, pp 207-208.

23. Stewart, *Faces of Power*, p 330.

24. As noted by Stewart, *Faces of Power*, p 330.

25. Keaveney says he is the second Phraates, Frye and Sampson say the third. Justin uses his name only, while Mayor and Plutarch avoid using his name at all.

26. Sampson, *Defeat of Rome*, pp 88-9.

27. Keaveney, Arthur, *Lucullus: A Life* (New York@ Routledge, 1992), p. 116.

28. Plutarch, *Lucullus*, 39.3.

29. Julian, *The Caesars*, 322.D.

30. Plutarch, *Cimon and Lucullus Compared*, I.5.

31. Pliny the Elder, *Natural History*, translated by H Rackham (London: Loeb Classical History, 1923), XXVI.

32. Nicholas Yalouris, *Searching for Alexander: An Exhibition* (New York: New York Graphic Society, 1980), p 10; See also Stewart, *Faces of Power*, p 76.

33. Peter Greenhalgh, *Pompey: The Roman Alexander* (Columbia University Press, 1981), p 11.

34. Sarolta A Takács, 'Alexandria in Rome', *Harvard Studies in Classical Philology*, Vol 97 (1995), p 264.

35. Greenhalgh, *Pompey*, p 14.

36. Merle Severy (ed), *Greece and Rome: Builders of Our World* (Washington DC: National Geographic Society, 1968), p 203.

37. Greenhalgh, *Pompey*, p 28.

38. Greenhalgh, *Pompey*, p 27.

39. Sampson, *The Defeat of Rome*, p 67.

40. Greenhalgh, *Pompey*, p 95: 'Where Sulla massacred and Crassus crucified, Pompey pardoned'.

41. N J DeWitt, 'Caesar and the Alexander Legend', *The Classical Weekly*, Vol 36, No 5, (November 1942), p 52.

42. Sallust, *Fragments of the Histories*, Vol 11, translated by John T Ramsey (Cambridge, MA: Loeb Classical Library, Harvard University Press, 2015), 3.84.

43. David F Graf, 'Athenodorus of Tarsus and Nabataea: The Date and Circumstances of His Visit to Petra', in *Studies in the History and Archaeology of Jordan X* (Amman: Department of Antiquities, 2009), pp 70-73.

44. Greenhalgh, *Pompey*, p 109.

45. Curtius, III.VIII. 22-24. Alexander's night march at Issus unnerved the Persians at dawn; Plutarch, *Alexander*, 24, Alexander provoked a night action during the siege of Tyre; see also Frontinus, *Strategems*, II.V.17 and Polyaenus, *Stratagems of War*, translated by R Shepherd (Chicago: Ares Publishers, 1974), IV.III.27.

46. Severy, *Greece and Rome*, p 212. Alexander vetoed the idea of a night attack at Gaugamela.

47. Plutarch, *Pompey*, 32.7-8.

48. Curtius, 6.4.25.

49. Greenhalgh, *Pompey*, p 118.

50. Pliny, *Natural History*, VI.19.51.

51. Pliny, *Natural History*, VI.19.52.

52. Plutarch, *Pompey*, 38.2.

53. Cassius Dio, *Dio's Roman History*, translated by Earnest Cary (London: Loeb Classical Library, Harvard University Press, 1954-61), 37.6.4-7.2.

54. Plutarch, *Alexander*, 21, and *Pompey*, 36. Alexander did however marry Barsine; see also Mayor, *The Poison King*, p 330.

55. Mayor, *The Poison King*, p 352.

56. Mayor, *The Poison King*, p 354; Curtius, V; Dio, 37.14.1-2.

57. Note: At the end of the American Civil War, the Union army marched through Washington DC on parade. It also took two days to pass in review.

58. Dio, 36.21.2.

59. Appian, *History of Rome*, Vol II. XII.117. Appian apparently did not believe that a cloak of such age could have survived.

60. Diodorus Siculus, *Library of History*, translated by C H Oldfather (London: Loeb Classical Library, 1963), 40.4. See also Brian Bosworth, 'Augustus, the Res Gestae and Hellenistic Theories of Apotheosis', *JRS*, Vol 89 (1999), pp 1–18.

61. Florus, I.XL.31.

62. Plutarch, *Pompey*, 46.1; Greenhalgh, *Pompey*, p 168.

63. Diodorus Siculus, XL.4.

64. Julian, *The Caesars*, 322.

65. Julian points this out in *The Caesars*.

66. Peter Green, *Classical Bearings*, pp 198–199.

67. Catullus, *The Poems of Catullus*, translated by F W Cornish (Berkeley: University of California Press, 2005), Poem 29.

68. Flavius Josephus, *Antiquities*, XIV.VI.2; Arthur Keaveney, 'The King and the War-Lords: Romano-Parthian Relations Circa 64-53 BC', *American Journal of Philology*, Vol 103, No 4 (Winter 1982), p 412. Gabinius (and later Crassus) supported Mithradates III against his brother Orodes II.

69. Plutarch, *Antony*, 3.

Chapter 3: Parthia Triumphant: Crassus and Antony

1. Plutarch, *Crassus and Nicias*, 5; Frontinus, *Stratagems*, IV.II.4.

2. Diodorus Siculus, 17.6.1-2.

3. Plutarch, *Alexander*, 15; Justin, *Epitome*, XI.6. Plutarch, Justin and the *Panegyrici Latini*, 12.5.1, estimate that Alexander began his campaign with roughly 40,000 infantry and 4,000 cavalry; Orosius, 131, says 32,000 infantry and 4,500 cavalry. Other sources give different numbers.

4. Zosimus, *Historia Nova*: The Decline of Rome, translated by James J Buchanan and Harold T Davis (San Antonio, TX: Trinity University Press, 1967), III.32.

5. Plutarch, *Crassus*, 16.2; see also Sampson, *Defeat of Rome*, 94.

6. Plutarch, *Crassus*, 17.4.

7. Josephus, *Antiquities*, XIV.VII.1.

8. Plutarch, *Crassus*, 19.3.

9. See Xenophon, *Anabasis*, the story of the 10,000 Greeks.

10. Plutarch, *Crassus*, 28, 1-2; Dio, 40.16.1-5; Florus, I.XLVI.4-5.

11. Plutarch, *Crassus*, 21.1-3.

12. Sampson, *The Defeat of Rome*, pp 107–110.

13. Arrian, *Anabasis Alexander*, translated by E Iliff Robson (Cambridge, MA: Loeb Classical Library, Harvard University Press, 1961), III.1.

14. Dio, 40.18.1; Florus, I.XLVI.6; see Sampson, *The Defeat of Rome*, p 108, for alternative possibilities such as the now-lost city of Thapsacus.

15. Curtius, IV.IX.12-13.
16. Curtius, IV.IX.13-14; Arrian, III.7-16.
17. Stoneman, *Alexander the Great*, pp 44-5; Lane Fox, *Alexander the Great*, p 217.
18. Polyaenus, IV.III.26: 'Alexander by a forced march endeavoured to gain the Tigris, before Darius'.
19. Hammond, N G L, *The Genius of Alexander the Great*, (Chapel Hill: The University of North Carolina Press, 1997), p 105; A B Bosworth, *Conquest and Empire: The Reign of Alexander the Great* (Cambridge: Cambridge University Press, 1988), p 79.
20. D Engels, '*Alexander's Intelligence System*', *The Classical Quarterly*, New Series, Vol 30, No 2 (1980), p 337. Engels argues that local guides deceived Alexander about the location of Darius' army when he crossed the Euphrates.
21. Sampson, *Defeat of Rome*, pp 122-3; Dio, 40.15-27; Plutarch, *Crassus*, 23.31.
22. For a description of the Parthian composite bow and its manufacture see Antony Karasulas, *Mounted Archers of the Steppe 600 BC–AD 1300* (Oxford: Osprey Publishing, 2004), pp 18-27.
23. Warry, *Warfare in the Classical World*, pp 208-209.
24. Pliny, *Natural History*, VI. 47. See also, George Rawlinson, *The Seven Great Monarchies Of The Ancient Eastern World*, *Volume 6: Parthia* (New York: J W Lovell, 1880).
25. That they were watching *The Bacchae* is a sign of the Hellenization of both men.
26. Zosimus, *Historia Nova*, III. 32.
27. Cicero, *Atticus*, V.XX; *Letters*, II.X.
28. Cicero, VI.I.XIV.
29. Suetonius, *Julius Caesar*, 44, translated by Michael Grant in *The Twelve Caesars*, (Middlesex: Penguin Classics, 1979).
30. Plutarch, *Caesar*, 11.3; see also Dio, 37.51.2; Suetonius, *Julius Caesar*, 7.
31. Peter Green, *Classical Bearings*, p 196.
32. Curtius, IV.iv.19: '*Gades ad Oceanum*'.
33. Spencer, *The Roman Alexander*, p 22.
34. Jona Lendering, 'The De Bello Gallico', *Ancient Warfare*, II.4 (2008); see also http://www.livius.org/caa-can/caesar/caesar_gallic_war00.html
35. Plutarch, *Caesar*, 23.2.
36. Ovid, *Metamorphoses*, XV: 745.
37. Conybeare, Edward, *Roman Britain*. II. G8 (London: Society for Promoting Christian Knowledge, 1903).
38. Catullus, Poem 29.
39. Lucan, *Pharsalia*, 8.
40. Lucan, *Pharsalia*, 8.3.
41. Cicero, *Atticus*, translated by E O Winstedt, VII.26.
42. For a discussion of Caesar's visit to Troy see Andreola Rossi, 'Remapping the Past: Caesar's Tale of Troy', *Phoenix*, Vol 55, No ¾ (Autumn-Winter 2001), pp 313-26.
43. Strabo, *Geography*, 13.1.27.

44. Plutarch, *Pompey*, 78–79; Lucan, *Pharsalia*, VIII. 610.

45. Lucan, *Pharsalia*, X.14–52. Gruen ignores Lucan in his attack on the *imitation*. For more on how Caesar's contemporaries viewed him see D Wardle, '"The Sainted Julius": Valerius Maximus and the Dictator', *Classical Philology*, Vol 92, No 4 (Oct1997), pp 323–45.

46. Velleius Paterculus, *Compendium*, II.41.1.

47. Julian, 322–325.

48. Diodorus Siculus, 1.4.6–7.

49. Aurelius Victor, *Epitome De Caesaribus*, translated by Thomas M. Banchich (Buffalo: Canisius College, 2009), 2.

50. Statius, *Silvae*, 1.1.84–87; Gruen, *Rome and the Myth of Alexander*, 188; Stewart, *Faces of Power*, p 397.

51. V Ehrenberg, 'Caesar's Final Aims', *Harvard Studies in Classical Philology*, Vol 68 (1964), p 151.

52. Cicero, *Atticus*, XIII.XXVII–XXVIII. These letters were written in May of 45 BC; See also Edith Hamilton's take on this letter, *The Roman Way*, p 75.

53. Cicero, *Atticus*, XIII.XXVIII.III.

54. Polybius, *Histories*, X.28–31.

55. Grainger, *Roman War of Antiochus the Great*.

56. Appian, *Civil Wars*, II.110.

57. Lane Fox, *Alexander the Great*, p 277.

58. Plutarch, *Caesar*, 61.

59. Plutarch, *Brutus*, 25.

60. Florus, II.XIII.94–95.

61. Appian, *Civil Wars*, II. 151; Stewart, *Faces of Power*, p 345.

62. Appian, *Civil Wars*, II. 149–152.

63. Michael Ivanovitch Rostovtzeff, *Rome* (New York: Oxford University Press, 1960), p 138.

64. Plutarch, *Brutus*, 53.4.

65. Plutarch, *Alexander*, 43; Curtius, V.

66. Michael Grant, *Cleopatra: A Biography* (New York: Dorset Press, 1972), p 110.

67. Arrian, *Anabasis*, 5.1–2.2.

68. Curtius, 7.9.15. Curtius notes that Alexander had observed a pile of rocks and sacred grove that marked the extent of Dionysus' travels.

69. Plutarch, *Antony*, 26.

70. Plutarch, *Alexander*, 2.1–2.

71. Velleius Paterculus, *Compendium*, I.6.5.

72. Plutarch, *Antony*, 4.

73. Plutarch, *Antony*, 60.2.

74. Plutarch, *Antony*, 28.

75. Arrian, *Anabasis*, VII.8; Plutarch, *Alexander*, 45.1. Plutarch notes that Alexander first wore Persian 'barbarian dress' when he was in Parthia.

76. Plutarch, *Antony*, 29.4.

77. Florus, II.XVIIII.6.
78. Plutarch, *Antony*, 33.4.
79. Plutarch, *Antony*, 34; see also Aulus Gellius, *Attic Nights*, translated by John C Rolfe (London: William Heinemann Ltd, 1961), 15.4.
80. William Shakespeare, *Antony and Cleopatra*, Act III. Scene I.
81. Plutarch, *Antony*, 37.4.
82. Curtius, VI.V.11.
83. Florus, 2.20.5; Eutropius, *The Breviarum ab Urbe Condita*, translated by H W Bird (Liverpool: Liverpool University Press, 1993), 7.6.2.
84. Plutarch, *Antony*, 50; for more on this battle see my article 'Mark Antony's Persian Campaign' in *Military History* (Nov. 2006) or at http://www.historynet.com/mark-antonys-persian-campaign.htm
85. Justin, XI.V.1-3; Frontin, II.XI.3. Frontinus explains how Alexander subdued Thrace.
86. Dio, 49.40.2-3.
87. Velleius Paterculus, *Compendium*, II. 82.
88. Pearson, *Lost Histories*, p 63.
89. Dio, 49.40.2-41.3, 50.3.
90. Grace H Macurdy, 'Iotape', *The Journal of Roman Studies*, Vol 26, Part 1 (1936), 40-42. Note: This Artavasdes was not related to the king of Armenia. Ironically, one of his sons would father two Parthian kings.
91. Plutarch, *Antony*, 58.4.
92. Velleius Paterculus, *Compendium II*, 84.
93. John M Carter, *The Battle of Actium: The Rise and Triumph of Augustus Caesar* (New York: Weybright & Talley, 1970), p 202.
94. Gruen, *Rome and the Myth of Alexander*, p 189.

Chapter 4: The Empire Strikes Back

1. Suetonius *Augustus*, 21.
2. Grant, M, *The Climax of Rome*, 21ff.
3. Suetonius, *Augustus*, 89; Plutarch, *Moralia*, translated by W C Hembold (Cambridge, MA: The Loeb Classical Library, 1939), 207.b; G W Bowersock, *Augustus and the Greek World* (Oxford: The Clarendon Press, 1965), p 33. For an example of Alexander's clemency see Polyaenus, IV.III.30.
4. Suetonius, *Augustus*, 18; Dio, 51.16.5.
5. Stewart, *Faces of Power*, p 80; Plutarch, *Alexander*, 15.8; Arrian, *Anabasis*, 1.12; The *Historia Augusta*, Probus, 1.2, also mention the visit to Achilles' tomb but not the lyre as does Aelian, *Varia Historia*, 9.38.
6. Suetonius, *Augustus*, 50; Stewart, *Faces of Power*, citing Pliny, 415 T-155 & T-156.
7. Robert Alan Gurval, *Actium and Augustus* (Ann Arbor: University of Michigan Press, 1998), pp 69-70; see also William M Murray, 'Octavian's Campsite Memorial

for the Actian War', *Transactions of the American Philosophical Society*, New Series, Vol 79, No 4 (1989), pp 4 and 124 and Chamoux, *Hellenistic Civilization*, p 28.

8. Pliny, *Natural History*, 34.48, 35.27, 93-94: see also Spencer, *The Roman Alexander*, p 130; and Stewart, *Faces of Power*, 224n.

9. Stewart, *Faces of Power*, p 190.

10. Suetonius, *Augustus*, 94.4-5.

11. Plutarch, *Moralia*, 207.c.

12. Edward N. Luttwak, *The Grand Strategy of the Roman Empire: From the First Century A.D. to the Third* (Baltimore: John Hopkins University Press, 1976), p 87.

13. Stewart, *Faces of Power*, p 96.

14. Suetonius, *Augustus*, 4.1.

15. Christopher Howgego, *Ancient History from Coins* (London: Routledge, 1995), p 69.

16. Josephus, *Wars of the Jews*, XX.1-3. The Antonia fortress which guards the Jerusalem Temple was named after Mark Antony.

17. E Badian, *Studies in Greek and Roman History* (New York: Barnes & Noble, 1964), p 172; also see Badian's *Publicans and Sinners: Private Enterprise in Service for the Roman Republic)* (Ithaca, NY: Cornell University Press, 1972) for details on Roman taxes; and Stewart, *Faces of Power*, p 90.

18. Stoneman, *Legends of Alexander*, Intro, xxviii-xxiv.

19. Duane W Roller, *Through the Pillars of Herakles: Greco-Roman Exploration of the Atlantic* (New York, Routledge, 2006), p 118.

20. Alaric Watson, *Aurelian and the Third Century* (London: Routledge, 1999), p 180.

21. Justin, XLII.5; Pat Southern, *Augustus* (London: Routledge, 1998), p 126.

22. Touraj Daryaee, *The Oxford Handbook of Iranian History* (Oxford: Oxford University Press, 2014), p 173.

23. Justin, XLII.5; Florus, XXXIIII.64.

24. For more on Augustan-era writers see Stewart, *Faces of Power*, pp 21-40.

25. Propertius, *The Elegies, Books I-IV*, edited by W A Camps (Cambridge: Cambridge University Press, 1965), III.4.4.

26. Horace, *The Odes and Epodes*, translated by Niall Rudd (Cambridge, MA: Harvard University Press, 2004), IV.15.6.

27. Virgil, *The Works of Virgil*, translated by John Conington (Philadelphia: David McKay Publishers, 1900), p 313.

28. Virgil, *Aeneid*, VI.794.

29. Ronald Syme, *History in Ovid* Oxford: Clarendon Press, 1978), p 49.

30. Bosworth, 'Augustus', *JRS*, p 14.

31. Ovid, *Ars Armatoria*, I.VI.177-181 in *The Love Books of Ovid; being the Amores, Ars Armatoria, Remedia Amoris, and Medicamina Faciei Feminea* translated by J Lewis May (New York: Willey Book Co. 1940). See also Syme, *History in Ovid*, pp 8-9; Compare this to Plutarch's observation of Crassus' intention above.

32. Ovid, I.VI.194.

33. Strabo, *Geography*, II.5.12.

34. Livy, 9.18; Morello, 'Livy's Alexander Digression', pp 62-85.

35. Hornblower, *Greek Historiography*, p 238.

36. Dio, 55.10.7; Augustus. *Res Gestae*. trans. by B. Bosworth, 23; Ovid. *Ars Amat*, I. 171-2.

37. Augustus, *Res Gestae Divi Augusti* 32.

38. Suetonius, *Augustus*, 45: for more on the sons of foreign kings educated at Rome see David Braund, *Rome and the Friendly King: The Character of the Client Kingship* (London: Croom Helm, 1984).

39. Josephus, *Antiquities*, xviii, 2–4.

40. Tacitus, *Annals*, 2.1-4.

41. Augustus, *Res Gestae*, 33.

42. Debevoise, 'Parthian Problems', pp 78-9; Grajetzki, *Greeks & Parthians*.

43. Lucan, 10. 45-52. For a different take on Lucan's meaning, see Spencer, *The Roman Alexander*, pp 112-15.

44. Watson, *Aurelian*, p 180.

45. Rostovtzeff, *Rome*, p 194.

46. Suetonius, *Gaius*, 1. These men had also served with Tiberius' popular nephew, Germanicus. Many blamed Tiberius for his death.

47. Colledge, *The Parthians*, p 48.

48. Suetonius, *Gaius*, 14.

49. Tacitus, *Annals*, II. 54; see also Aalders, '*Germanicus und Alexander Der Grosse*', p 383.

50. Tacitus, *Annals*, II. 60. This Egyptian Heracles is also mentioned by Herodotus, II.43.

51. Tacitus, *Annals*, II. 58-9; see also Velleius Paterculus, II.101.1. It is interesting to note that during Germanicus' stay in Syria, a young Jesus of Nazareth was growing up in nearby Judea.

52. Tacitus, *Annals*, II.71.

53. Aalders, '*Germanicus und Alexander Der Grosse*', pp 382-384.

54. Tacitus, *Annals*, VI.31.

55. Dio, 59.27.3. Dio has quite a different take on this incident to Suetonius.

56. Josephus, *Antiquties*, xviii.4.4.

57. Note: There was precedent. Octavian was the great nephew of Caesar.

58. Tacitus, *Annals*, 52; also Antony A Barrett, *Caligula: The Corruption of Power* (New Haven: Yale University Press, 1989), p 146.

59. Dio, 59.17.11.

60. S J V Malloch, 'Gaius' Bridge at Baiae and Alexander-Imitatio', *The Classical Quarterly*, Vol 51, No 1 (2001), pp 206-217.

61. Compare the descriptions of the Bacchic procession of Alexander in Arrian, *Anabasis*, 7. 67.1-8, and Curtius, 9.10.24-8, with those of Caligula's procession in Dio, 59.17.5-6 and Suetonius, *Caligula*, 19.2. For Caligula's age see Barrett, *Caligula*, p 214.

62. Dio, 59.25.1-3: 'And when he reached the ocean, as if he were going to conduct a campaign in Britain…'

63. Lendering, Jona, http://www.livius.org/ga-gh/germania/praetorium_agrippinae.html, abstracted from his book, co-authored with Arjen Bosman, *Edge of Empire: Rome's Frontier on the Lower Rhine* (Zutphen: Karwansaray BV, 2013).

64. Suetonius, *Caligula*, 55.3; Arrian, *Anabasis*, V.19.4.

65. Dio, 59.26-28.

66. Plutarch, *Moralia*, Sayings of Spartans: Damis; Aelian, *Varia Historia*, II.19; see also John Ferguson, *The Religions of the Roman Empire* (Ithaca: Cornell University Press, 1970), p 89.

67. Pliny, *Natural History*, 35.27 and 35.93-94; Spencer, *The Roman Alexander*, pp 93 and 130-131; Stewart, *Faces of Power*, pp 365-6.

68. Tacitus, *Annals*, XII, 10.

69. Frye, *Heritage of Persia*, p 211.

70. Frye, *Heritage of Persia*, p 222.

71. Dio, 60.21.

72. See Spencer, *The Roman Alexander*, p 73; Seneca, *Concerning Benefits*, 2.15.1-16.2.

73. J S Crawford, 'A Portrait of Alexander the Great at the University of Delaware' , *American Journal of Archaeology*, Vol 83, No 4, p 480.

74. Michael Grant, *Emperor in Revolt: Nero* (New York: American Heritage Press, 1970), pp 237-8.

75. Hornblower, *Greek Historiography*, pp 234-5.

76. Carlo Maria Franzero, *The Life and Times of Nero* (London: Alvin Redman Ltd, 1954), p 132.

77. Tacitus, *Annales*, XV 24-30.

78. Grant, 228; Dio, 63.5.

79. E M Sandford, 'Nero and the East', *Harvard Studies in Classical Philology*, Vol 48. (1937), pp 81-3.

80. Dio, 63.8.

81. Suetonius, *Nero*, 19.

82. Seneca, *Naturales Quaestiones*, VI.8.3.

83. Lucan, 10.272-275; Spencer, *The Roman Alexander*, p 160.

84. Dio, 62.18.

85. Tacitus, *Annals*, XV.31.

86. Suetonius, *Domitian*, 2.

87. Bennett, Julian, *Trajan Optimus Princeps: A Life and Times*, p 188.

88. Statius, *Thebaid*, 8.286-93; also see A S Hollis' analysis of this passage in 'Octavian in the Fourth Georgic', *The Classical Quarterly*, New Series, Vol 46, No 1 (1996).

89. This pass was first fortified against northern barbarians by Alexander the Great. See Procopius, *History of the Wars*, translated by H B Dewing (London: Harvard University Press, 1954), I.x.9.

90. Gibbon, Edward, *Decline and Fall*, Ch 1.

91. F A Lepper, *Trajan's Parthian War* (London: Oxford University Press, 1948), pp 156-72.

92. Antony R Birley, *Hadrian : the Restless Emperor*, (New York: Routledge, 1997), p 65.

93. Theodor Mommsen, *A History of Rome Under the Caesars*, (New York: Routledge, 1996), p 550, n 737.

94. See Lepper, *Trajan's Parthian War*, pp 28-9, for problems in dating Trajan's campaign.

95. Birley, *Hadrian*, p 69. See also Dio, 68.19.2.

96. Julian, 333.A.

97. Fronto, *Preamble to History*, 18.

98. Fergus Millar, *The Roman Near East 31 BC–AD 337* (London: Harvard University Press, 1996) p 101.

99. See R P Longden, 'Notes on the Parthian Campaigns of Trajan', *The Journal of Roman Studies*, Vol 21, (1931), p 13, n 5.

100. Dio, 68.21.4.

101. Stewart, *Faces of Power*, reading Albrecht Wirth, 'The Tale of the Kings Daughter in the Besieged Town', *American Anthropologist*, Vol 7, Issue 4 (Oct 1984), points out that when Plutarch wrote his *Life of Alexander* he was writing for a public enthralled by the conquests of Trajan, 19; see also Mommsen, *Rome Under the Caesars*, p 339.

102. Longden, 'Notes on the Parthian Campaigns of Trajan', analyses the reasons for Trajan's war and gives a comprehensive study of the emperor's actions in the east. He does not mention the symbolic significance of Trajan at Gaugamela.

103. Fronto, *Preamble to History*, 4.

104. Lepper, *Trajan's Parthian War*, pp 207-208. See also Diodorus, XVII. 64.3 and Arrian, XVI, for Alexander's march from Gaugamela to Babylon.

105. Dio, 68.29.1; see also Lepper, *Trajan's Parthian War*, p 10.

106. Birley, *Hadrian*, p 73.

107. Touraj Daryaee, '*Imitatio Alexandri* and its Impact on Late Arsacid, Early Sasanian and Middle Persian Literature', *Electrum*, Vol 12, (2007), p 91.

108. Lepper, *Trajan's Parthian War*, p 172; quoting F Cumont in *Anatolian Studies*, (1923), 114 f, the original French: *'il n'est pas douteux que l'annexion de ces deux "états-tampons" ait eu pour but de permettre la réalisation d'une œuvre qui devait assurer la suprématie de Rome sur la Grand Arménie... Cette conquéte préparée par les ingénieurs des Flaviens fut obtenue sans peine par les légions de Trajan.*

109. Dio, 68.30.1.

110. David Potter in 'The Inscriptions on the Bronze Heracles from Mesene: Vologeses IV's War with Rome and the Date of Tacitus' "*Annals*"', *Zeitschrift für Papyrologie unde Epigraphik*, Bd 88 (1991), pp 277-90, suggests that it was the other way around, that the Jewish revolt inspired the Parthian resistance; Birley, *Hadrian*, p 74, thinks it likely that Vologeses could have convinced the Jews of Cyrene to

'open a second front'; Julian Bennett, *Trajan: Optimus Princeps: A Life and Times* (Bloomington: Indiana University Press, 1997), p 201, thinks the two simultaneous revolts could have been either 'design or accident'; while Stewart Perowne, *Hadrian* (New York: W W Horton, 1960), p 139, and Lepper, *Trajan's Parthian War*, only note that they occurred at the same time; Eusebius, *Ecclesiastical History* (London: Loeb Classical Library, 1980), VI.II, does not make the connection.

111. For more on this see Stephen A Stertz, 'Marcus Aurelius as Ideal Emperor in Late-Antique Greek Thought', *The Classical World*, Vol 70, No 7 (Apr-May 1977), pp 433-9.
112. Graham Webster, *The Roman Imperial Army*, (Totowa, NJ: Barnes & Noble, 1985), p 65.
113. Birley, *Hadrian*, p 75; *Historia Augusta*, Hadrian, IV. 9.
114. *Historia Augusta*, Hadrian, XXI.10-13.
115. Birley, *Hadrian*, p 131.
116. Birley, *Hadrian*, pp 164 and 239.
117. Dio, 69.11.2-4.
118. Arrian, 7.23.8; Aelian, *Varia Historia*, 7.8.
119. D A Russell and N G Wilson, *Menander Rhetor: a Commentary* (New York, Clarendon Press, 1981), p 57.
120. Andrew Chugg, 'The Sarcophagus of Alexander the Great', *Greece & Rome*, Second Series, Vol 49, No 1 (Apr 2002), p 25.
121. Corbulo did station troops on the banks of the Euphrates River to threaten invasion but their presence there was a bluff to keep the Parthians guessing.

Chapter 5: Marcus Aurelius: Unintended Consequences

1. Marcus Aurelius, *Meditations*, translated by George Long (Chicago: University of Chicago, 1952) 6.24.
2. Colledge, *The Parthians*, p 167.
3. *Historia Augusta*, 9.6.
4. *Historia Augusta*, 9.6.
5. Antony R Birley, *Marcus Aurelius: A Biography* (London, Routledge, 2000), p 114.
6. James H Oliver, 'Marcus Aurelius: Aspects of Civic and Cultural Policy in the East', *Hespera Supplements*, Vol 13 (1970), p 93; Helmut Nickel, 'The Emperor's New Saddle Cloth: The Ephippium of the Equestrian Statue of Marcus Aurelius', *Metropolitan Museum Journal*, Vol 24 (1989), p 20.
7. Marcus Aurelius, *Meditations*, 3.3.
8. Stewart, *Faces of Power*, 44.
9. See W W Tarn, 'Alexander Helios and the Golden Age', *The Journal of Roman Studies*, Vol 22, Part 2 (1932), pp 135-160; and M H Fisch, Alexander and the Stoics, *The American Journal of Philology*, Vol 58, No 2 (1937), pp 129-151; see also Stewart, *Faces of Power*, pp 14-15, for a discussion of the Stoics and Peripatetic school of Philosophy

10. Fergus Millar, 'Emperors, Frontiers and Foreign Relations, 31 BC to AD 378', *Britannia*, Vol 13 (1982), 5.

11. Dio, 71.1.2.

12. Birley, *Marcus Aurelius*, p 121.

13. Dio, 71.2.1.

14. Lucian, *Alexander*, translated by Paul Turner in *Satirical Sketches* (Baltimore: Penguin Books, 1962).

15. *Historia Augusta*, Aurelius, 8.6; Fronto. *Preamble*, 12. Fronto warned against the sloth of the Syrian legions.

16. Marcus Aurelius, *Meditations*, 1.11.

17. Fronto, *Preamble*, 7.

18. Glanville Downey, 'Libanius' Oration in Praise of Antioch (Oration XI)', *Proceedings of the American Philosophical Society*, Vol 103, No 5 (15 Oct 1959), p 662; see also John Malalas, *The Chronicle of John Malalas: A Translation*, translated by Elizabeth Jeffreys et al, (Melbourne: Australian Association for Byzantine Studies,1986), p 125.

19. *Historia Augustus*, Verus, 7.10. Panthea earned a mention in *The Meditations* of Aurelius, 8.37.

20. Eutropius, 8.10.

21. Birley, *Marcus Aurelius*, p 158.

22. Eutropius, 8.10.

23. Eutropius, 8.12.

24. Peter Christensen, *The Decline of Iranshahr: Irrigation and Environments on the History of the Middle East 500 BC to AD 1500* (Copenhagen: Museum Tusculanum Press, 1993), pp 79-80.

25. J F Gilliam, 'The Plague under Marcus Aurelius', *American Journal of Philology*, Vol 82, No 3 (July 1961).

26. Lepper, *Trajan's Parthian War*, p 12.

27. Birley, *Aurelius*, pp 129-30; Fronto, *Preamble*, 10-18.

28. C R Haines, 'Some notes on the text of Fronto', *Classical Quarterly*, Vol 9, No 1 (Jan 1915), p 52.

29. Birley, *Marcus Aurelius*, pp 185-8.

30. *Historia Augusta*, Avidius Cassius, 10.1. Avidius named one of his daughters Alexandria.

31. *Historia Augusta*, 8.5; Birley, *Marcus Aurelius*, pp 130 and 189.

32. *Historia Augusta*, 19.12.

33. Julian, *Letter to Themistius*, 253A.

34. *Historia Augusta*, Caracalla, 5.5. Compare the bust of Commodus at the Capitoline Museum in Rome with that of Alexander at the Aarhus University in Denmark.

35. Athenaeus, 12.537.f; Pearson, *The Lost Histories*, p 63; see also Herodian, *History of the Roman Empire*, translated by Edward C Echols (Berkeley, University of California Press, 1961), 1.14.8.

36. *Historia Augusta*, *Commodus*, 9. 4–5; see also Herodian, 1.14.8.
37. Cecil H Smith, 'A Bronze Bust of Commodus', *The Burlington Magazine for Connoisseurs*, Vol 13, No 65 (Aug 1908), pp 252–56.
38. *Historia Augustus*, Marcus, 28.1.

Chapter 6: The Severans: Father and Son Invade Iraq

1. Dio, 75.3.2–3.
2. Antony R Birley, *Septimius Severus: The African Emperor* (London: Routledge, 1999), pp 135–6; Dio, 75.6.2a.
3. Herodian, 3.1.2.
4. Freya Stark, *Alexander's Path* (Woodstock, NY: The Overlook Press, 1988), p 6; David Magie, *Roman Rule in Asia Minor* (Princeton: Princeton Legacy Library, 2015), p 671.
5. Dio, 75.7.4; Plutarch, *Alexander*, 20.8.
6. *Historia Augusta*, Severus, 16.1.
7. Al-Tabarī, *The History of al-Tabarī, Vol IV: The Ancient Kingdoms*, translated by Moshe Perlmann (Albany: State University of New York Press, 1999), p 97.
8. Birley, *Septimius Severus*, p 136.
9. Philostratus, *Apollonius*, 2.33.
10. Birley, *Septimius Severus*, p 130.
11. Malalas, XII.18.
12. *Historia Augusta*, Caracalla, 2.1–2.
13. Justin, XI.V.
14. Dio, 78.7.1.
15. Andrew Runni Anderson, 'Alexander's Horns', *Transactions and Proceedings of the American Philological Association*, Vol 58 (1927), p 100. Busts of Alexander as Helios are housed in the Capitoline Museums in Rome and the Archaeological Museum of Rhodes.
16. Karsten Dahmen, 'Alexander in Gold and Silver: Reassessing the Third Century AD Medallions from Aboukir and Tarsos', *American Journal of Numismatics*, Second Series, 20, (2008), pp 493–546.
17. Stewart, *Faces of Power*, p 76.
18. Herodian, 4.7.4–5.
19. Herodian, 4.8.1.
20. Herodian, 4.7. 2; see also Dio, 78.7.1.
21. *Historia Augusta*, Caracalla, 4.10.2.9.
22. Dio, 78.7.2.
23. Herodian, 4.8.2–3.
24. David S Potter notes this in *The Roman Empire at Bay* (London: Routledge, 2004), p 143.
25. Herodian, 4.8.9.
26. Victor, *Epitome*, Caracalla, 4.

27. Stewart, *Faces of Power*, p 92.
28. Herodian, 4.9.3; see also Potter, *Roman Empire at Bay*, p 144.
29. Dio, 78.12.2.
30. Al-Ṭabarī, *The History of al-Ṭabarī, Vol V: The Sasanids, the Byzantines, the Lakmids*, translated by Clifford & Bosworth (Albany: State University of New York Press, 1999), p 98.
31. Frye, *Heritage of Persia*, p 237.
32. Herodian, 4.11.2.
33. Herodian, 4.14.6.
34. *Historia Augusta*, Caracalla, 4.10.6-7.
35. Glenn Barnett, 'Father and Son Invade Iraq', *Ancient Warfare* (Dec 2008) for more details on the Parthian wars of Septimius Severus and Caracalla.
36. Lucan, 10.48-52.

Chapter 7: The Sasanians

1. Zonaras, *The History of Zonaras*, translated by Thomas Banchich (London: Routledge, 2011), p 41.
2. Stoneman, *Legends of Alexander*, x; for the text see J W McCrindle, *Ancient India; As Described in Classical Literature* (Westminster: Archibald Constable, 1901), pp 150-155.
3. For the complete text see: http://www.sdstate.edu/projectsouthasia/upload/The-Itinerary-of-Alexander-the-Great.pdf.
4. Suetonius, *Domitian*, 13.
5. Watson, *Aurelian*, p 188.
6. *Historia Augusta*, 16.4. On the other hand Aurelius Victor claims that Aurelian was the first, *Epitome*, 35.5.
7. Watson, *Aurelian*, p 181.
8. A D Lee, *Information and Frontiers: Roman Relations in Late Antiquity* (Cambridge: Cambridge University Press, 1993), p 41.
9. Frye, *Heritage of Persia*, pp 236-7.
10. Parvaneh Pourshariati, *Decline and Fall of the Sasanian Empire: The Sasanian-Parthian Confederacy and the Arab Conquest of Iran*, (London: I B Tauris, 2009), pp 47-53. Pourshariati devotes a chapter to the Parthian clans active in Sasanian times. See also Frye, *Heritage of Persia*, pp 239-40.
11. Pourshariati, *Decline and Fall*, pp 56-7.
12. Agathias, IV.24.1.
13. Fan Hong and J A Mangan (eds.), *Sport in Asian Society: Past and Present* (London: Routledge, 2002), p 312.
14. Eutropius, 8.23; Orosius, 348.
15. Touraj Daryaee, *Sasanian Persia, The Rise and Fall of an Empire* (London: I B Tauris, 2009), p 70.

16. Daryaee. '"*Imitatio Alexandri*" and its impact', p 92; Nixon and Rodgers, *Panegyrici Latini*, pp 89-97.

17. *Alexandre le Grand en Iran, Le Dārāb Nāmeh d'Abu Tāher Tarsusi* by Abu Tāher Tarsusi, reviewed by: Evangelos Venetis, *Iranian Studies*, Vol 39, No 3 (Sep 2006), pp 456-9; The *Karnamak-e Ardeshir* says that Alexander is from 'Arum' probably meaning Rome.

18. Charles F Horne, *The Sacred Books and Early Literature of the East. Volume VII: Ancient Persia* (New York: Parke, Austin, & Lipscomb, 1917), pp 225-53.

19. Pourshariati, *Decline and Fall*, pp 33-4, fn. 132.

20. Pourshariati, *Decline and Fall*, p 431.

21. Touraj Daryaee, www.dabirjournal.org, *Alexander and the Arsacids in the manuscript MU29*, 2015, Vol 1, No 1.

22. Daryaee, *Sasanian Persia*, pp 2 and 85.

23. William L Hanaway, 'Anāhitā and Alexander', *Journal of the American Oriental Society*, Vol 102, No 2 (Apr-Jun 1982), p 287.

24. Abu Mohammad Bin Yusuf, *Sikandar Nāma, e Barà*, translated by H Wilberforce Clarke (London: W H Allen & Co, 1881), pp 118-29.

25. Ferdowsi, *Shahnameh*, XX.

26. Bighami, Muammad ibn Amad, *Love and War: Adventures from the Firuz Shah Namah of Sheikh Bighami*, translated by William L Hanaway (Ann Arbor: Scholars Facsimiles and Reprints, 1974) p 7. There is also a tradition which has Sasanian King Bahrām V (Gōr) travelling to India; see also François de Blois, garšāsp-nāma, *Encyclopædia Iranica*, Online, Feb. 2, 2012.

27. Bighami, *Love and War*, Intro, pp 5-7.

28. Pourshariati, *Decline and Fall*, p 321.

29. Daryaee, *Sasanian Persia*, pp 77-8; Frye, *Heritage of Persia*, p 247.

30. Daryaee, *Sasanian Persia*, pp 75-77.

31. Dio, 80.18.1.

32. Herodian, 6.2.1-2; Dio, 80.4.1-2; Zonaras, XII.15; Potter, *Roman Empire at Bay*, p 223.

33. *Historia Augusta*, Severus Alexander, 5.1. Dio has another version for the naming of Alexander, 80.17.

34. Herodian, 5.7.3.

35. *Historia Augusta*, Severus Alexander, 35.1.

36. Aelianus is also credited by the *Encyclopædia Iranica* with preserving some of the writings of Ctesias of Cnidus which shed light on the Achaemenid era.

37. *Historia Augusta*, Severus Alexander, 35.2.

38. *Historia Augusta*, Severus Alexander 64.1-3; and Stewart, *Faces of Power*, p 50.

39. *Historia Augusta*, Severus Alexander, 11.1-5.

40. *Historia Augusta*, Severus Alexander, 25.5-9 and 39.1.

41. *Historia Augusta*, Severus Alexander, 50. 4.

42. Watson, *Aurelian*, p 181.

43. Herodian, 6.4.4-6.

44. Festus, *Breviarium*, translated at http://www.attalus.org/translate/festus.html.
45. *Historia August*, Severus Alexander, pp 53-4.
46. Sykes, *A History of Persia*, Vol 1, pp 395-6.
47. Herodian, 6.5.1-9.
48. Herodian, 6.5.8.
49. *Historia Augusta*, Severus Alexander, pp 56.3-6.
50. *Historia Augusta*, Severus Alexander, 56.7.
51. Herodian, 6.7.1.
52. Beate Dignas & Engelbert Winter, *Rome and Persia in late Antiquity: Neighbours and Rivals*, p 155.
53. Daryaee, *Sasanian Persia*, p 46.
54. Sykes, *A History of Persia*, p 431; see also Wirth, 'Tale of the King's Daughter'.
55. Al-Tabarī, *History, Volume V: The Sasanids, the Byzantines, the Lakmids*, translated by C E Bosworth (Albany: State University of New York Press, 1999), p 828.
56. George Rawlinson, *The Seventh Great Oriental Monarchy*, pp 51-52; Vahan M Kurkjian, *A History of Armenia* (New York: Armenian General Benevolent Union of America, 1958), XVIII.115.
57. Catholic Encyclopedia, http://www.newadvent.org/cathen/07023a.htm.
58. Kurkjian, *History of Armenia*, XVIII.115.

Chapter 8: Shapur I: King of Kings

1. Alan Bowman, Avril Cameron and Peter Garnsey (eds), *The Cambridge Ancient History. Volume 12: Crisis of Empire AD 193-337* (Cambridge: Cambridge University Press, 2005), p 40; Warwick Ball, *Rome in the East: The Transformation of an Empire* (London: Routledge, 2001), p 120; Shapur Shahbazi, Shapur I i, *Encyclopædia Iranica*, online, 20 July 2002.
2. Al-Tabarī, *History, Vol V*, pp 823-5.
3. Michael H Dodgeon and Samuel NC Lieu, *The Roman Eastern Frontier and the Persian Wars AD 226-363* (London: Routledge, 1994), pp 46-7. For more on Shapur's coins see *e-Sasanika*, An Exceptional Gold Coin of Shapur I, Vol. 7. 2009.
4. Cohen, A, *Everyman's Talmud*, (New York: E. P. Dutton & Co, 1949), p 288.
5. Babylonian Talmud, *Sanhedrin* 98a. See *Zechariah* 9: 9-10 for the origin story of the donkey. See also *Revelations* 6.2.
6. Matthew Canepa, *Two Eyes of the Earth*, pp 76-7. Canepa cites German scholar H von Gall.
7. Daryaee, *Sasanian Persia*, pp 99-100, 118.
8. Daryaee, *Sasanian Persia*, p 70.
9. Richard Stoneman, *Palmyra and its Empire: Zenobia's Revolt Against Rome* (Ann Arbor: The University of Michigan Press, 1992), p 95.

10. Eutropius, 9.2. Victor, *Epitome*, 27.7–8:7. However Ammianus Marcellinus wrote that the doors of the temple were open in 357 when Constantius II visited Rome to celebrate a triumph (16.10.1).

11. Stoneman, *Palmyra*, p 93. Quoted from the Naqsh-e-Rustam inscriptions.

12. Porphyry, *On the Life of Plotinus*, (Cambridge, MA: Harvard University Press, 1966), Ch 3.

13. *Historia Augusta*, The Three Gordians, 26. 6.

14. *Historia Augusta*, The Three Gordians, 27. 2.

15. Shahbazi, Shapur I i, *Encyclopædia Iranica*, online, July 2002. See also Canepa, *Two Eyes of the Earth*, p 259n; For a discussion of Gordian's death see: http://judithweingarten.blogspot.com/2009/11/persian-no-spin-zone.html.

16. Zosimus, I.

17. Zonaras, XII.17.

18. Ammianus Marcellinus, 23.5.7; Eutropius, 9.2.3. The site of the tomb is not known today.

19. Bowman et al (ed), *Cambridge Ancient History, Vol 12*, p 40; Ball, *Rome in the East*, p 120; Shahbazi, Shapur I i, *Encyclopaedia Iranica*, online. The Sasanian rock carving at Naqsh-e-Rustam is our only source for this battle.

20. Daryaee, *Sasanian Persia*, p 7; Stoneman, Palmyra, pp 93–4.

21. Ammianus Marcellinus, 23.5.3.

22. Ammianus Marcellinus, 20.2.2.

23. Zosimus, I. 27.

24. Clark Hopkins, *The Discovery of Dura Europos* (New Haven: Yale University Press, 1979); Stoneman, *Palmyra*, pp 104 and 242–6.

25. Malalas, XII.26.

26. Malalas, XII. 26.

27. Ferdowsi, *Shahnameh*, 6.23.2. The *Shahnameh* claims he had 70,000 men with him. Stephen Williams, in his book *Diocletian and the Roman Recovery*, p 21, thinks these estimates are exaggerated.

28. Zosimus, I.i.33.

29. Kaveh Farrokh, *Sassanian Elite Cavalry AD 224–642* (Oxford: Osprey Publishing, 2005), p 45; Christensen, *Iranshahr*, p 109.

30. Gibbon, *Decline and Fall*, Ch 10, n 135.

31. Zonaras, XII, 20.

32. Stoneman, *Palmyra*, p 94. The story of Valerian's flaying and stuffing comes from the early Christian writer Lactantius in his work *Demortibus Persecutorum*, 5. He graced Constantine's court and described the gruesome deaths of the pagan emperors who persecuted the church. His accuracy is suspect. Agathias hints at this cruelty by saying that it 'is vouched for by the testimony of several historians'; 4.23.3 and 4.23.7.

33. Zosimus, I. 36.

34. *Historia Augusta*, Tyranni Triginta, 14.4.
35. *Historia Augusta*, Tyranni Triginta, 14.6; see also Stewart, *Faces of Power*, p 162.
36. Frank L Holt, *Alexander the Great and the Mystery of the Elephant Medallions* (Berkeley: University of California Press, 2005), p 3.
37. Most historians discount the assertion in the *Historia Augusta* that the Romans tried to get Valerian back. See *Historia Augusta*, The Two Valerians, 3.1.
38. Canepa, *Two Eyes of the Earth*, pp 80–81.
39. Ferdowsi, *Shahnameh: The Epic of the Kings*, 20.4. The *Shahnameh* attributes the building of a dam in Iran to Alexander.
40. Frye, *Heritage of Persia*, p 243; see also Al-Tabarī, *History*, Vol V, p 827-8. Stoneman, *Palmyra*, p 94 calls it a 'bridge'.
41. For more on ancient Palmyra see Stoneman, *Palmyra*.
42. Gibbon, *Decline and Fall*, Vol I, X.IV.
43. *Historia Augusta*, The Two Valerians, 4.2-4.
44. *Historia Augusta*, The Two Valerians, 4.2; Zonaras, XII.23.
45. Stoneman, *Palmyra*, p 106.
46. Zosimus, I.39.
47. Dodgeon and Lieu, *The Roman Eastern Frontier*, pp 67-87; Isidore Epstein, *Judaism: A Historical Perspective* (Baltimore: Penguin Books, 1959), p 124.
48. Historia Augusta, The Two Valerians, 4.2.
49. Stoneman, *Palmyra*, p 113.
50. Zosimus, I.44.2.
51. Gibbon, *Decline and Fall*, Vol I, X.IV, n 154.
52. H L Havell (trans), *Longinus On The Sublime* (London: Macmillan, 1890), Introduction.
53. Eunapius, *Lives of the Philosophers and Sophists*, translated by Wilmer C. Wright (Loeb Classical Library, 1921), Introduction.
54. Geoffrey Chaucer, *Canterbury Tales,* The Monk's Tale, 120 (modern translation). Chaucer also tells the story of Alexander in The Monk's Tale.
55. Roland Smith, 'The Casting of Julian the Apostate in the likeness of Alexander the Great', *Histos*, 5 (2011), p 50, fn 24; Andrew Stewart, 'Alexander in Greek and Roman Art', in Joseph Roisman (ed), *Brill's Companion to Alexander the Great*, (Leiden, Brill, 2003), pp 89-104.
56. Eutropius, 9.13.
57. Victor, 35.2; Smith, 'The Casting of Julian the Apostate', p 50.
58. Victor, 35.6.
59. Howgego, *Ancient History from Coins*, pp 126-7.
60. Zosimus, I.50-51; also see Stoneman, *Palmyra*, pp 169-70.
61. *Historia Augusta*, Tyranni Triginta, 30.24-6.
62. *Historia Augusta*, Aurelian, 33-4.
63. Watson, *Aurelian*, p 79.
64. Victor, 35.5; Stoneman, *Palmyra*, p 186.

65. Watson, *Aurelian*, p 188.
66. *Historia Augusta*, Aurelian, 35.4. Watson, *Aurelian*, pp 103–4, on the other hand does not believe that he was on the march to a new Persian war.

Chapter 9: Diocletian: Roman Revival

1. Eutropius, 9.19.
2. *Historia Augusta*, Probus, 20.1.
3. Zonaras, XII. 30.
4. Al-Tabarī, *History, Vol 5*, p. 45.
5. Frye, *Heritage of Persia*, p 249; see also MacKenzie, 'Katir's Inscription at Naqshe' Rajab', http://www.cais-soas.com/CAIS/Languages/pahlavi/kartir_inscription_rajab.htm
6. Festus, 64.6–11; Eutropius, 9.19.1.
7. *Historia Augusta* Carus, Carinus and Numerian, pp 8–9; Victor, 38.3; Eutropius, 18.
8. *Historia Augusta*, 9.1.
9. Omar Khayyám, *Rubáiyát*, XIX.
10. Carus' son Numerian briefly ruled as emperor. He was better known as a poet. In an extant work he wrote that he would, 'sing of our sea-board beneath the twin boundaries of our world'. By this he meant all the lands between the eastern and western oceans. As we have seen it was a common theme in Rome. See 'The Cynegetica by Nemesianus', The Loeb Classical Library, 1935.
11. Malalas, XII. 37.
12. Kurkjian, *History of Armenia*, XVIII.
13. Kurkjian, *History of Armenia*, XVIII. 115.
14. Daryaee, *Sasanian Persia*, pp 10–11.
15. Eutropius, 9.24.
16. Kurkjian, *History of Armenia*, XVIII.116.
17. Eutropius, 9.24–25. Other accounts vary on the distance Galerius had to run.
18. Timothy D Barnes, *Constantine and Eusebius* (Cambridge, MA: Harvard University Press, 2006), p 17.
19. Dodgeon and Lieu, *Roman Eastern Frontier*, p 127, quoting Festus, 25, 65, 12–66, 5; see also Eutropius, IX. 25.
20. Eutropius, 9.25.
21. For a study of the panels of this arch see Margret S. Pond Rothman, 'The Thematic Organization of the Panel Reliefs on the Arch of Galerius', *American Journal of Archaeology*, Vol 81, No 4 (Autumn 1977), pp 427–54.
22. *Historia Augusta*, Carus, Carinus and Numerian, 9.3.
23. Nixon and Rodgers, *Panegyrici Latini*, 68. The reference to 'the race of Hercules' refers directly to Alexander.
24. Bowman et al, *Cambridge Ancient History*: Vol 12, p 81.

25. Williams, *Diocletian*, p 84.
26. Dodgeon and Lieu, *Roman Eastern Frontier*, p 134.
27. Festus, 25.3; Malalas, XIII.16-21.
28. Festus, 131; quoting Petrus Particius, *Fragments*, 13 FGH IV, pp 188-9. Particius is our main ancient source for these negotiations.
29. Jerome, *Chronicon*, s.a. 304.
30. Victor, Constantius, 17.
31. John Holland Smith, *Constantine the Great* (New York: Scribner's and Sons, 1971), p 8; Eutropius, IX. 26; Theophanes, *Chronicon*, 5793.
32. From the Egyptian Supreme Council of Antiquities: http://www.sca-egypt.org/eng/SITE_Pompey's_Pillar.htm.

Chapter 10: Shapur II: The Great One

1. Al-Tabarī, *History, Vol V*, p 898.
2. Malalas, 13.1.
3. Eusebius, *Life of Constantine*, translated by Averil Cameron and Stuart G Hall (Oxford: Clarendon Press, 1999), IV.8-13.
4. Eusebius, *Constantine*, I.8.
5. Michael Tierney, 'Constantine the Great and his City', *Studies: An Irish Quarterly Review*, Vol 23, No 89 (Mar 1934), pp 59-70.
6. Comstock, Mary B, 'Roman Medallions and Contorniates', *Boston Museum Bulletin*, pp 35-6.
7. David Potter, *Constantine the Emperor*, (Oxford: Oxford University Press, 2013), p 207. See also Dodgeon and Lieu, *Roman Eastern Frontier*, p 130.
8. Nicholas J Saunders, *Alexander's Tomb: The Two-Thousand Year Obsession to Find the Lost Conqueror* (New York: Basic Books, 2007), pp 109-110.
9. Orosius, 138.
10. Augustine of Hippo, *The City of God*, translated by Henry Betteson (London: Penguin, 2004), IV.4.
11. Potter, *Roman Empire at Bay*, pp 469-70.
12. Although we know about it from other writers, this book has not survived. Potter, *Roman Empire at Bay*, p 470.
13. Stoneman, *Legends of Alexander*, Intro, p xi, n 12.
14. Daryaee, *Sasanian Persia*, p 15.
15. A. Tafażżolī, 'Adur Narseh', *Encyclopædia Iranica*, online, 15 Dec 1983.
16. Touraj Daryaee, 'Shapur II', *Encyclopædia Iranica*, online, 20 July 2009.
17. Pourshariati, *Decline and Fall*, p 56.
18. C E Bosworth, 'Arabs and Iran in the pre-Islamic period', *Encyclopædia Iranica*, online, 10 Aug 2011. See also Touraj Daryaee, 'Shapur II', *Encyclopædia Iranica*, for details of the Arab raids on Fars and Shapur's retaliation.
19. Kurkjian, *History of Armenia*, XXXVI.

20. Pirouz Mojtahed-Zadeh, *Security and Territoriality in the Persian Gulf: A Maritime Political Geography* (London: Routledge, 1999), p 163; Daryaee, *Sasanian Persia*, pp 46-7.
21. Bosworth, 'Arabs and Iran in the pre-Islamic period', *Encyclopædia Iranica*, online, 2011.
22. Pourshariati, *Decline and Fall*, pp 334-5.
23. Frye, *Heritage of Persia*, p 241.
24. Dodgeon and Lieu, *Roman Eastern Frontier*, p 147; Malalas, 13.3. See also Samuel N C Lieu and Dominic Montserrat, *Constantine: History, Historiography and Legend* (London: Routledge, 1998), pp 160 and 186. They quote Byzantine sources including the *Chronicle of John of Nikiou* and the *Annals of Georgius Cedrenus*.
25. Eusebius, *Constantine*, I. 57.
26. Eusebius, *Constantine*, IV.62.4.
27. Eusebius, *Constantine*, I.57.
28. Julian, *Orations*, 1.18.b.
29. Singara was briefly occupied by Trajan. See Dio, 68.22.
30. Freya Stark, *Rome on the Euphrates: The Story of a Frontier* (New York: Harcourt, Brace & World, 1967) p 215.
31. Dodgeon and Lieu, *Roman Eastern Frontier*, pp 176-8; Anonymous, *Itinerarium Alexandri*, 1-11.
32. Robin Lane Fox, 'The Itinerary of Alexander', *The Classical Quarterly*, New Series, Vol 47, No 1 (1997), p 246.
33. Festus, 27.
34. Eutropius, 10.10.
35. Julian, *Orations*, I.22.
36. Libanius, *Libanius: Selected Works*, translated by A Norman (William Heinemann, 1969), LIX. 6075; Dodgeon and Lieu, *Roman Eastern Frontier*, pp 155-7.
37. Dignas and Winter, *Rome and Persia*, p 89; This night battle was so rare that it was mentioned in several ancient sources including Festus, Libanius, Julian, Eutropius, Jerome, Orosius, Socrates Scholasticus and others.
38. Festus, 27.
39. Julian, *Orations*, I. 22. Julian refers to Constantius crossing the Tigris.
40. Libanius, LIX.99-120.
41. Kirkjian, *History of Armenia*, 103. In the Middle East a crippled or maimed man was (and still is) ineligible for kingship.
42. Michael Grant, *The Roman Emperors* (New York: Barnes & Noble, 1997), p 242.
43. Ammianus Marcellinus, 17.5.1.

Chapter 11: Julian: The Soul of Alexander

1. Socrates Scholasticus, *Historia Ecclesiastica*, 3.21.7. This Socrates was a Christian historian who wrote during the reign of Theodosius. He had a low opinion of Julian.

2. Libanius, 132.
3. Ammianus Marcellinus, 17.11.2. See also Zosimus, III.
4. Ammianus Marcellinus, 17.1.
5. Ammianus Marcellinus, 17.5.5.
6. Ammianus Marcellinus, 18.6.22.
7. Ammianus Marcellinus, 18.7.1-6.
8. Ammianus Marcellinus was an eye witness to the siege of Amida. He is our main source for this battle. See books 18 and 19. The following is based on his accounts.
9. Ammianus Marcellinus, 19.2.4.
10. Ammianus Marcellinus, 19.1.7.
11. Daryaee, 'shapur II', *Encyclopædia Iranica*, online, 20 July 2009.
12. Ammianus Marcellinus, 20.6.
13. Julian, *Epistle ad Themistium*, 253D.
14. Malalas, 13.17.
15. Eutropius, 10.15.
16. Libanius, 17.17; Dodgeon and Lieu, *Roman Eastern Frontier*, p 192.
17. For a historiographic summary of Alexander's influence on Julian see Smith 'The Casting of Julian the Apostate "in the likeness" of Alexander the Great'.
18. Julian, *Orations*, I.119.
19. Ammianus Marcellinus, 25.4.15.
20. Nixon and Rodgers, *Panegyrici Latini*, III.II.6.6.
21. Robin Lane Fox, 'The Itinerary of Alexander', p. 249; Socrates Scholasticus, 3.2.1; Cicero had camped there also.
22. Julian, *The Caesars*, Vol II, 326a.
23. Polymnia Athanassiadi, *Julian and Hellenism: An Intellectual Biography* (Oxford: Clarendon Press, 1981), p 194; Arrian, *Anabasis*, VII.16.5-6; Appian, *The Histories*, II.153.
24. Socrates Scholasticus, 3.21.
25. Harry Turtledove, *The Chronicle of Theophanes: Anni Mundi 6095-6305 (A.D. 602-813* (Philadelphia: University of Pennsylvania Press, 1982), p 121.
26. Ammianus Marcellinus, 23.3.5; Zosimus, 3.12.5. Zosimus claimed that the number was closer to 18,000.
27. Malalas, 13.21; Zosimus, 3.13.2.
28. For a more complete telling of Julian's invasion see Jan den Boeft (ed), *Philological and Historical Commentary on Ammianus Marcellinus XXIV* (Leiden: Brill, 2002).
29. Den Boeft, *Commentary on Ammianus Marcellinus*, XXIV.7.2; Eutropius, 10.14.
30. Ammianus Marcellinus, 24.7.4-6; Zosimus, 3.26.3.
31. Libanius, 18.260-61.
32. Ammianus Marcellinus, 25.3; Zosimus, 3.29.1.
33. Malalas, 13.23.
34. Al-Tabarī, *History, Vol V*, pp 842-843.

Chapter 12: The Sasanian wars with Byzantium: The waning of Alexander

1. St John Damascene, *Barlaam and Ioasaph*, I. 3-4.
2. Grant, *Roman Emperors*, p 263.
3. Ammianus Marcellinus, 30.2.
4. Nixon and Rodgers, *Panegyrici Latini*, pp 458-9.
5. Russell and Wilson, *Menander Rhetor*, pp 92-93.
6. Claudian, *Panegyric on the Fourth Consulship of Honorius*, translated by Maurice Platnauer, (London: William Heinemann Ltd, 1963), pp 255-60.
7. Claudian, *Panegyric*, VIII. 395-405.
8. Socrates Scholasticus, 5.16.
9. For more on this form of imitating Alexander see Anthony Kaldellis, *Procopius of Caesarea: Tyranny, History and Philosophy at the end of Antiquity* (Philadelphia: University of Pennsylvania Press, 1984), Ch 4.
10. Alan Cameron, *Circus Factions: Blues and Greens at Rome and Byzantium* (Oxford: Clarendon Press, 1976), p 68. See footnotes 2 & 3.
11. Richard Stoneman, *The Book of Alexander the Great: A Life of the Conqueror* (London: I B Tauris, 2011), xxv.
12. Russell and Wilson, *Menander Rhetor*, pp 16-17, quoting Pacatus Drepanius, *Panegyrici Latini*, II.XII.
13. Shahbazi, 'Sasanian dynasty', *Encyclopædia Iranica*, online, 2005. The length of these negotiations reminds us of the 'Iran Nuclear Deal' of our own time.
14. O Klíma, 'bahrām (2)', *Encyclopædia Iranica*, online, 24 August 2011.
15. Daryaee, *Sasanian Persia*, p 21.
16. Geoffrey Greatrex and Samuel N C Lieu, *The Roman Eastern Frontier and the Persian Wars AD 363-628* (London: Routledge, 2007), pp 31-2.
17. Procopius, 1.2, 1-10; Agathias, 4.25; Daryaee, *Sasanian Persia*, p 22.
18. Pourshariati, *Decline and Fall*, pp 66-7. Ferdowsi calls the animal a 'water horse', *Shanamah*, Yasdagird, 7.
19. Pourshariati, *Decline and Fall*, 59; Daryaee, *Sasanian Persia*, p 22. See also Shahbazi, 'yazdegerd I', *Encyclopaedia Iranica*, online, for details on this king and an extended bibliography.
20. Socrates Scholasticus, 8.8; Theodoret, *Ecclesiastical History*, XXXVII.
21. Daryaee, *Sasanian Persia*, 78.
22. Pourshariati, *Decline and Fall*, pp 67-71.
23. For more on the war of 421-422 see Geoffrey Greatrex, 'The two Fifth-Century Wars between Rome and Persia', *Florilegium*, 12 (1993), pp 1–14; Socrates Scholasticus, 7.18 is our best ancient source for this war.
24. Ammianus Marcellinus, 25.1.12-13; Shahbazi, 'army i. Pre-Islamic Iran', *Encyclopædia Iranica*, online, 2011.
25. Daryaee, 'yazdegerd II', *Encyclopædia Iranica*, online, 2012.

26. Procopius of Caesarea, in *History of the Wars*, I.III, said of this branch of Huns: 'They are the only ones among the Huns who have white bodies and countenances which are not ugly'.

27. *The Chronicle of Pseudo-Joshua the Stylite*, translated by Frank R Trombley and John W Watt (Liverpool: Liverpool University Press, 2000), pp 9–11. Defences against the northerners included the 'Caspian Gates', a series of forts and walls first established by Alexander the Great; Procopius, 1.4.13-16.

28. Procopius, 1.7.1.

29. Greatrex and Lieu, 63; See also Procopius, 1.10.11-12.

30. Note: Turkish place names like Erzurum that contain the letters 'rum' indicate a connection with Rome.

31. Greatrex and Lieu, *Roman Eastern Frontier*, pp 63-7; also Zachariah of Mitylene, *Historia Ecclesiaca*, VII.3-4; Procopius, 1.7.17-19.

32. Greatrex and Lieu, *Roman Eastern Frontier*, p 68.

33. Greatrex and Lieu, *Roman Eastern Frontier*, p 69.

34. Greatrex and Lieu, *Roman Eastern Frontier*, p 71; Zachariah of Mitylene, VII.5.

35. John the Lydian, *De Magistratibus*, III. 53.

36. Greatrex and Lieu, *Roman Eastern Frontier*, pp 74-5; Zachariah of Mitylene, VII.6; Procopius, 1.10.13-15.

37. For the Mazdakite rebellion see Dignas and Winter, *Rome and Persia*, p 99.

38. Ian Hughes, *Belisarius: The Last Roman General* (Barnsley: Pen & Sword Books, 2009), Intro.

39. Gibbon, *Decline and Fall*, IV.41.

40. Procopius, 2.2.13-15.

41. Procopius, 1.8.

42. Procopius, 1.14.22-30.

43. Greatrex and Lieu, *Roman Eastern Frontier*, p 92; Geoffrey Greatrex, *Rome and Persia at War 502-532* (Prenton: Francis Cairns Publications, 1988), pp 193-212.

44. Greatrex, *Rome and Persia at War*, p 232 n 21.

45. Dignas and Winter, *Rome and Persia*, p 112.

46. Also known to the Arabs as the 'Year of the Elephant'. See the Qur'an, Surah 105.

47. J A S Evans, *Procopius* (New York: Twayne Publishers, 1972), p 104; Procopius, 4.16.12-16.

48. Procopius, 2.16-19.

49. Frye, *Heritage of Persia*, p 259; Glanville Downey, *Ancient Antioch* (Princeton: Princeton University Press, 2015), pp 252-3.

50. Walter Kaegi, *Heraclius, Emperor of Byzantium* (Cambridge: Cambridge University Press, 2003), p 87, n117. For more on the destruction of Antioch see Glanville Downey's, *Ancient Antioch*.

51. Greatrex and Lieu, *Roman Eastern Frontier*, pp 108-110.

52. Theophanes Confessor, 321.

53. Rawlinson, III.63.
54. Meander Protector, *Fragments 6.1-6.3*, translated by R C Blockey.
55. Simocatta, iii.1.1-iii.18.14.9. 4.
56. Photius, *Bibliotheca* or *Myriobiblon*, Codex 64, edited by N G Wilson. Photius, a ninth-century writer and cleric gives us a second-hand account. The original work, attributed to Theophanes of Byzantium, is lost.
57. Photius, *Bibliotheca*, Codex 64; Greatrex and Lieu, *Roman Eastern Frontier*, pp 142–145.
58. Simocatta, iii.1.1-iii.18.14.11.4.
59. Simocatta, iii.1.1-iii.18.14.12.10.
60. Elishē, *History of Vardan and the Armenian War*, translated by R Thompson, pp 31-32; see also Simocatta, iii.1.1 – iii.18.14.14; Greatrex and Lieu, *Roman Eastern Frontier*, pp 156–158.
61. Simocatta, iii.1.1- iii.18.14.15. 2.
62. Simocatta, iii.1.1-iii.18.14.15.10.
63. Simocatta, iii.1.1-iii.18.14.16.2.
64. Photius, *Bibliotheca*, Codex 65.
65. Simocatta, iii.1.1- iii.18.14.9.1-12; Al-Tabarī, *History, Vol V*, p 994.
66. For more on Choban, see Shahbazi, 'bahrām (II)', *Encyclopaedia Iranica Bibliotheca*, online, 24 August 2011; and Pourshariati, *Decline and Fall*, pp 126-29.
67. Simocatta, iv.1.1-iv.16.28.13.1-8.

Chapter 13: Heraclius and Khusrow II: Greek Tragedy

1. Al-Tabarī, *History, Vol V*, pp 1003.
2. Gibbon, *The Decline and Fall*, XLVI. I.
3. Simocatta, VIII.15.7.
4. Downey, *Ancient Antioch*, pp 268-9.
5. Kaegi, *Heraclius*, p 85, n 109.
6. Kaegi, *Heraclius*, p 79, n 78; see also http://www.tertullian.org/fathers/antiochus_strategos_capture.htm
7. Al-Tabarī, *History, Vol V*, p 1002.
8. Ja'far Subhani, *The Message* (Karachi: Islamic Seminary Publications, 2006), Ch 3, n 24.
9. *The Quràn*, translated by M H Shakir (Elmhurst: Tahrike Tarsile Quran, 1993), 30.2-3.
10. Kaegi, *Heraclius*, p 12.
11. Mary Whitby, 'The Devil in Disguise: The End of George of Pisidia's Hexaemeron Reconsidered', *Journal of Hellenic Studies*, Vol 115 (1995), pp 115-129. Whitby argues that the poetry of George of Pisidia was political in nature, purposely favouring Heraclius.

12. Gerrit J Reinink and Bernard H Stolte, *The Reign of Heraclius (610-641) Crisis and Confrontation* (Leuven: Peeters, 2002), pp 81-94.
13. Irfan Shahid, 'The Iranian Factor in Byzantium during the Reign of Heraclius', *Dumbarton Oaks Papers*, Vol 26 (1972), pp 297-8.
14. Theophanes, *Chronicles*, 13-15, does not mention Issus.
15. For a study of the location of the Gaugamela battlefield see A M Devine, 'The Battle of Gaugamela: A Tactical and source-critical study', *The Ancient World*, Vol XIII (Aug 1986), pp 87-116.
16. Kaegi, Walter, *Heraclius*, p 186.
17. Henry Smith Williams et al, *The Historians' History of the World* (New York: Encyclopaedia Britannica, pp 166-7). Even Shahid agrees that the emperor's exploits on Dorkon shows a comparison between Alexander and Heraclius. Footnote 754.
18. Canepa, *Two Eyes of the Earth*, pp 147-9.
19. Graeme Wood, 'What ISIS Really Wants', *The Atlantic* (March 2015).

Conclusion

1. Aelian, *Varia Historia*, 12.26.
2. Shahid, 'The Iranian Factor', argues that Heraclius never conquered Persia but that is not the point. He didn't have to.
3. See Stoneman, *The Book of Alexander the Great*.

Bibliography

Africa, T W, 'The Opium Addiction of Marcus Aurelius', *Journal of the History of Ideas*, Vol. 22, No. 1 (Jan–March 1961), pp 97–102.

Aalders, G J D, '*Germanicus Und Alexander Der Grosse*', *Historia: Zeitschrift für Alte Geschichte*, Vol. 10, No. 3 (July 1961), pp 382–384.

Abu Mohammad Bin Yusuf, *Sikandar Nāma,e Barà*, trans. H. Wilberforce Clarke, (London: W H Allen & Co, 1881).

Agathias, *Greek Anthology*, T E Page et al (eds), translated by W R Paton, (Cambridge, Massachusetts: Harvard University Press, 1916).

Al-Tabarī, *The History of al-Tabarī. Vol IV: The Ancient Kingdoms*, translated by Moshe Perlmann (Albany: State University of New York Press, 1987).

Al-Tabari, *The History of al-Tabarī, Vol V: The Sasanids, the Byzantines, the Lakmids*, translated by Clifford E. Bosworth (Albany: State University of New York Press, 1999).

Anderson, Andrew Runni, 'Alexander's Horns', *Transactions and Proceedings of the American Philological Association*, Vol. 58 (1927), pp 100–122.

Anderson, William B, 'Contributions to the Study of the Ninth Book of Livy', *Transactions and Proceedings of the American Philological Association*, Vol. 39 (1908), pp 89–103.

Appian, *History of Rome*, translated by Horace White et al (New York: The Macmillan Co, 1912).

Arrian, *Anabasis Alexander*, translated by E. Iliff Robson (Cambridge MA: Loeb Classical Library, Harvard University Press, 1961).

Athanassiadi, Polymnia, *Julian and Hellenism: An Intellectual Biography* (Oxford, Clarendon Press, 1981).

Athenaeus, *The Deipnosophists*, translated by Charles Burton Gulick (London: W. Heinemann Ltd, 1927).

Attaleates, Michael, *The History*, translated by Anthony Kaldellis, Dumbarton Oaks Medieval Library 16 (Cambridge, MA: Harvard University Press, 2012).

Augustine of Hippo, *The City of God*, translated by Henry Bettenson (London, Penguin, 2004).

Aurelius, Marcus, *Meditations*, translated by George Long (Chicago: University of Chicago, 1952).

Badian, E, *Studies in Greek and Roman History* (New York: Barnes & Noble, 1964).

Badian, E, *Publicans and Sinners: Private Enterprise in Service of the Roman Republic*, Ithaca, NY: Cornell University Press, 1972).

Ball, Warwick, *Rome in the East: The Transformation of an Empire* (London, Routledge, 2001).

Barnes, Timothy D, *Constantine and Eusebius* (Cambridge, MA: Harvard University Press, 2006).

Barnett, Glenn, 'Mark Antony's Persian Campaign', *Military History* (Nov 2006).

Barnett, Glenn, 'Father and Son Invade Iraq', *Ancient Warfare* (Dec 2008).

Barnett, Glenn, and Arnold Blumberg, 'Seeking the Knockout Blow: A History of Asymmetric Warfare', *Ancient Warfare* (Oct 2009).

Barnett, Glenn, and Arnold Blumberg, 'Emperor Julian's Invasion of Mesopotamia', *Military History* (June 2005).

Barrett, Antony A, *Caligula: The Corruption of Power* (New Haven: Yale University Press, 1989).

Bennett, Julian, *Trajan: Optimus Princeps: A Life and Times* (Bloomington: Indiana University Press, 1997).

Bighami, Muhammad ibn Ahmad, *Love and War; adventures from the Firuz Shah Namah of Sheikh Bighami*, translated by William L Hanaway (Ann Arbor: Scholars Facsimiles & Reprint, 1974)

Bieber, Margarete, 'The Portraits of Alexander the Great', *Greece & Rome,* Vol. 12, No. 2 (Oct. 1965).

Birley, Antony R, *Marcus Aurelius: A Biography* (London: Routledge, 2000).

Birley, Antony R, *Septimius Severus: The African Emperor* (London: Routledge, 1999).

Birley, Antony R, *Hadrian : the Restless Emperor* (New York: Routledge, 1997).

Boeft, Jan den, *Philological and historical commentary on Ammianus Marcellinus XXIV* (Leiden: Brill, 2002).

Bosworth, A B, *Conquest and Empire: The Reign of Alexander the Great* (Cambridge: Cambridge University Press, 1988).

Bosworth, Brian, 'Augustus, the Res Gestae and Hellenistic Theories of Apotheosis', *The Journal of Roman Studies*, Vol. 89 (1999), pp 1-18.

Bowder, Diana, *Who Was Who in the Roman World* (New York: Washington Square Press, 1980).

Bowersock, G W, *Augustus and the Greek World* (Oxford: The Clarendon Press, 1965).

Braund, David, *Rome and the Friendly King: The Character of the Client Kingship* (London: Croom Helm, 1984).

Cadoux, T J, 'Marcus Crassus: A Revaluation', *Greece & Rome*, Second Series, Vol. 3, No. 2 (Oct 1956), pp 153–61.

Caesar, Julius, *The Conquest of Gaul*, translated by S A Handford (Harmondsworth, Middlesex: Penguin Books, 1980).

Cameron, Alan, *Circus Factions: Blues and Greens at Rome and Byzantium* (Oxford: Clarendon Press, 1976)

Canepa, Matthew, *The Two Eyes of the Earth: Art and Ritual of Kingship between Rome and Sasanian Iran* (London: University of California Press, 2009).

Carter, John M, *The Battle of Actium: The Rise and Triumph of Augustus Caesar* (New York: Weybright & Talley, 1970).

Cassius Dio, *Dio's Roman History*, translated by Earnest Cary (London: Loeb Classical Library, Harvard University Press, 1954–1961).

Catullus, Gaius Balerius, *The Poems of Catullus* (Berkeley: University of California Press, 2005).

Chamoux, Francois, *Hellenistic Civilization*, translated by Michel Roussel (Oxford: Blackwell Publishing, 2003).

Christensen, Peter, *The Decline of Iranshahr: Irrigation and Environments in the History of the Middle East, 500 B.C. to A.D. 1500* (Copenhagen: Museum Tusculanum Press, 1993).

Chugg, Andrew, 'The Sarcophagus of Alexander the Great?', *Greece & Rome*, Second Series, Vol. 49, No. 1 (April, 2002), pp 1–26.

Cicero, Marcus Tullius, *Letters to Atticus* (London: Loeb Classical Library, Harvard University Press, 1970).

Cicero, Marcus Tullius, *The Letters to His Friends* (London: Loeb Classical Library, Harvard Press, 1927).

Claudian, *Panegyric on the Fourth Consulship of Honorius*, translated by Maurice Platnauer (London: William Heinemann Ltd, 1963).

Cole, Juan, *Napoleon's Egypt: Invading the Middle East* (New York: Palgrave Macmillan, 2007).

Colledge, Malcolm, *The Parthians* (New York: Fredrick A Praeger, 1967).

Comstock, Mary B, 'Roman Medallions and Contorniates', *Boston Museum Bulletin*, Vol. 66, No. 343 (1968), pp 28–40.

Conybeare, Edward, *Roman Britain*, II, G8 (London: Society for Promoting Christian Knowledge, 1903).

Crawford, J S, 'A Portrait of Alexander the Great at the University of Delaware', *American Journal of Archaeology*, Vol 83, No 4 (Oct, 1979), pp 477–81.

Croke, Brian, 'Poetry and Propaganda: Anastasius I as Pompey', *Greek, Roman, and Byzantine Studies*, 48 (2008).

Curtius Rufus, Quintus, *History of Alexander*, Vols I & II, translated by John C Rolfe (Cambridge MA: Loeb Classical Library, Harvard University Press, 1962).

Dahmen, Karsten, 'Alexander in Gold and Silver: Reassessing the Third Century AD Medallions from Aboukir and Tarsos', *American Journal of Numismatics*, Second Series, 20 (2008), pp 493-546.

Daryaee, Touraj, '*Imitatio Alexandri* and its impact on Late Arsacid, Early Sasanian and Middle Persian Literature', *Electrum*, Vol 12 (2007), pp 89-97.

Daryaee, Touraj, *Sasanian Persia: The Rise and Fall of an Empire* (London: I.B.Tauris, 2009).

Daryaee, Touraj, *The Oxford Handbook of Iranian History* (Oxford: Oxford University Press, 2014).

Debevoise, Neilson, 'Parthian Problems', *The American Journal of Semitic Languages and Literatures*, Vol 47, No 2 (Jan 1931), pp 73-82.

Devine, A M, 'The Battle of Gaugamela: A Tactical and source-critical study', *The Ancient World*, Vol XIII (Aug 1986), pp 87-116.

DeWitt, N J, 'Caesar and the Alexander Legend', *The Classical Weekly*, Vol 36, No 5 (2 November 1942), pp 51-53.

Dignas, Beate, and Engelbert Winter, *Rome and Persia in Late Antiquity: Neighbours and Rivals* (Cambridge: Cambridge University Press, 2007).

Diodorus Siculus, *Library of History*, translated by C H Oldfather (London: Loeb Classical Library, 1963).

Dodgeon, Michael H, and Samuel N C Lieu, *The Roman Eastern Frontier and the Persian Wars AD 226-363* (London: Routledge, 1994).

Downey, Glanville, 'Libanius' Oration in Praise of Antioch (Oration XI)', *Proceedings of the American Philosophical Society*, Vol 103, No 5 (15 Oct 1959), pp 652-86.

Downey, Glanville, *Ancient Antioch* (Princeton: Princeton University Press, 2015).

Ehrenberg, V, 'Caesar's Final Aims', *Harvard Studies in Classical Philology*, Vol 68 (1964), pp 149-61.

Encyclopædia Iranica, Online edition (New York, 1996-).

Engels, D, 'Alexander's Intelligence System', *The Classical Quarterly*, New Series, Vol 30, No 2 (1980), pp 327-40.

Epstein, Isidore, *Judaism: A Historical Perspective* (Baltimore: Penguin Books, 1959).

Erskine, Andrew, 'Greek Gifts and Roman Suspicion', *Classics Ireland*, Vol 4 (1997).

Eusebius, *Ecclesiastical History* (London: Loeb Classical Library, 1980).

Eusebius, *Life of Constantine*, translated by Averil Cameron and Stuart G Hall (Oxford: Clarendon Press, 1999).

Eutropius, *The Breviarium ab Urbe Condita*, translated by H W Bird (Liverpool: Liverpool University Press, 1993).

Evans, J A S, *Procopius* (New York, Twayne Publishers, 1972).

Farrokh, Kaveh, *Sassanian Elite Cavalry AD 224-642* (Oxford: Osprey Publishing, 2005).

Farrokh, Kaveh, *Shadows in the Desert: Ancient Persia at War* (Oxford: Osprey Publishing, 2007).

Ferdowsi, *The Epic of the Kings: Shahnameh the National epic of Persia*, translated by Reuben Levy (Chicago: University of Chicago Press, 1967).

Ferguson, John, *The Religions of the Roman Empire* (Ithaca: Cornell University Press, 1970).

Florus, Lucius Annaeus, *Epitome of Roman History*, translated by E S Forster, Cambridge MA: Harvard University Press, 1929).

Fisch, M H, 'Alexander and the Stoics', *The American Journal of Philology*, Vol 58, No 2 (1937), pp 129-51.

Franzero, Carlo Maria, *The Life and Times of Nero* (London: Alvin Redman Limited, 1954).

Frontinus, Sextus Julius, *The Stratagems, and the Aqueducts of Rome*, translated by Charles E Bennett et al (Boston: Harvard University Press, 1961).

Fronto, Marcus Cornelius, *Correspondence*, translated by H R Haines (Cambridge: Harvard University Press, 1920).

Frye, Richard N, *The Heritage of Persia* (Costa Mesa: Mazda Publishers, 1993).

Frye, Richard N, *Iran*, (London: Allen & Unwin, 1954).

Gawlikowski, M, 'Thapsacus and Zeugma the Crossing of the Euphrates in Antiquity', *Iraq*, Vol 58 (1996), pp 123-33.

Gellius, Aulus, *Attic Nights*, translated by John C Rolfe (London: William Heinemann Ltd, 1961).

Gibbon, *The Decline and Fall of the Roman Empire* (New York: Alfred A. Knopf, 1994).

Gilliam, J F, 'The Plague Under Marcus Aurelius', *AJP*, Vol 82, No 3 (July 1961).

Graf, David F, 'Athenodorus of Tarsus and Nabataea: The Date and Circumstances of His Visit to Petra', in *Studies in the History and Archaeology of Jordan X* (Amman: Department of Antiquities, 2009).

Grainger, John D, *The Roman war of Antiochos the Great* (Leiden: Die Deutsche Bibliothek, 2002).

Grajetzki, Wolfram, *Greeks & Parthians in Mesopotamia and Beyond* (London: Bristol Classical Press, 2011).

Grant, Michael, *From Alexander to Cleopatra: The Hellenistic World* (New York: Collier Books, 1990).

Grant, Michael, *Cleopatra: A Biography* (New York: Dorset Press, 1972).

Grant, Michael, *Emperor in Revolt: Nero* (New York: American Heritage Press, 1970).

Grant, Michael, *Roman History from Coins* (Cambridge: The University Press, 1968).

Grant, Michael, *The Roman Emperors* (New York: Barnes and Noble, 1997).

Grant, Michael, *The Climax of Rome* (Boston: Little Brown and Co, 1968).

Greatrex, Geoffrey, *Rome and Persia at War 502-532* (Prenton: Francis Cairns Publications, 1988)

Greatrex, Geoffrey and Samuel N C Lieu, *The Roman Eastern Frontier and the Persian Wars AD 363-628* (London: Routledge, 2007).

Green, Peter, 'Caesar and Alexander: Aemulatio, imitatio, comparatio', *American Journal of Ancient History*, 3 (1978), pp 1-26.

Green, Peter, *Classical Bearings: Interpreting Ancient History and Culture* (Berkley: University of California Press, 1998)

Greenhalgh, Peter, *Pompey: The Roman Alexander* (Columbia: University of Missouri Press, 1981).

Gruen, Erich S, *The Hellenistic World and the Coming of Rome*, Vols 1 & 2 (Berkeley: University of California Press, 1984).

Gruen, Erich S, 'Rome and the Myth of Alexander', in T W Hillard et al (eds), *Ancient History in a Modern University* (Grand Rapids: William B. Eerdmans Publishing, 1998).

Gurval, Robert Alan, *Actium and Augustus* (Ann Arbor: University of Michigan Press, 1998).

Hagerman, C, 'In the Footsteps of the "Macedonian Conqueror": Alexander the Great and British India', *International Journal of the classical tradition*, Vol 16 (2009).

Haines, C R, 'Some notes on the text of Fronto', *Classical Quarterly*, Vol 9, No 1 (Jan 1915), pp 50-54.

Hamilton, Edith, *The Roman Way* (New York, W W Norton & Co, 1932).

Hamilton, J R, *Plutarch: Alexander, A Commentary* (Oxford: The Clarendon Press, 1969).

Hammond, N G L, *The Genius of Alexander the Great* (Chapel Hill: The University of North Carolina Press, 1997).

Hanaway, William L, 'Anāhitā and Alexander', *Journal of the American Oriental Society*, Vol 102, No 2 (Apr-Jun 1982), pp 285-95.

Hanaway, William L, *Love and War: Adventures from the Firuz Shāh Nāma of Sheikh Bighamī*, Persian Heritage Series, 19 (New York: UNESCO, 1974).

Hannestad, Niels, 'Imitatio Alexandri in Roman Art', in *Alexander the Great. Reality and Myth* (Rome: L'Erma di Bretschneider,1993).

Havell, H L, *Longinus on the Sublime* (London, MacMillian, 1890).

Herodian, *History of the Roman Empire*, translated by Edward C Echols (Berkeley: University of California Press, 1961).

Historia Augusta, translated by David Magie (Cambridge: Loeb Classical Library, 1924).

Holliday, Peter, 'Roman Triumphal Painting: Its Function, Development, and Reception', *The Art Bulletin*, Vol 79, No 1 (March 1997), pp 130–47.

Hollis, A S, 'Octavian in the Fourth Georgic', *The Classical Quarterly*, New Series, Vol 46, No 1 (1996), pp 305–8.

Hollis, AS, 'Statius' Young Parthian King ('Thebaid' 8.286–93)', *Greece & Rome*, Second Series, Vol 41, No 2 (Oct 1994), pp 205–12.

Holt, Frank L, *Alexander the Great and the Mystery of the Elephant Medallions* (Berkeley, University of California Press, 2005).

Hong, Fan, and J A Mangan (eds), *Sport in Asian Society: Past and Present* (London: Routledge, 2002)

Hopkins, Clark, *The Discovery of Dura Europos* (New Haven, Yale University Press, 1979)

Horace, *Odes and Epodes*, translated by Niall Rudd (Cambridge, Mass: Harvard University Press, 2004).

Hornblower, Simon (ed), *Greek Historiography* (Oxford: Clarendon Press, 1994).

Horne, Charles F, *The Sacred Books and Early Literature of the East, Vol VII*: Ancient Persia (New York: Parke, Austin, & Lipscomb, 1917)

Howgego, Christopher, *Ancient History from Coins* (London: Routledge, 1995).

Hughes, Ian, *Belisarius: The Last Roman General* (Barnsley, Pen and Sword, 2009).

Josephus, Flavius, *Complete Works* (Ann Arbor: Kregel Publications, 1983).

Julian, *Works*, translated by Wilmer Cave Wright (Cambridge, MA: Harvard University Press, 1949-61).

Justin, *Epitome of The Philippic History of Pompeius Trogus*, translated by John Yardley (Oxford: Oxford University Press, 1997).

Juvenal, *The Satires of Juvenal*, intro. A F Cole (New York: Putnam's Sons, 1906)

Kaegi, Walter Emil, *Heraclius, Emperor of Byzantium* (Cambridge: Cambridge University Press, 2003).

Kaldellis, Anthony, *Procopius of Caesarea: Tyranny, History and Philosophy at the end of Antiquity* (Philadelphia: University of Pennsylvania Press, 1984).

Kaldellis, Anthony (editor and translator), *The Byzantine Family of Michael Psellos* (Notre Dame, University of Notre Dame, 2006).

Karasulas, Antony, *Mounted Archers of the Steppe 600 BC – AD 1300* (Oxford: Osprey Publishing, 2004).

Keaveney, Arthur, *Lucullus: A Life* (New York: Routledge, 1992).

Keaveney, Arthur, *Sulla: The Last Republican* (New York: Routledge, 1982).

Keaveney, Arthur, 'The King and the War-Lords: Romano-Parthian Relations Circa 64-53 BC', *The American Journal of Philology*, Vol 103, No 4 (Winter 1982), pp 412-428.

Khayyám, Omar, *The Rubáiyát*, translated by Robert Graves and Ali Shah (Garden City, NY: Doubleday, 1968).

Kurkjian, Vahan M, *A History of Armenia* (New York: Armenian General Benevolent Union of America, 1958).

Kühnen, Angela, *Die imitatio Alexandri in der Römischen Politik* (Münster: Rhema Verlag, 2008).

Lane Fox, Robin, *Alexander the Great* (London: The Dial Press, 1974).

Lane Fox, Robin, *The Search for Alexander* (Boston: Little Brown & Co, 1980).

Lane Fox, Robin, 'The Itinerary of Alexander: Constantius to Julian', *The Classical Quarterly*, New Series, Vol 47, No 1 (1997), pp 239-252.

Langford, Julia, *Becoming Alexander: Caracalla, Imperial Self-Presentation and the Politics of Inclusion*, unpublished paper delivered at the 2012 APA Annual Meeting in Philadelphia on 5 February 2012.

Lee, A D, *Information and Frontiers: Roman Relations in Late Antiquity* (Cambridge: Cambridge University Press, 1993).

Lendering, Jona, 'The De Bello Gallico', *Ancient Warfare*, II.4 (2008).

Lepper, F A, *Trajan's Parthian War* (London: Oxford University Press, 1948).

Lieu, Samuel N C, and Dominic Montserrat (eds), *Constantine: History, Historiography and Legend* (London: Routledge, 1998).

Livius, Titus (Livy), *The Rise of Rome*, translated by T J Luce (New York: Oxford University Press, 1998); translated by B O Foster (Cambridge: Harvard University Press, 1929).

Longden, R P, 'Notes on the Parthian Campaigns of Trajan', *The Journal of Roman Studies*, Vol 21 (1931), pp 1-35.

Lucan, *The Civil War (Pharsalia)* , translated by J D Duff (London: Heinemann, 1962).

Lucian, *Dialogues of the Dead: Philip and Alexander*, translated by M D Macleod, Loeb Classical Library Vol VII (Cambridge, MA: Harvard University Press, 1961).

Lucian, *Satirical Sketches*, translated by Paul Turner (Baltimore: Penguin Books, 1962).

Luttwak, Edward N, *The Grand Strategy of the Roman Empire: From the First Century A.D. to the Third* (Baltimore: John Hopkins University Press, 1976).

Macurdy, Grace H, 'Iotape', *The Journal of Roman Studies*, Vol 26, Part 1 (1936).

Magie, David, *Roman Rule in Asia Minor* (Princeton: Princeton Legacy Library, 2015).

Malelas, John, *The Chronicle of John Malelas*, translated by Elizabeth Jeffreys et al (Melbourne: Australian Association for Byzantine Studies,1986).

Malloch, S J V, 'Gaius' Bridge at Baiae and Alexander-Imitatio', *The Classical Quarterly*, Vol 51, No 1 (2001), pp 206-217.

Marcellinus, Ammianus, translated by Walter Hamilton as *The Later Roman Empire* (London: Penguin, 1986).

Mayor, Adrienne, *The Poison King: The Life and Legend of Mithradates* (Princeton: Princeton University Press, 2010).

McCrindle, J W, *Ancient India: As Described in Classical Literature* (Westminster: Archibald Constable, 1901).

McJannet, L, 'Antony and Alexander: Imperial Politics in Plutarch, Shakespeare, and Some Modern Historical Texts', *College Literature*, 20, No 3 (Oct. 1993), pp 1–18.

Memnon, 18.2, Codex 224, *Photius: Bibliotheca* (© Les Belles Lettres, Paris) Rene Henry, (ed) Roger Pearse

Millar, Fergus, *The Roman Near East* (London: Harvard University Press, 1996).

Millar, Fergus, 'Emperors, Frontiers and Foreign Relations, 31 B. C. to A. D. 378', *Britannia*, Vol 13 (1982), pp 1–23.

Minns, Ellis H, 'Parchments of the Parthian Period from Avroman in Kurdistan', *Journal of Hellenic Studies*, Vol 35 (1915), pp 22–65.

Mommsen, Theodor, *A History of Rome Under the Caesars* (New York: Routledge, 1996).

Morello, R, 'Livy's Alexander Digression (9.17-19): Counterfactuals and Apologetics', *The Journal of Roman Studies*, Vol 92 (2002), pp 62–85.

Murray, William M, 'Octavian's Campsite Memorial for the Actian War', *Transactions of the American Philosophical Society*, New Series, Vol 79, No 4 (1989), i–172.

Nepos, Cornelius, *Hannibal*, translated by J C Rolfe (London: Harvard University Press, 1960).

Nickel, Helmut, 'The Emperor's New Saddle Cloth: The Ephippium of the Equestrian Statue of Marcus Aurelius', *Metropolitan Museum Journal*, Vol 24 (1989), pp 17–24.

Nixon, C E V, and Barbara Saylor Rodgers, *In Praise of Later Roman Emperors: The Panegyrici Latini* (Berkeley: University of California Press, 1994).

Oliver, James H, 'Marcus Aurelius: Aspects of Civic and Cultural Policy in the East', *Hesperia Supplements*, Vol 13 (1970), pp 1–168.

Omidsalar, Mahmoud, *Iran's Epic and America's Empire: A Handbook for a Generation in Limbo*, edited by Laurence Vogt, unpublished manuscript.

Orosius, Paulus, *Seven Books of History against the Pagans*, translated by Irving Raymond (New York: Colombia University Press, 1936).

Ovid, *The love books of Ovid; being the Amores, Ars amatoria, Remedia amoris and Medicamina faciei feminea*, translated by J Lewis May (New York: Willey Book Co, 1940).

Pastor, L B, 'Marius' Words to Mithridates Eupator (Plut. Mar. 31.3)', *Historia: Zeitschrift für Alte Geschichte*, Vol 48, No 4, 4th Quarter, (1999).

Pearson, Lionel, *The Lost Histories of Alexander the Great* (Chico: Scholars Press, 1983).

Perowne, Stewart, *Hadrian* (New York: W W Horton, 1960).

Philostratus, *The Life of Apollonius of Tyana*, translated by F C Conybeare. (London: Harvard University Press, 1969).

Plautus, Titus Maccius, *Mostellaria*, edited by Frank R Merrill (London: Macmillan, 1972).

Pliny the Elder, *Natural History*, translated by H. Rackham (London: Loeb Classical Library, 1923).

Plutarch, *Lives*, translated by Bernadotte Perrin (Cambridge: Harvard University Press, 1962).

Plutarch, *Moralia*, translated by W C Helmbold (Cambridge, MA: The Loeb Classical Library, 1939).

Polyaenus, *Stratagems of War*, translated by R Shepherd (Chicago: Ares Publishers, 1974).

Polybius, *The Histories*, translated by W R Paton (Cambridge, MA: Harvard University Press, 1954).

Porphyry, *On the Life of Plotinus* (Cambridge, Harvard University Press, 1966).

Potter, David, *Constantine the Emperor* (Oxford, Oxford University Press, 2013).

Potter, David, *The Roman Empire at Bay* (London, Routledge, 2004).

Potter, David, 'The Inscriptions on the Bronze Heracles from Mesene: Vologeses IV's War with Rome and the Date of Tacitus' "Annales"', *Zeitschrift für Papyrologie und Epigraphik*, Bd 88 (1991), pp 277-90.

Pourshariati, Parvaneh, *Decline and Fall of the Sasanian Empire: The Sasanian-Parthian Confederacy and the Arab Conquest of Iran* (London: I.B.Tauris, 2009).

Procopius, *History of the Wars*, translated by H B Dewing (London: Harvard University Press, 1954)

Propertius, Sextus, *Elegies, book I-IV*, edited by W A Camps (Cambridge: Cambridge University Press, 1965).

Pseudo-Callisthenes, *The Greek Alexander Romance*, translated by R. Stoneman (London: Penquin Books, 1991)

Quràn, The, translated by M H Shakir (Elmhurst: Tahrike Tarsile Quran, 1993).

Rawlinson, George, *The Seven Great Monarchies Of The Ancient Eastern World, Volume 6: Parthia* (New York: J W Lovell, 1880).

Reinink, Gerrit J, and Bernard H Stolte, *The Reign of Heraclius (610-641) Crisis and Confrontation* (Leuven: Peeters, 2002).

Roller, Duane W, *Through the Pillars of Herakles: Greco-Roman exploration of the Atlantic* (New York: Routledge, 2006).

Rossi, Andreola, 'Remapping the Past: Caesar's Tale of Troy (Lucan "BC" 9.964-999)', *Phoenix*, Vol 55, No ¾ (Autumn–Winter 2001), pp 313-26.

Rostovzeff, Michael Ivanovitch, *Rome* (New York: Oxford University Press, 1960).

Rostovzeff, Michael Ivanovitch, *The Social and Economic History of the Roman Empire* (Oxford, The Clarendon Press, 1957).

Rostovzeff, Michael Ivanovitch, *Iranians and Greeks in Southern Russia*, (Oxford: The Clarendon Press, 1922).

Rubincam, C, 'A Tale of Two "Magni": Justin/Trogus on Alexander and Pompey', *Historia: Zeitschrift für Alte Geschichte*, Vol 54, No 3 (2005), pp 265–74.

Russell, D A, and N G Wilson, *Menander Rhetor: A Commentary* (New York, Clarendon Press, 1981)

Sallust, *Fragments of the Histories*, Vol II, translated by John T Ramsey (Cambridge, MA: Loeb Classical Library, Harvard University Press, 2015).

Sampson, Gareth C, *The Defeat of Rome in the East: Crassus, the Parthians, and the Disastrous Battle of Carrhae, 53 BC* (Philadelphia: Casemate, 2008).

Sanders, Lionel J, 'The Dionysian Narrative of Diodorus 15', *Hermes*, Vol 116, No 1, 1st Quarter (1988), pp 54–63.

Sanford, E M, 'The Career of Aulus Gabinius', *Transactions and Proceedings of the American Philological Association*, Vol 70 (1939), pp 64–92.

Sandford, E M, 'Nero and the East', *Harvard Studies in Classical Philology*, Vol 48 (1937), pp 75–103.

Saunders, Nicholas, J, *Alexander's Tomb: The Two-Thousand Year Obsession to Find the Lost Conquerer* (New York, Basic Books, 2007).

Scullard, Howard Hayes, *Scipio Africanus: Soldier and politician* (Ithaca: Cornell University Press, 1970).

Seltman, Charles, *Greek Coins* (London: Methuen & Co., 1965).

Seneca, *Naturales Quaestiones*, translated by Thomas Corcoran (Cambridge: Harvard University Press, 1972).

Severy, Merle (ed.), *Greece and Rome: Builders of Our World* (Washington DC: National Geographic Society, 1968).

Shakespeare, William, *Antony and Cleopatra* (New York: Barnes & Noble, 1994).

Shuckburgh, Evelyn Shirley, *A History of Rome to the Battle of Actium* (New York: Macmillan and Co, 1894).

Simocatta, Theophylact, *The History of Theophylact Simocatta*, translated by Michael & Mary Whitby (Oxford: Clarendon Press; New York: Oxford University Press, 1986).

Smith, Cecil H, 'A Bronze Bust of Commodus', *The Burlington Magazine for Connoisseurs*, Vol 13, No 65 (Aug 1908), pp 252-257.

Smith, John Holland, *Constantine the Great* (New York: Scribner's and Sons, 1971).

Smith, Rowland, 'The Casting of Julian the Apostate "in the likeness" of Alexander the Great: A topos in antique historiography and its modern echoes', *Histos*, 5 (2011), pp 44-106.

Sordi, Marta, '*Alexandro Magno e l'eredita disiracusa*'. *Aevum*, 57 (1983), pp 19-23.

Southern, Pat, *Augustus* (London: Routledge, 1998).

Speidel, M P, 'Valerius Valerianus in Charge of Septimius Severus' Mesopotamian Campaign', *Classical Philology*, Vol 80, No 4 (Oct 1985), pp 321-6.

Spencer, Diana, *The Roman Alexander: Reading a Cultural Myth* (Exeter: University of Exeter Press, 2003).

Stark, Freya, *Rome on the Euphrates: The Story of a Frontier* (New York, Harcourt, Brace & World, 1967)

Stark, Freya, *Alexander's Path* (Woodstock, NY: The Overlook Press, 1988).

Statius, *Thebaid: A song of Thebes*, translated by Jane Wilson Joyce (Ithaca: Cornell University Press, 2008).

Stertz, Stephen A, 'Marcus Aurelius as Ideal Emperor in Late-Antique Greek Thought', *The Classical World*, Vol 70, No 7 (Apr-May, 1977), pp 433-9.

Stewart, Andrew, *Faces of Power: Alexander's Image and Hellenistic Politics* (Berkeley: University of California Press, 1993).

Stoneman, Richard, *Legends of Alexander the Great* (London: Everyman, 1994).

Stoneman, Richard, *Alexander the Great* (London: Routledge, 1997).

Stoneman, Richard, *Palmyra and its Empire: Zenobia's Revolt against Rome* (Ann Arbor: The University of Michigan Press, 1992).

Stoneman, Richard, *The Book of Alexander the Great: A Life of the Conqueror* (London: I.B. Tauris, 2011).

Strabo, '*The Geography of Strabo*', Vol I, translated by Horace Leonard Jones (Chicago: Loeb Classical Library, 1917).

Subhani, Ja'far, *The Message* (Karachi, Islamic Seminary Publications, 2006).

Suetonius, *The Twelve Caesars* (Middlesex, UK: Penguin Classics, 1979).

Swain, Simon, et al, *Severan Culture* (Cambridge: Cambridge University Press, 2007).

Sykes, Sir Percy, *A History of Persia* (Oxford: Clarendon Press, 1922).

Syme, Ronald, *History in Ovid* (Oxford: Clarendon Press, 1978).

Tacitus, *The Annals of Imperial Rome*, translated by Michael Grant (Middlesex: Penguin Books, 1987).

Takács, Sarolta A, 'Alexandria in Rome', *Harvard Studies in Classical Philology*, Vol. 97 (1995), pp 263-276.

Tarn, William Woodthorpe, 'Alexander Helios and the Golden Age', *The Journal of Roman Studies*, Vol 22, Part 2 (1932), pp 135-60.

Tarn, William Woodthorpe, 'Alexander, Cynics and Stoics', *The American Journal of Philology*, Vol 60 (1939), pp 41-70.

Thucydides, *History of the Peloponnesian War*, translated by Steven Lattimore (Indianapolis: Hackett Publishing Co, 1998).

Tierney, Michael, 'Constantine the Great and his City', *Studies: An Irish Quarterly Review*, Vol 23, No 89 (Mar. 1934).

Tröster, M, 'Roman Hegemony and Non-State Violence: A Fresh Look at Pompey's Campaign against the Pirates', *Greece & Rome*, Vol 56, No 1 (Apr. 2009), pp 14–33.

Turtledove, Harry, *The Chronicle of Theophanes: Anni Mundi 6095-6305 (A.D. 602-813)* (Philadelphia: University of Pennsylvania, 1982)

Velleius Paterculus, *Compendium of Roman History*, translated by Frederick W Shipley (London: Loeb Classic Library, 1924).

Victor, Aurelius, *Epitome De Caesaribus*, translated by Thomas M Banchich (Buffalo: Canisius College, 2009).

Virgil, *The Works of Virgil*, translated by John Connington (Philadelphia: David McKay Publishers, 1900).

Virgil, *The Aeneid*, translated by W F Jackson Knight (Baltimore: Penguin Classics), 1971.

Wardle D, '"The Sainted Julius": Valerius Maximus and the Dictator', *Classical Philology*, Vol 92, No 4 (Oct 1997).

Wardman, A E, 'Plutarch and Alexander', *The Classical Quarterly*, Vol 5, No ½, (Jan-Apr 1955), pp 96-107.

Warry, John, *Warfare in the Classical World* (New York: Barnes & Noble, 1998).

Watson, Alaric, *Aurelian and the Third Century* (London: Routledge, 1999).

Wilcox, Peter and Angus McBride, *Rome's Enemies 3: Parthians and Sasanid Persians* (London: Osprey Publishing, 1991).

Webster, Graham, *The Roman Imperial Army of the First and Second Centuries* (Totowa, NJ: Barnes & Noble, 1985).

Williams, Derek, *The Reach of Rome: A history of the Roman Imperial Frontier 1st-5th Centuries AD* (New York: St Martin's Press, 1996).

Williams, Stephen, *Diocletian and the Roman Recovery* (London, B T Batsford Ltd, 1985).

Williams, Henry Smith, et al, *The Historians History of the World* (New York, Encyclopedia Britannica, 1907)

Wirth, Albrecht, 'The Tale of the King's Daughter in the Besieged Town', *American Anthropologist*, Vol 7, issue 4 (Oct 1894).

Wroth, Warwick, *A Catalogue of The Greek Coins of the British Museum: The Coins of Parthia* (Chicago: Argonaut Inc, 1967).

Yalouris, Nicolas, et al, *Searching for Alexander: An exhibition* (New York: New York Graphic Society, 1980).

Zonaras, *The History of Zonaras*, translated by Thomas Banchich (London, Routledge, 2011).

Zosimus, *Historia Nova: The Decline of Rome*, translated by James J Buchanan and Harold T Davis (San Antonio, TX: Trinity University Press, 1967).

Index